# PRAISE FOR *THE LONG RUN*

"*The Long Run* is the real deal. Armed with heart, wisdom, grit, and wit, Matt Long kicked death right in the ass and came roaring back to life. If you want a lesson in believing in yourself, in fighting back against all odds, buy this book—*before* they make the movie."

—**DENIS LEARY,** comedian, actor, writer, and creator
of the television drama *Rescue Me*

"Some runners inspire, and some are inspired by others. Matt Long does both. His love of life, family, and friends, and his true passion for sport, make this an incredibly courageous comeback story."

—**JOAN BENOIT SAMUELSON,** 1984 Olympic gold medalist
and winner of the Boston Marathon

"Matt's story is one of inspiration and perseverance. He is unwilling to allow a horrible tragedy to stand between him and the finish line. There are powerful lessons here for any athlete."

—**DEAN KARNAZES,** champion runner and bestselling
author of *Ultramarathon Man* and *RUN!*

"To aim high is glorious; to achieve your goal when starting from the bottom—that's the mark of a champion. And that's Matt Long. I promise not to complain about my Achilles tendinitis anymore!"

—**BILL RODGERS,** winner of the Boston and New York City marathons

"*The Long Run* is a deeply human testament to the healing power of family, friends, and community. This book will move you, and not just metaphorically: It got me running again."

—**STEVE RUSHIN,** award-winning journalist and author of *The Pint Man*

"I've met some truly uncommon athletes over the years, but Matty Long's trial by fire is in a class by itself. Read his story and you'll believe; not just in him, but in the ~~power we all have to change~~ our lives for the better."

—**MARY CARILLO,**

"At a time when millions of Americans are jobless and some are losing their homes, it's good to remember that some of us are winning tough battles—and, like Matt Long, applying every bit of grit and courage we have."

—**GERRI WILLIS**, host of *The Willis Report*

"He's one of the most inspiring human beings on earth. He proves that no comeback is—or ever should be—too daunting."

—*Men's Health*, Top Ten Men of the Year

"Like Long himself, his memoir is full of the heartfelt can-do attitude sure to appeal to the Iron Man in everyone."

—*Publishers Weekly*

"You will be moved, inspired . . . transfixed and amazed at the real-life twists and turns that [Matt Long] has overcome."

—*The Huffington Post*

"The book is open and honest—at times, almost painfully so—and readers will be horrified by Long's ordeal and inspired by his determination to get back as much of himself as he could."

—*Booklist*

"Read this book. It will inspire you to do what you love to do, regardless of how unattainable that goal may seem."

—*The Poughkeepsie Journal*

# THE LONG RUN

# THE
# LONG
# RUN

## A NEW YORK CITY FIREFIGHTER'S TRIUMPHANT COMEBACK FROM CRASH VICTIM TO ELITE ATHLETE

# MATT LONG
### with CHARLES BUTLER

RODALE.

First published in hardcover by Rodale Inc. in 2010
This paperback edition published in 2011

Rodale books may be purchased for business or promotional use
or for special sales. For information, please write to:
Special Markets Department, Rodale, Inc.,
733 Third Avenue, New York, NY 10017

Printed in the United States of America
Rodale Inc. makes every effort to use acid-free ♾, recycled paper ♻.

Book design by Christopher Rhoads

**The Library of Congress has cataloged the hardcover edition as follows:**

Long, Matt.
    The long run / Matt Long with Charles Butler.
        p.    cm.
    ISBN-13: 978–1–60529–246–5   hardcover
    ISBN-10: 1–60529–246–X   hardcover
    1. Long, Matt.   2. Runners (Sports)—United States—Biography.
3. Traffic accident victims—United States—Biography.   4. Firefighters—
New York (State)—New York—Biography.   I. Butler, Charles.   II. Title.
GV1061.15.L64A3   2010
796.42092—dc22
                                        2010022293

Paperback ISBN  978–1–60961–179–8

**Distributed to the trade by Macmillan**

2   4   6   8   10   9   7   5   3   1   paperback

We inspire and enable people to improve their lives and the world around them.
www.rodalebooks.com

*Dedicated to*
*Mom, Dad, and my brothers and sisters*

*And to*
*Sarah, Leah, Ben, and Mom*

# Contents

# A NOTE ON THE PAPERBACK EDITION

This September 11 marks the tenth anniversary of a fateful day in America's history, and mine. But like many of my fellow firefighters in the New York City Fire Department, I try not to reminisce too much about that day.

That's why this coming anniversary is a milestone that I initially looked toward apprehensively. What I mean is, each year, right around Labor Day, the media and the public start talking about what "a beautiful, sunny morning" September 11, 2001, was in New York City until the attacks on the World Trade Center shattered everything. And then they start sharing memories of where they were when the first reports of the attacks came in. Well, for me there was nothing beautiful about that day, and truthfully I'd rather not remember where I was for most of it. But in light of the news this past spring regarding the demise of Osama bin Laden, I expect that *maybe* this anniversary will be a little easier to handle than I had anticipated. Usually on September 11 I attend a Mass with firefighters from Engine 58, Ladder 26 at St. Monica's Church on Manhattan's Upper East Side. The Mass is offered for Lieutenant Robert Nagel, a member of Engine 58 before he died on September 11. This September 11, I once again plan to attend the Mass and say a prayer for Lieutenant Nagel. But this year, for the first time since the days after the attack, I may return to lower Manhattan, to Ground Zero, and say a prayer there, and remember.

━━━━━━━━

As you'll discover when you read *The Long Run*, a little over four years after 9/11, on December 22, 2005, I met with a challenge that more directly impacted my life than even being in the path of crumbling skyscrapers did. The eventual aftermath of my accident deepened a truth that 9/11 initially formed within me: Today, after all I have been through and all I have suffered, I try to make each moment memorable, and lasting, and positive for myself and for those I meet. After all I have been through, I can't have it any other way.

I wake each day motivated by two words: I Will. They help me when the challenges of life stack up. With this tenth anniversary of 9/11 in sight, I suggest that you look back *a little* at the events of that day. But mostly look forward and to what We Will do to make the lives of our friends and families, neighbors and strangers, more memorable, lasting, and positive in the days ahead. We can't have it any other way.

—*Matt Long, August 2011*

# 1

# THE CHASE IS ON

As I stood there on that unusually warm November morning, looking all around me, everything seemed to say *New York*.

I was a row or so back from the starting line of the 2005 New York City Marathon, with the Manhattan skyline, shrouded in a dank, soupy fog, rising off in the distance beyond New York Harbor. Nearby, my teammates, 150 or so New York City firefighters, were doing their final stretches and giving each other one last command: *Beat the cops, okay, beat the NYPD*. Any second, Frank Sinatra would be blaring over the loudspeakers, so that every last one of the 37,597 runners about to take off from Staten Island via the Verrazano-Narrows Bridge for a 26.2-mile race through the city's four other boroughs could hear—what else?—"New York, New York."

Like I said, everything seemed to say New York.

But all I could think about was Boston.

*Boston?* What had gotten into me? I was a New Yorker, born and raised in Brooklyn, with the accent to prove it. When I used to have hair, I combed it like Tony Manero, John Travolta's character in

*Saturday Night Fever;* my sisters, Eileen and Maureen, called me John Revolting. Now I lived in midtown Manhattan, where I was a firefighter with Ladder Company 43 in East Harlem, and on this marathon day, to remember all my fellow firefighters who died on September 11, 2001, I had stenciled "343" on my left arm. I also owned three bars in Manhattan, and if needed I could tell you where to go for the best Manhattan clam chowder, Brooklyn lager, or New York strip in the city. I had nothing against Boston—in fact, I was a huge Bill Buckner fan, and I'd have a beer with Denis Leary any day of the week. But New York was my town.

Still, at that moment I couldn't get that other city out of my mind.

"Hey, Matty? Matty? How you feeling?"

"Shane, I'm good, bro. I'm good. How about you?"

"I'm ready. Just keep the pace, Matty, keep the pace."

To me it sounded like Shane McKeon, a training partner and another firefighter on the starting line, was saying, "Keep the faith." In a way, he was. He was reminding me to stay steady. *Keep the pace.* If I could click off 26.2 miles at a pace of about seven minutes and 15 seconds per mile, that would get me to the finish line in Central Park in three hours and 10 minutes. And that would easily beat my best-ever marathon time by nearly 40 minutes. And, if everything went right, that would give me a shot at finishing among the top 10 firefighters running on this day, which would help us in our annual race-within-a-race against the police department.And best of all, that would win me a prized spot in next year's Boston Marathon.

And that's why I had Beantown on the brain. I wanted to run the most famous race of all. *Boston.*

They've been staging the Boston Marathon every April since 1897, and for most of those years only a select crowd gets to take part. To earn an official race entry, you need to nail a pretty demanding time based on your age. So, at 39, I had to run a 3:15 marathon. Boston race officials allow a 59-second grace period, but not a second more. I didn't want to chance a close call, so a few weeks earlier I told Shane that I would go out a bit faster—I'd aim for a 3:10 finish, giving myself a five-minute cushion.

Whatever it took to make it to Boston, I was game.

Still, even with my plan in place I knew there were no guarantees when it came to a race like a marathon. The day's weather could trip you up, and today's temperatures were expected to rise to the mid-60s, scorching for late fall. I also worried that I might feel flat after so many weeks of intense training; I had been running upwards of 50 miles a week since May. And then there was the fact that I was still relatively new to the competitive running scene. Just two years ago I was a firefighter with a sore back and a triple chin; without really noticing, I had packed an extra 35 pounds on my five-foot-ten frame. I was up to 212 pounds, and behind my aching back friends were calling me Beer Belly Matty and Fatty Long. But then I found religion—or I should say running, as well as biking and swimming. In other words, I found the world of triathlons.

Egged on by my friend Noel Flynn, I trained through the winter of 2004 for my first triathlon—a 1.5-kilometer swim, 40-kilometer bike, and 10-kilometer run—that spring. When I completed it, I couldn't wait for the next one. And the one after that. I got addicted to the competition and the training and the camaraderie among the athletes I met at different events. I joined a triathlon club. I tracked my mile-split times and my heart rate after every workout. I logged the number of miles I put on my running shoes, retiring a pair when it hit 300. I consumed nutrition books. I started preaching that *bagels are not your friends* at family parties. I cut back on my beer intake—a huge concession for a guy who owns bars. And I started racing every chance I could. In 2004, my first full year of training, I did 14 triathlons of different lengths, and traveled everywhere from Long Island to New Jersey to Texas to do them. The adrenaline rush from the training and the competing was like nothing I had ever experienced—except maybe the rush of running to a fire with my ladder company. And all the work paid off in other ways as well: I dropped to 175 pounds, and the backache disappeared for good. Suddenly, I was in the best shape of my life.

Then I made the ultimate commitment: I signed up for an Ironman, an event that can make waste of even the best athlete over the course of a 2.4-mile swim, 112-mile bike, and 26.2-mile run. It was in Lake Placid, New York, in July 2005, four months before the New York City Marathon. My training buddies thought I was nuts. "Matty, what's the rush?" Frank Carino, a close friend and fellow firefighter, asked one day after we did a long, hard training run together. Frank had attempted his first Ironman only after competing in smaller ones for five years. "The Ironman can take a huge toll on your body. You can build up slowly, you know."

"Frank, I know, but the thing is, I love this stuff—even when it hurts."

No, there was no talking me out of it. On July 26 I did my first Ironman, finishing in 11 hours and 18 minutes, and in 279th place out of about 2,000 finishers. I did the marathon leg—the third and final one—in three hours and 44 minutes, nearly nine minutes faster than my last solo marathon seven years earlier. A pretty good showing, I thought. "Pretty good?" Frank said after we were done. "That was fantastic. Matty, you've got to slow down, you're catching up to me. You're definitely going to Kona someday."

He was talking about Kona, Hawaii, site of the annual Ironman World Championship. Frank had qualified for the first time with his race in Lake Placid. For me, Kona would be a goal come 2006. First, I had to make it to Boston.

I looked at my watch: 10:09 a.m. One minute until the cannon blast to start the marathon. Just then, John McLaughlin, an FDNY lieutenant who once ran this race in well under three hours, shouted to me.

"Hey, Matt, what are you looking to do today?"

"Three-ten, John," I shouted back.

"Three-ten. Sounds good to me. Why don't you run with me?"

Huh? He wasn't part of my marathon game plan. I had run hundreds of miles with Noel and Shane and Frank over the past few months. But none with John McLaughlin. Besides, he was faster than me; he could throw me off pace. "Hey, thanks, John, but just go ahead. Enjoy."

"Come on, Matt. Come out with me; we'll do it together."

"Thanks, bro, but I'm planning on running the first two miles kind of slow, maybe at 7:45 pace. That way I won't die later."

"What? How are you going to run 3:10 doing that? You're crazy."

Just then, BOOM! The race was on, and John was gone.

Every year on Marathon Sunday, the television crews covering the race show an overhead shot of the Verrazano-Narrows as the mass of runners crosses the two-mile span into Brooklyn. From that vantage point, the runners look like a collection of colorful bugs, inching their way toward some unknown spot. But when you're actually on the bridge, among so many people, it feels more like you're part of an oversize rugby scrum—with bodies bumping, elbows bashing, shoulders colliding, and feet tripping over feet and more feet. It can also seem like one massive, slow-moving, no-end-in-sight traffic jam. The weird thing? You don't hear many runners complaining. And why should they? They're running the *New York City Marathon*, the biggest race in the world, and perhaps the biggest block party, too. They know that once they make it over the bridge and into Brooklyn, a line of spectators will stretch—virtually unbroken—for the next 24 miles, whooping them on until the finish line in Central Park. For sheer spontaneous citywide enthusiasm, nothing beats Marathon Day in New York. Nothing.

Once I made it over the bridge and had a little more running room, I pushed myself to get on my planned pace. I made my way up Fourth Avenue and through the Bay Ridge section of Brooklyn. My mom and dad still lived in this neighborhood after raising nine kids—yes, we were one big Irish Catholic family. The day before, Mom had said she and Dad would be out cheering for me, so I told her I would look for them, but I warned her: There would be no time for a family reunion this morning.

At around mile three I met up with Jason Brezler, a young probationary officer I knew from the FDNY training academy. Since March, I had been on temporary leave from my firehouse in East Harlem and detailed to the academy's physical fitness unit. Everyone in the FDNY refers to the academy as the Rock, maybe because it's on 22 run-of-the-mill acres of Randall's Island, the strip of land on the East River that most New Yorkers pay little attention to. It's also where probies like Brezler go for six months of basic training in the ways of becoming a firefighter. They learn everything from how to haul fire hoses up a dozen flights of stairs to crawling through narrow, smoky tunnels while breathing in purified air through a mask. And they learn how to save lives, including their own.

Since the first day of probie school, Brezler had stood out as a hardworking, levelheaded kid. He told me at one point that he was a graduate of the U.S. Naval Academy and had been stationed with the Marines in Iraq and Afghanistan before signing up with the FDNY. Now he was running his first New York City Marathon.

"How you feeling, Brezler?"

"Good, sir. How are you doing, sir?"

"So far, so good. Three miles down, right?"

"Yes, sir."

For the better part of the next seven miles, through the heart of Brooklyn, Jason and I ran together, not saying much, just settling into a zone. And keeping to our pace.

It was at the Rock that I first started training with Shane and two other firefighters who worked in the fitness unit, Tommy Grimshaw and Larry Parker. Three or four days a week we would meet at 6 a.m., two hours before the probies arrived, and get our workouts in. We were a foursome for the decades. I covered the thirties while Shane, at 28, had the twenties. He was an anomaly as a runner: a hulking six-foot-six, 230-pound former college baseball player who could bang out mile repeats at six minutes a pop. He was hoping to break the three-hour mark in the marathon for the first time. Larry, 42, was known throughout the FDNY as the Fireman Ironman. He had competed in triathlons for years and ran his own training camp for aspiring Ironmen. He regularly finished the marathon among the top five firefighters. And then there was Tommy. At maybe five foot six, with sandy brown hair and darting eyes, Tommy, 55, looked more like a high school English teacher than a firefighter. But he was as tough as his raspy Queens accent. He had run nearly every New York City Marathon since 1978 and had finished each one in four hours or better.

Back in the summer, we pledged that we would each qualify for Boston—and then we trained together to make sure we all did.

Some days the four of us ran long, some days we ran hard, and some days we did both. On Monday, for instance, we might do 12 miles, with eight of them at a six-minute, 15-second clip. On Tuesday, an easy eight-miler. Friday was the killer: an 18- or 19-mile long run during which Shane or Larry would "drop the hammer" at certain intervals; they'd take a seven-minute-per-mile pace and jam it to 6:30 for a mile or two.

For the first few weeks, whenever Shane dropped the hammer, I would fall behind him by several hundred yards, catching up only when he slowed down. But as we came to the final month of marathon training, the gap had lessened—and Shane noticed. "Matt, you're pushing it, my man," he said after one run. "I wouldn't be surprised if you're one of our top 10 guys on marathon day. You've come a long way in a short time, bro."

As Jason and I made our way through Brooklyn, and with the heat rising, I knew I would not be dropping any hammer on the kid today. Instead, at the end of each mile, I made a point to check in on him. "Jason, that mile was a little too fast." "Jason, that one was a little too slow." "Jason, don't worry about that guy passing us; let him go. You're doing fine." But just before finishing mile 10, when we were in Brooklyn's Williamsburg section, Jason no longer looked himself.

"Matt, it's my stomach," he said. "I'm jumping out for a few minutes."

"Anything I can do for you, Brez?"

"No, no. I'll catch up to you."

"Okay, I'll be on the right side of the road the whole way. Look for me—or I'll look for you at the finish."

I had 16 miles to go, and I was surrounded by hundreds of runners, but I saw no one I knew. Not Shane or Larry or Tommy. Not even John McLaughlin. Now I was on my own.

Running up First Avenue on Marathon Day is like roaming the French Quarter on Fat Tuesday. From miles 16 to 18, it's one big cocktail of cheers, laughter, music, and screams coming from rowdy spectators lined up three deep on each side of the avenue. The people float out of the bars and restaurants that seem to cover every inch of every block from 60th Street to 96th Street. The Yorkville Brewery and Tavern. Finnegans Wake. American Trash. I knew them well. They were friendly rivals to Third & Long, Turtle Bay, and M.J. Armstrong's, the three pubs I had opened with my brother Jimmy and some friends over the years. If all went according to plan, I would end up at Third & Long tonight. The bar was hosting a marathon party for the firefighters, where we hoped to be toasting a victory over the cops, and recouping a lot of lost calories.

But I had a long way to go before I could think of anything colder than Gatorade. I hit the 18-mile mark at 92nd Street in two hours and 12 minutes, 90 seconds off my 3:10 pace. *No problem*, I told myself, *I still have the cushion.* A few blocks up, parked on 103rd Street, was 43 Truck, my rig. I had been stationed at the nearby firehouse—Engine 53, Ladder 43—since graduating from the Rock 12 years earlier. Some of the guys from the house were up on the truck rooting for me, and razzing me, as I came by.

"Yo, Matty, you're looking great," I heard John Kelly yell. "Especially your legs."

"Matt, we'll see you tonight at Third & Long," Kevin Torrey shouted. "That is, if you're not still running!"

I smiled, but I didn't look back. I just gave them a wave and kept going. I could take their heat. We had been together a long time. Kelly, Torrey, and six or seven others were known in the firehouse as the Cronies, firefighters who worked well together putting out fires, and putting everyone at ease the rest of the time.

Through East Harlem and then through the Bronx, I still felt strong. I never hit the wall—that point when the body just wants to stop after running so many miles and dealing with so much pain. I remembered the wall well from the first marathon I did nine years earlier. Back then, I didn't run the race with the right purpose; I didn't prepare properly for all the physical and mental demands that come with exerting yourself for that long and over that distance. The result? The wall crushed me that day.

But not today.

As I moved down Fifth Avenue through miles 22 and 23, making my way toward Central Park, I saw two runners up ahead in fire-red singlets, just like the one I was wearing. *Damn*, I said to myself, *I'm gaining on some firefighters*. I passed one of them, Paul Franco, with three miles to go, and another, Kevin White, a half a mile later. *How many more firefighters were ahead of me?* I wondered.

I ripped into the park for the final two-plus miles. When I came to the mile 24 marker, I was right on my pace, or so I thought. That's when I saw Frank Carino, in a red shirt and khaki shorts, on the side of the road, jumping up and down. He hopped into the race and started running alongside of me, all pumped up.

"John McLaughlin! He's right in front of you!"

"What?"

"John McLaughlin! He's right in front of you! I can't believe this!"

"Frank, how many firefighters are ahead of me? What place is McLaughlin in?"

"He's fourth, Matt. Fourth!"

Fourth? That meant I was fifth. Forget about top 10. I was already top five. And John McLaughlin was now in sight.

"Matt, you're doing awesome," Frank kept telling me. "Awesome!"

Actually, at that point, with less than two miles to go, I was starting to feel the hurt. My quads were shredded, and I was breathing harder and harder. It seemed like I was slowing down, so I asked Frank if I was on 3:10 pace. Frank had been an accountant before he became a firefighter, and he always prided himself on doing calculations fast.

"Matt, you're doing awesome. You're going to break 3:10; you're going to break 3:10. Just keep going."

A few yards later, Frank and I spotted a guy in an FDNY running shirt stretching his hamstring on the side of road. We kept running. "Holy crap, holy crap! You just passed John McLaughlin!" Frank yelled to me. "You got to be kidding me!" He was hysterical.

As we finished mile 25, I said, "Frank, I'm really hurting." But Frank didn't say anything. He just kept jogging next to me, staring at his watch.

Suddenly, he said, "Matt, listen."

"What?"

"Remember I told you that you had plenty of time, that you're breaking 3:10? Uh, I made a mistake."

"What?"

"I got a little excited. You better move it. You're closer to 3:15."

"What the . . . ? Are you kidding me?"

Frank just yelled, "Go, go, go!" and trailed off.

I turned up Central Park South for the final mile and laid down the hammer. I was afraid to look at my watch; what it said didn't matter. The official time was at the finish line, and I had to get there, pronto. My legs turned over faster than at any time that I could remember; my mind went on hold. For those few minutes, I didn't think. I just ran.

Until I crossed the line in 3:13:56.

I was going to Boston.

My brother Jimmy was waiting for me at the finish line. He's a firefighter, too. I was drenched in sweat, but I still gave him a hug. "How did we do?" I asked him.

"You guys are going to beat the cops again, Matt," Jimmy said with a huge grin. "That's five times in a row, bro."

"And where did I place?"

"Fourth," he said. "How the hell did that happen?"

I just smiled.

Later, when I saw Frank at the postrace party at Third & Long, he sprinted to me. "Oh, my God, Matty, I'm so sorry!"

I let him off the hook. I was too pumped. "Hey, it's all right, Frank. I qualified for Boston; that's all that counts."

And so did Shane, Larry, and Tommy; we were *all* going to Boston. That night we sat at the bar telling stories about the race, laughing, and, with the aches of the day still fresh, plotting out our training plans for the race in April. We decided to dial back the long runs until after Christmas. "Hey, my body could use a break after a year like this," I told the guys. Larry, the Fireman Ironman, suggested that through the end of the year we do shorter runs and meet a couple of times a week for some easy, early morning pool workouts. That sounded good to everyone. We clinked our beers and ordered one more round.

We also agreed that in Boston, we would all run in our red FDNY shirts and keep the pace, together.

# 2

# BROKEN FRAMES

When you're in the bar business in Manhattan, the holiday season is itself a marathon. A nonstop, madcap run of parties and happy hours that linger into closing time—or at least you hope it does. You can make your rent for the first few months of the new year with a booming couple of weeks.

That's why it was nice to taper the training some after the marathon and concentrate on the bars and the good times they offered. And not just for the guests. You see, one of the perks of owning a bar is that every night you have a chance to host a party, and I was always up for that job. On the Saturday before Christmas, for instance, I had 60 members of my triathlon club down to M.J. Armstrong's for our year-end bash. It was nice seeing everyone in something other than biker shorts and bathing caps, and fueling up on Guinness instead of Gatorade. Frank Carino came, and even though there was snow on the ground, we spent most of the night making plans for next summer's Ironman. Then, the following night, we had our annual staff holiday party at Third & Long. Simple formula there: Open bar starts at 3 p.m., and it keeps going until the last person surrenders.

But the event that made my holidays was one where I did nothing but show up. It was Dinner at Debo's, as I liked to call it. Debo is Mark DiBenedetto, an old friend who, along with his wife, Amy, throws one of the more impressive parties of the season. They have 30 or so people over to their Chelsea apartment, break out the good china, dip into the wine collection, and serve up the juiciest pan-roasted lamb chops the world has to offer. Dinner at Debo's was always a classy way to break up the hectic days before Christmas.

Little could Mark and Amy have known, though, just how chaotic New York City would be the night of that year's dinner, December 21.

A day earlier, the 35,000 men and women who operate the city's massive transit system had gone on strike, shutting down all bus and subway service and leaving New Yorkers on edge. Kids scrambled to get to school, and commuters from the outer boroughs had to walk miles, some over bridges and along highways, to make their way to work. And forget about driving into Manhattan. Things got so bad that Mayor Michael Bloomberg restricted midtown streets to cars with four passengers or more during rush hour.

The city was in a virtual lockdown, a hostage to a maddening, traffic-jamming, no-end-in-sight transit strike that was making eight million New Yorkers more uptight than usual. And getting in the way of their holiday plans. Including mine.

Debo lived about two miles from my apartment in midtown. Catching a cab the night of their party proved impossible, so along with a buddy, Sean Scott, I walked downtown. The distance didn't bother me; it was more the bitter cold that had invaded the city that week. Temperatures had sunk into the teens. When I walked into his apartment with Sean, Debo rushed over. "Hey, guys, you made it. What can I get you to kill that chill?"

"A ticket to Florida, Debo," I told him, "and a glass of Pinot Noir."

Needless to say, the party was worth the frigid walk, and it was still going strong when I decided to head home just after midnight. When I made my way downstairs and to the street, I pulled on my ski cap. It seemed even colder now. Fortunately, the traffic had let up a bit, and I grabbed a cab. The taxi moved easily through the streets, heading uptown, past stores and office buildings all decorated for the holidays. For a moment, at least, a little bit of sanity had returned to New York.

I checked the voice mail on my cell phone. Two messages. "Matty, I know you're out tonight, bro," came the first one. It was Shane. "Just a reminder. We're on for a 6 a.m. swim tomorrow. You, Tommy, Larry, and me. See you then, and don't be late. *I know you were out tonight.*"

The second one was from Noel Flynn. "Matt, just double-checking about tomorrow night. We're all set. We're meeting at the China Grille for dinner and drinks. Okay, it will be a great way to get the holidays rolling. See you tomorrow, buddy. Should be a fun one."

I smiled as I put away the phone. A few minutes later the cab pulled up to my apartment on East 48th Street, between Second and Third Avenues. I got out and with a vicious gust of wind rushing through the street, I quickstepped toward my building's entrance. I was cold and tired. And tomorrow promised to be another day of running around and having fun.

Just the way I liked it.

━━━━━━━━

The alarm went off, and my eyes glanced at the clock: *5:15.* Short night's sleep, long day ahead. No rolling over. The guys would bust my chops all day if I were late for our workout. I crawled out of

bed and flipped on the TV to get the latest on the transit strike
and what it might mean for my commute. The anchorwoman, looking way too pretty for this hour of the morning, delivered the news
I was hoping not to hear. "Representatives for the city and transit
workers are due back at the bargaining table this morning, but right
now, New York, get set for day three of Transit Strike 2005."

*Damn*, I thought, *this should be a fun commute.*

For the first two days of the strike, I had worked with the probies at one of the FDNY's training facilities in Manhattan. But this
morning I needed to be out at the Rock, and I had to meet Shane
and the guys in less than an hour. Most days I would just drive to
work, but with the driving restrictions in place, I wouldn't be able
to get back into the city during the afternoon rush hour. So that
option was out. I could run the four miles to the Rock, but with the
TV weatherman now saying, "It's 26 degrees, with a wind that
makes it feel a lot colder," I knew it wasn't the day for a run.

That left just one thing to do: take my bike.

I usually avoided biking to the Rock. The Triborough Bridge,
which connects Manhattan to Randall's Island, was typically cluttered with garbage and broken glass that could easily ruin a tire or
take a rider down. Today I had no choice. I went over to the wall of
my living room where my Trek 2200 hung on its rack. I bought it
two years earlier when I first got into triathlon training. It was
plenty of bike for a beginner triathlete. A sleek black-and-blue steel
model outfitted with a carbon-fiber fork, it had aero bars on it for
the triathlon and a forward-angle seatpost to let me ride more
aggressively. When I later got even more into training and competing, I upgraded to a Cervélo P3, and the 2200 became my training
bike. It was about to get an unscheduled workout.

I rolled the Trek out of my apartment and toward the elevator.
I was wearing the warmest winter biking gear I could find: a Gore-

Tex jacket overlaying two long-sleeved shirts, Gore-Tex pants, and a pair of biking gloves. I also had a ski hood pulled over my head and around my chin. A knapsack with a change of clothes was slung over my back.

I came down the elevator and said good morning to Berto, the doorman on duty at that hour.

"Matt, you're a tough man to bike in this kind of weather," Berto said as he held the door open. "Stay warm, be careful."

"I hear you, bro. See you tomorrow."

I stepped out onto 48th Street and adjusted my bike helmet. I climbed onto the bike and started pedaling toward Third Avenue. It was still dark outside and bitterly cold.

━━━━━━━

At that hour, just about 5:45 a.m., Third Avenue looked like it did on most mornings when I would head to the Rock. Light from the office buildings and restaurants lining nearly every block helped to shed some contrast on the predawn darkness. The five lanes across the avenue were already busy, with cabs and delivery trucks streaming by, heading north. No tie-ups, everything moving in the pre–rush hour. A normal day, in a sense.

I had cycled up Third Avenue hundreds of times over the years, sometimes in the midafternoon, sometimes in the middle of the evening, but mostly on weekend mornings on the way to Central Park for a workout with members of my triathlon club. And I had never had a problem.

That's not to say biking in Manhattan is a walk through a small-town library. It's a blur of lights, colors, attractions, and distractions. A cascade of shrill noises, obnoxious sounds, screams and sirens, backfires, taunts, whistles. You're constantly on the lookout for potholes, car doors opening, and old ladies crossing the street. It tests every sense and reflex—a video game come to life. It's at times thrilling and mesmerizing. And fun. But it's also scary and dangerous because it's *not* a video game. Your guard must be up every second for what may suddenly get in your way. There are trucks, buses, cabs, limos, cop cars, and, as I well knew, fire engines, all with drivers in a hurry. You have timid drivers from the suburbs, unsure of themselves amid the constant flow. You have combative drivers, recklessly maneuvering the lanes as if they were racing Matchbox cars on a kid's bedroom floor.

You have other cyclists, too. On one extreme there are the commuters, who tend to be more conservative, cordial to other riders and drivers. They're riding in work clothes, maybe even a suit and tie, and hoping not to break a sweat. They stop at every red light, waiting obediently for a green. Then you have the messengers who ride their bikes all day, every day, throughout the city. They're superskilled, swerving in and out of traffic, with carrying cases slung across their backs. They zip in and out of lanes, around idling cars, through packs of people crossing streets. They often ignore red lights, dashing through intersections with maybe only a glance to see if a car might be coming from their left or right. They can be a major pain in the ass.

When I biked in Manhattan, I fell somewhere between these extremes. Usually I wasn't in a desperate hurry; my rush came when my training buddies and I would do timed circuits of the park's six-mile loop. But I was no angel, either. I did my share of pushing the traffic laws. If I were waiting for a light to turn green and saw no cars approaching the crossing, then, yes, I would get a jump on the light. I was a New Yorker. My DNA gave me the green light. And now, after two years of intense training on the bike—upwards of 150 miles per week—I felt confident on the city streets.

I settled into my commuting pace, a comfortable 18 miles per hour or so, as I rode along the right-hand side of Third Avenue, a few feet from the curb. I moved just fast enough to keep pace with the traffic lights. If I stayed at this rate, I wouldn't need to slow down until I hit 125th Street, where I would turn right toward the Triborough Bridge. Cars and trucks and taxis passed on my left. I biked by Smith & Wollensky, the popular steakhouse on 49th Street. Outside of my bars, Smith & Wolly's had been my regular haunt for years; after dinner tonight with Noel, I'd probably stop in for a nightcap. I biked by my favorite Starbucks. They knew me in there for my regular order, a Grande Soy Mocha. When I got to 51st Street, a UPS truck passed me on my left. *This must be a brutal time of year for those guys,* I thought.

Everything moved easily. A transit strike was crippling New York, but at that hour you wouldn't have known it in this slice of the city.

I stayed along the curb and pedaled, one more workout ahead of me, one more day of work, one more party tonight. Things were going according to plan. In no time at all, I'd be at the Rock.

A second later, I disappeared.

———

People have asked me if I saw it coming. If I saw anything of what soon would turn me and my world upside down. And I tell them that I didn't see anything, or at least I don't think I did. But I'm not sure, because that moment, and many moments that preceded it, and so many that followed it, never existed, or at least they don't exist in the memories I hold. They are the broken frames of my life. And while I've tried to patch them together by talking to those people who soon were at the scene and those who later saved my life, and by reading accounts of everything that the newspapers wrote, and by poring through the hundreds of notes and messages people left for me outside my hospital bedroom, and by pleading with my family and friends for every detail they could offer, and even years later, when I finally had the stomach for it, by watching video taken from surveillance cameras of the actual accident scene, so little comes back. I can't remember what I did.

When I try to recall that moment, my brain won't let me.

All I can assume, and what the doctors have told me, is that the impact was so sudden and traumatic that my brain just shut down and, mercifully, spared me the memories. My body was about to endure a gruesome invasion. Hellish. My mind didn't need a 3-D picture of it.

What I have learned of that moment and the weeks that immediately followed comes from the conversations I've had with many of these people. I wish I could say everything I'm about to write is 100 percent accurate. I know it can't be. People's memories get fuzzy; they go dark sometimes.

I should know.

═══════════

The bare facts: As I rode up Third Avenue, a 52-seat passenger bus chartered to transport employees of Bear Stearns to work during the transit strike was heading in the same direction but was in the center lane of the avenue, two lanes to my left. Just as I was about to cross 52nd Street, the bus made a sudden and sweeping right turn. The sequence of events happened so quickly—fires take longer to ignite—that all I had a chance to do before I collided with the bus was raise my left arm to shield myself. It did no good.

I hit the bus on its right side, near the front passenger entrance. Instead of ricocheting backward from the impact, my body and bike got run over by the bus, somehow getting squeezed between the eight-inch gap separating the bus's undercarriage and the street's blacktop. I was trapped beneath a 40,000-pound bus, dead center, about two feet behind the front axle, enmeshed with the bike and gored through my anus and up through my midsection by the bike's seatpost. I was alive and, according to the first people on the scene, moaning, but I was also spewing deep red, coagulated blood from the opening in my lower abdomen. It poured out of me so quickly that by the time the first rescue responders had arrived, a puddle of blood had collected on the southeast corner of 52nd Street.

I was bleeding to death.

In addition to the bus driver, a 30-year-old man from Albany, New York, who police would later cite for making an illegal right turn from the center lane instead of from the avenue's designated bus lane, an NYPD officer happened to be nearby. He immediately radioed for help. Within five minutes four officers from the NYPD Emergency Service Unit arrived. One of the officers, Detective Charles King, was stunned when he first looked under the bus and saw me. "It was like someone got hit by a train," King told a reporter, "but at a slower speed."

King went to the front of the bus with a set of hydraulic lifts, which can raise as many as five tons in a matter of seconds. In the meantime, Detectives Ralph Logan and Charlie Raz started shimmying under the bus. They found me, groaning one second, unconscious the next. "It was like he and the bike were one and the same," King reported. I was a mess. While the seatpost protruded from my midsection, one handlebar was wedged into the bus's metal underbelly. Even when King raised the bus with the lifts, the bike remained stuck in the sheet metal of the bus. Logan and Raz shouted for a battery-operated saw to extract the bike from the bus, and from me.

While they sawed, the detectives faced another problem: the

blood that continued to pour from me. "As we tried to take the bike out," Logan said, "we were slipping around his blood; it was like an oil slick. It got to the point where I had to put my feet on the bottom of the bus just to keep from slipping." Besides the blood from the fissure in my midsection, more came from my left leg, where both my femur and tibia had broken through the skin.

As the detectives continued to saw, firefighters from Engine 8, Ladder 2, located on East 51st Street, just three blocks from my apartment, arrived. Through the years I had become friendly with some of the guys there. I would often stop by to use their gym equipment or grab a drink of water on my way back from a run in the park. But under the bus that morning, wrapped up in the frame of the bike and with a helmet and ski mask covering most of my face, it was impossible to identify me at first glance.

Firefighter Donal Buckley steadied one end of the bike as Logan sawed. When they finally got the bike free from under the bus carriage, I moaned the word *fireman*, which caught Buckley off guard. But that's all I said. The ESU crew then delicately dislodged the seatpost from my body. The blood continued to spout, but it could have been worse; later, Logan told someone that my bike shorts acted as a compression bandage and held me together.

It took about five minutes for the detectives to free me. They rolled me onto a backboard, then lifted me from under the bus and onto a gurney. An ambulance was already there. The paramedics immediately put bandages around my opened abdomen, trying to stanch the bleeding. It continued to be deep red, oxygenated blood, a sign of serious internal bleeding. "We could tell that his pelvis and lower extremities were really messed up," Logan said.

At this point I was drifting in and out, but I managed to say *forty*. This time Buckley took a closer look at my face; this time something clicked.

"Hey," Buckley blurted out, "it's Matty Long, from Ladder 43."

Months later, Buckley would tell a friend of mine, "You know, in a situation like that, you just go through the steps—one, two, three, four—however you were trained, that's what you go through. That's all you're concerned about. You're not worried about who the person is, initially. But when he said he was a fireman, you know, you kind of pushed it up a little bit."

The detectives and the firefighters knew they couldn't do much for me at that point. Logan barked to the paramedics, "Let's not play games. This guy needs a hospital." The ambulance raced off.

---

Just after 6 a.m., when I hadn't arrived at the Rock, Shane starting calling my cell phone and giving me the business. "Get out of bed, you bum!" he joked in the first message he left.

Typically, we gave someone a five-minute grace period before we took off for our workout—and then made the guy feel miserable once we got back. We would high-five each other and say, "Oh, what a great workout, too bad you missed it." Whatever it took to tweak him. But that morning the guys decided to hang back and wait for me. Tommy didn't have a good feeling.

"Matt's never late," he said. "Let's give him five more minutes."

Five minutes turned into 10, then 30. Finally, at 6:40, the phone rang in the locker room. Larry grabbed it. "Matty's been in an accident!" he yelled out to Tommy and Shane. "He got hit by a bus!"

That was all the news they heard for a while. They waited, assuming I wasn't badly hurt, that I simply was riding along, a bus got too close and bumped me, and I just went into a parked car and flipped off my bike.

If only that had been the case.

# 3

# BROOKLYN, USA

My brother Jimmy was the first one in my family to receive a call about the accident, around 6:15 a.m. He was at his home in Queens, just getting up to go to work; his wife, Pam, was still asleep. Jimmy had joined the FDNY in the winter of 1994, six months after I had, and spent his first nine years at a firehouse in midtown Manhattan. He injured his foot one day when responding with his company to a fire in a high-rise apartment building, and while recovering he took a temporary job in the department's public communications office. Growing up, Jimmy always told me he never wanted a desk job—"I don't want to go to work in a jacket and tie," he'd say—but it turned out he did his temp job, briefing senior FDNY officials on department issues or dealing with inquiries from the media, so well that his boss asked him to stay on. So now every day he went to work in, yes, a jacket and tie and took calls like this one.

It came from a captain in my firehouse, Eugene Kananowicz—K-9, as we affectionately called him. K-9 told Jimmy that he didn't know much, except that I had been in an accident and was being taken to New York–Presbyterian Hospital/Weill Cornell Medical Center on the Upper East Side of Manhattan. The only thing K-9 added was that it might be a good idea if Jimmy got up to the hospital. Actually, that's what Jimmy would do whenever a firefighter got hurt, either respond to the scene or to the hospital so he could communicate information back to the family and the press. Of course, now he was dealing with an accident involving his brother.

As Jimmy got dressed, K-9 called again. This time he told Jimmy that I had suffered a broken leg. And that's when Jimmy knew I was in trouble. There's a protocol in the fire department, as Jimmy was well aware of, that when first relaying information about an injured firefighter, you say you don't know much, you spare the details. You want to give the sense that nothing is seriously wrong. But when K-9 told Jimmy that I had a broken leg, my brother knew to read between the lines. He knew it was more than that.

He picked up his pace getting out the door, but before leaving for the hospital he called our parents, Mike and Eileen Long. They lived about 20 minutes from Jimmy. He told Dad what he knew: I had been in an accident and was headed to the hospital—with a broken leg. "Don't worry," he said to Dad. "I have a department car coming to pick you and Mom up and get you to the hospital. I'll meet you there."

Ten minutes later an FDNY cruiser, its lights flashing, pulled up in front of my folks' house. Mom and Dad got into the car but were told by the officer that they couldn't leave until the police escort arrived. "An escort? What for?" Mom wanted to know. "He only has a broken leg." Seconds later the NYPD cruiser appeared. The two cars took off, sirens blaring, toward Manhattan.

Mom looked at Dad, worried. "Mike, this doesn't seem right. All this for a broken leg?"

They met the old-fashioned way: in an ice cream parlor, over a hot fudge sundae. It was 1961 and Mike Long, 21 at the time and just back from service with the U.S. Marines, worked the counter at the corner ice cream store on Fulton Street, in the Cypress Hills section of Brooklyn. He looked like a marine, six feet tall with broad shoulders, a closely cropped haircut, and thick hands. One afternoon Eileen Dougherty, just 20, a tiny brunette with curls, walked into the shop with some friends. She had grown up in the neighborhood, a couple of blocks from the soda shop. Eileen ordered a sundae with vanilla ice cream, no whipped cream, and she and the marine, dressed in a white shirt and apron, got to talking. She kept coming in, and he kept talking to her, until he finally asked her out. Two years later they were married in Blessed Sacrament Church.

And then all hell broke loose.

First came Michael, a year or so after their wedding. Then I showed up on September 3, 1966. Perhaps as a sign of things to come, I brought a little drama to my arrival. Mom had yet to have a contraction, but my head kept pushing against the wall of her belly, flooring her with pain. She was in such agony that the obstetrician finally had to induce her. As Mom likes to remind me, "You were in a rush from the moment you were born."

Apparently, my delivery didn't discourage her from having more kids, because over the next 14 years she had another seven: Jimmy, Robert, Eileen, Maureen, Chris, Frank, and, the last, Eddie. Yes, count them up. The nine Long kids. All we were missing was a designated hitter and we could have fielded a team in the American League.

By nature, it seems, I was an extrovert. As a toddler I ran around the house, bopping from one thing to the next. Mom often tells the story of the time when I was three and she left Michael and me alone to play in the living room while she worked in the kitchen. Michael quietly lay on the floor playing with his cars and coloring while I bounced from chair to chair, climbing over the couch, knocking over a lamp, and pestering our tiny pet turtle, which otherwise would have been sleeping in its glass bowl. Finally, Mom got so annoyed at the racket I was making that she rushed into the living room, catching me as I was throwing the tiny reptile back in its bowl. She looked into the bowl, then screamed, "Oh, my God!" The turtle's head and feet were missing. Mom looked at me as I smacked my mouth shut. She thought I had decapitated it and went hysterical. It was only after a couple of hours, and when the turtle finally poked his head out, that Mom could finally calm down.

I was a rambunctious, impulsive, fast-talking kid who couldn't sit still, which may explain why I never became a big reader. Concentrating even for the length of a Hardy Boys chapter took a kind of effort and patience that I just didn't have. In fact, my fifth-grade teacher got so frustrated with my lack of reading skills that she made me do the year over. Today some doctor would say I suffered from ADD. He might be right. But in my own eyes, I was just a happy-go-lucky kid looking to make the most out of every day: having fun, playing sports, and keeping up with my siblings. And being part of a family the size of the Osmonds forces you to step lively. Everyone was rushing somewhere: Michael to cross-country practice, Eileen to a softball game, Jimmy and me to a basketball tournament. Dinner was another free-for-all. We joke now that Eddie, the youngest of us, is also the tiniest—we called him the Runt— because by the time the food made its way down to him, not much was left. And at the dinner table, with 11 voices trying to be heard, good manners and niceties often were ignored; we each built up our lightning-quick deliveries by trying to out-talk everyone else at the table.

Until I was 15, we lived in Cypress Hills, in a neighborhood of mostly Irish Catholic families just like ours. Small, two-story row houses filled the blocks, and when the weather was warm kids played ball in the street until it was pitch-black while their parents and grandparents hung out on their porches trying to catch a breeze from the passing elevated J train. It was small-town USA in big old Brooklyn, New York, and it seemed everyone knew every-one, and everyone knew the Longs, the ones with all the kids and the dad who ran one of the most popular spots around.

Talk about being born with a silver spoon. Our dad made *ice cream* for a living. The store, which Dad and his brother Tom bought from the owner, who originally had hired Dad, looked very much like Arnold's Drive-In from *Happy Days*. A cheerful spot filled from breakfast through 11 p.m. with infants, kids, teenagers, moms and dads, retirees, cops, schoolteachers, priests, nuns, you name it— everyone enjoying time together and simple, all-American food and desserts. As you pushed through the wood-framed entrance with "Long's Ice Cream Parlor" scripted on the plate glass, the first thing you noticed was a long, orange Formica counter where you could grab a seat on a stool that spun in circles. Everything behind the counter gleamed: the stainless-steel freezer filled with ice cream, the stainless-steel dispensers holding the different flavored syrups and toppings, and the stainless-steel soda fountains that dis-pensed root beer for the floats and seltzer for Brooklyn's famous egg creams. From the counter you could look through a small window and into a tiny kitchen where Dad or Uncle Tom or one of the full-time employees manned a small grill, preparing burgers and sand-wiches. Past the counter were eight booths with high-back benches, ideal for four people but, more often than not, crammed with twice that many. And, in the very back, was a 60-song jukebox whose menu of tunes turned over every two weeks or so. The jukebox seemed to be on all the time, playing pop songs from the '60s and '70s. Dad only shut it down on Sundays when the church crowd came in or when disco caught on and he couldn't take some of the more risqué songs. Donna Summers's "Love to Love You, Baby" didn't get much play in Long's Ice Cream.

But while you might first come to Long's for the atmosphere, you came back for the ice cream—rich, thick, and homemade, whipped daily in the store's basement. Dad didn't offer 31 or 47 or 69 different flavors. He kept it to the basics and the favorites: chocolate, vanilla, strawberry, and every now and then some rum raisin or cherry vanilla or mint chip. But what he may have been missing in variety he made up for in taste. Dad would always say the quality of the ice cream depended on the percentage of fat in the buttermilk. The higher, the tastier. He didn't skimp. Today the cholesterol cops would be on his case, but back then all he wanted was happy customers who would keep returning. And if the ice cream didn't satisfy a sugar craving, then you went up to the candy counter near the cash register. For every holiday, Mom and Aunt Anke decorated all the chocolates—the chocolate Easter bunnies, the chocolate Thanksgiving turkeys, the chocolate Santas.

Long's Ice Cream was the nucleus of our neighborhood. Families came in after school, after ball games, after the movies. If your curfew was 10 p.m. and you called your mom and said, "We're going to Long's," more often than not she would say, "Okay, you can stay out a little later," because you would just be drinking cherry Cokes, eating french fries, and listening to the jukebox. It was familiar, fun, and safe. And it was a great place for us to grow up. Every Sunday after Mass we went there for breakfast. We had our birthday parties there, with ice cream cakes Mom and Dad would make. After a basketball game, win or lose, that's where the team ended up. It became a second home.

At home, everything seemed to move along without a hitch. Mom had dinner on the table every night, 6:30 sharp, and when we went off to school in the morning, the lunches were ready. We could look up to the bleachers during a game we were playing and know Mom or Dad would be watching and cheering. Sure, there were times when they let us have it for some screwball thing we did—once, I tried to see what it would be like to light tissue paper with a match and ended up burning a hole in the living room rug, which didn't go over too well—but in a house with more going on in it than in the Oval Office, they put up a good front and more often than not kept their cool.

Of course, we were young and busy and not privy to their conversations or the bills that came in, and not sharp enough to know that life isn't just a double scoop of cherry vanilla. In hindsight I should have realized that—but, again, I was just a kid. I couldn't see that you don't get rich owning a small ice cream parlor no matter how busy it might be, and especially when you have nine kids to feed and put through Catholic school and fit with a new pair of sneakers before every basketball tryout. But Mom and Dad never let us know when things got tight. Only much later, when I had grown up and moved out, did Mom share the story of the time Dad came to her at the start of the week with a $10 bill. "Eileen," he said, "try and make it last 'til Friday." That week, Mom reminded me, we had spaghetti almost every night. "Italian food, Matthew, went a long way with our big family."

And when you own a corner ice cream parlor, you don't stop thinking about work at 5 p.m. or when Friday night arrives, like other dads do. Owning a small business is a full-time, seven-days-a-week job; sure, you might not be at the store every minute, but you can never forget about it. By the late 1970s, our part of Cypress Hills was changing, and not for the better. Regular customers started to move out of the neighborhood, and a couple of times the store was broken in to. Finally, after 21 years, Dad and Mom realized it was time to close down the ice cream parlor and move out of Cypress Hills. In 1982, during my first year of high school, we moved to Bay Ridge, and Dad opened a liquor store. A new start, but some of the same old challenges: making rent, attracting customers, and keeping up with his nonstop family.

Adding to all this was that Dad, even before I was born, had become heavily involved in New York state politics. He held strong beliefs about individual rights and the role—the limited role—government should play in people's lives. He just felt that if you worked hard, good things would come your way, and that they then shouldn't be taxed away by the government. In 1964, Barry Goldwater's run for president prompted Dad and Mom to join the state's Conservative Party. Over time Dad took on more party roles and responsibilities, and he became more involved in pushing a Conservative agenda in the city and the state. He didn't have hundreds of like-minded people at his front stoop offering to help out; he was a square peg in far-left New York City. At the start it often was just Dad and Mom going door to door, passing out fliers or hosting dinners to drum up support. And the defeats came more often than the wins. Over the years, he's said to me more than once, "Matt, I don't know. Sometimes I feel like I'm just tilting at windmills."

But he never got down, or at least he never showed it. He never wavered in his beliefs or commitments. And that's one thing I often found so refreshing about Dad. A lot of people, especially these days, don't agree with his politics. Even I, who generally back his agenda, quibble with some of his planks. But I will never fault him for his commitment. Maybe it came from being Catholic and learning to live by all the Church's rules; he and Mom, to this day, never miss Sunday Mass. Or maybe it has something to do with going into the Marines—that was his college. The Marines taught him to never show his weaknesses, even when he might have wanted to.

Or maybe that's just who he was.

I must have inherited something from him, because I took a fighter's attitude with me wherever I went. One day when I was 10 or so, a friend had a boxing tournament in his basement. In the first match I faced my brother Michael, two years older and two inches taller. I had him begging for mercy in less than a minute. On the basketball court, I wasn't afraid to find the opposing team's best player and get in his face and let him know that if he was going to beat me to the basket, he'd better be damn fast, because he wasn't going to get around me by finessing or bullying me. If he tried, then look out for my shoulder.

Yes, I could be a tough, headstrong kid, confident in my abilities—sometimes too confident. Thankfully, Dad was there to straighten me out. One time I came home after a high school basketball game in which I didn't see any playing time. Back then my head was bigger than my game; I thought I deserved a healthy amount of court time, maybe even to start. (Only later did I realize that I was really just a short, slow-footed guard with a marginal jump shot.) After this latest Did Not Play, I stormed into the house and shouted at my parents, "This is bullshit. I'm quitting."

Now, Dad didn't play much basketball growing up. He didn't know about pick-and-rolls and how to play weak-side defense. Still, he sat me down and said, "You're part of a team, Matthew. You go to practice, you practice hard, and you may get a break. But by going to practice and practicing hard, your team gets better. So if the coach is playing what he thinks is the best five, then that's what the coach is doing. And then after the season, if you decide you don't want to play next year, fine. But you made a commitment to the team, and you don't quit on them. You never quit."

At the time I thought he was only talking about basketball.

---

The paramedics raced down 52nd Street before taking a left and heading north up First Avenue. Within five minutes the ambulance pulled into the emergency entrance of New York–Presbyterian, on York Avenue and 68th Street. Through the years I had been in the hospital visiting injured firefighters plenty of times. If you ever got hurt on the job, the hope was that you would end up at New York–Presbyterian. The hospital is affiliated with both Columbia and Cornell medical schools, so the doctors are among the finest in the country. Plus its burn unit, as a lot of firefighters have discovered, offers some of the best treatment in the city.

But today I wasn't paying a social call. I was dying.

The paramedics rushed me into the emergency room, where the medical staff—at that hour it was mostly interns and residents—immediately realized what a disaster I was. Blood gushed from multiple tears in my body, the packs that the paramedics had placed around my open gut having already become worthless to stanch the hemorrhaging. An almost uninterrupted ribbon of red on the floor marked my path from the hospital entrance to the triage room. As the ER team tried to repack my wounds and stem the bleeding, the chief resident on duty paged the hospital's chief trauma surgeon, Dr. Soumitra Eachempati, who got the alert as he was walking to the hospital from his home, three blocks south. When he heard how dire I was, Dr. Eachempati didn't hesitate. "Get him to the OR. I'll meet you there. I'm five minutes away."

The next call went out to Dr. Dean Lorich, the hospital's chief orthopedic surgeon. Already it had become clear that the extent of my shattered bones and the hemorrhaging they were causing were life threatening and needed immediate attention. But unlike Dr. Eachempati, Dr. Lorich faced an exasperating battle getting to the hospital—with the transit strike once again to blame. He lived with his wife and two young daughters on Park Avenue and East 96th, the demarcation line below which cars with fewer than four passengers were prohibited from traveling. When he came down to the street from his apartment, Dr. Lorich first told two police officers his situation. "I'm a surgeon at New York–Presbyterian. I've got a guy dying. I need a cab to get me there right away."

But the cops looked at him blankly, until one of them said, "Sorry, Doc, rules are the rules. No exceptions."

Dr. Lorich was incensed. "You're joking, right?"

"Sorry, Doc, can't break the rules."

Dr. Lorich tried to enlist three strangers to get in a cab with him but had no luck. With options running out, he called his wife, pregnant and on bed rest, and told her to hustle downstairs with the two girls. They would fill out the four-seat requirement and drive with him to the hospital.

I had already been moved to the operating room by the time Jimmy arrived at the hospital, but he didn't know that when he rushed into the ER. He searched for me, with no luck. Finally he found a nurse. "I'm looking for Matt Long," Jimmy told her. "He came in a few minutes ago. He's a fireman."

The nurse at first didn't pay much attention to Jimmy—a bit surprising, because he stands an imposing six foot four. She just pointed to an area where some other firefighters already were waiting.

"No, you don't understand. I'm his brother," Jimmy followed up.

That must have triggered something because the nurse now looked at Jimmy. "I'm sorry. I'm very sorry. We're doing all we can for your brother," she said. "But, please, I've got to tell you—the shape he is in is as bad as it gets."

Jimmy shook when he heard that. Then he turned to his left, to a large room with a curtain half closed. He looked in and saw blood everywhere. On the floor, on the walls, on the medical equipment. He turned back to the nurse.

"Was that his room?"

She nodded.

Jimmy stammered. "My parents will be here shortly," he told her. "Can you please have that cleaned up before they get here?"

Mom and Dad arrived a few minutes later. The blood was gone.

# 4

## "WE CAN'T STOP THE BLEEDING"

It was just past 7 a.m. and two dozen doctors, residents, anesthesiologists, nurses, x-ray technicians, and interns were jammed inside the wide, rectangular operating room on the third floor of New York–Presbyterian. By now both Dr. Eachempati and Dr. Lorich had arrived. I lay in the middle of the room, unconscious on a table, bleeding through more holes than a rotted garden hose. They didn't know me or anything about me.

They didn't know that I was a New York City firefighter, a 12-year veteran of Ladder 43 in East Harlem. The best job I ever had, or ever would. You chased down fires and other trouble in big, shiny red rigs, and then, when the job was done, you headed back to the firehouse, played cards, watched TV, shot pool, planned the night's dinner, and pulled whatever prank you could to keep the other guys loose while you waited for the next call to come in. Because you always knew the next call was coming.

And the doctors didn't know that I was one of the Cronies. The senior men gave us that tag when we came to the house in the mid-'90s as young firefighters—and then became the best of friends. When we weren't on the job, we ran around together long after our shifts had ended. Pat Ginty, Tommy Corrigan, Pat Cleary, John Kelly, John Duffy, Kevin Torrey, Matty Long. *Have fun, will travel.* That was us. We played golf together, shot hoops together, skied together. Most of all, we bar-hopped around Manhattan together, staying out late and laughing all night long and looking out for the girls we might marry someday. I probably tried harder than all of the Cronies to find her. "There goes Matty again," the guys would say when they saw me chatting someone up, "casting his line out into the pond." They were lucky. They each would find the person they wanted to be with. So far, I hadn't. Maybe that's why they called me Matty Lonely.

And I'm sure these doctors didn't know about the bars I owned in the city, like Third & Long. I opened that place with Jimmy before we became firefighters. At the time I didn't have a job or much money. I was only 25 and mostly just bartending at spots around the city. Mom tried to talk me out of it. "Matt, you're a college grad. You don't need to be involved with bars," she told me. Two years later, with Jimmy and me playing bartender, bouncer, host, party planner, promoter, and dishwasher, the bar was an East Side success story. Friends from around the city stopped in, then told their friends. The place did great, especially on weekends, when the young crowd would come in for a pop before they headed to the clubs downtown, and then they would drop by for a nightcap on their way home. We liked to say that Third & Long was the place where the evening started and the night ended.

And they wouldn't have known about the Christmas dinner my sister Maureen would be hosting in a couple of days and that her house would be filled with 30 or more Longs. Moms, dads, brothers, sisters, grandparents, great-grandparents, sons, daughters, nephews, nieces. I would carve the turkey because I always carved the turkey. And then we'd play Secret Santa, passing out the gifts and laughing over who got the cheapest one.

And they didn't know that right about now I should be finishing up my last laps with Shane, Tommy, and Larry at the pool. On the way back we'd stop for coffee. Then fix breakfast in the small kitchen at the Rock. On a tiny burner I'd make omelets and oatmeal with nuts and bananas and apples. And they didn't know that the four of us would be running the Boston Marathon this coming April, and then I would start training for my next Ironman in July. I planned to use all the tips Frank Carino had given me to shave an hour off my previous Ironman time, and that would be enough to qualify for the Ironman World Championship in Kona. Only 1,700 or so people qualify each year. And I would be one of them, because that was my goal. Some friends called me the Hurricane because they never knew what I was going to do next. My family called me Matty Take Charge because I got things done. I planned to be in Kona for the World Championship next October. Because that was what I wanted to do.

No, these doctors knew none of this. And it didn't matter.

All they knew was what they saw. My body—a bloody, butchered, expiring mess. One doctor whispered that it looked as if a bomb had exploded inside my stomach. With all the blood that continued to pour out of me, these medical people figured I'd go into cardiac arrest at any moment. They wondered what state my brain was in, and wondered if I had become a vegetable already.

One doctor said I could die in seconds.

═══════════

Dr. Eachempati, as the hospital's chief trauma surgeon, took the lead in managing the proceedings. Most trauma injuries are caused by a blunt mechanism—a person gets hit by a car or is hurt when hitting the ground, say, after a fall from a ladder. The other kind of trauma is less common but often more severe. These are penetrating injuries, when someone is shot or stabbed. I won the daily double. My body had been clobbered by a 40,000-pound bus moving at upwards of 25 miles per hour; it also had been ruptured by my bike's seatpost.

The doctors assessed the damage: compound fracture of the left femur and tibia, broken left foot, broken right shoulder, all of which could have been caused by the initial collision with the bus. The more life-threatening issues had to do with the injuries around and inside my abdomen and midsection. When the bike's seatpost penetrated, it split my entire perineum down the middle, reaming through a core of eight inches of soft tissue. I was open from the base of my penis down to my anus, and my rectum had been torn. My intestines swelled so much that they bulged through the opening in my gut. The wound was so massive that the doctors could basically stick their hands through the hole into my abdomen and straight down to my anus. Bone and soft tissue should have been in the way. They were gone.

With the injury to my rectum, the stool that usually collects there seeped into my pelvis, which only caused another complication. The doctors figured I would likely need a colostomy to divert my stool and prevent massive pelvic infection, but at that point I was far too unstable to undergo such a procedure. My right pelvis, where many major arteries flow in and out of and where such nerves as the sciatic and pudendal connect through from the spine and to the legs, had been stretched and torn. A gloppy cesspool, a quagmire of my body's waste products and the blood dislodged from all these multiple injuries, collected in the remains of my pelvis. As best as they could, the doctors attempted to stop the bleeding in some of the more obvious and external wounds. But the internal ruptures, where it was more difficult to detect an egress point and where clots could begin forming, posed a delicate and dire challenge. My blood pressure, normally 110 over 70, had dropped to a dangerously low 70 over 40.

The various medical teams from orthopedics, neurology, and urology tried to patch me up, control the bleeding, and save my organs. Dr. Eachempati kept packing and compressing the blood vessels in my pelvis. Dr. Lorich and his orthopedic residents decided to put external fixators on my broken tibia and femur to stabilize those bones, planning to treat them at a later date. They set the pelvis with as much speed as they could. Then the doctors put in a suprapubic catheter to divert my urine because my urethra was completely disrupted.

As these doctors did their parts, anesthesiologists stationed at the top of the table kept me resuscitated and monitored my blood pressure. After an hour in the OR, I already had gone through six units of blood and needed more. As quickly as the nurses pumped one unit into me—each unit took about five to ten minutes—I required another one. The longer I bled, the longer the holes in my body—from the massive rupture in my abdomen to the microscopic internal tears—remained susceptible to infection. And it meant my heart had to work harder to keep circulating whatever blood I did have. I was on the clock, and the clock kept ticking.

That's when Dr. Eachempati made the decision to move me from the OR to interventional radiology. When surgeons can't stop the bleeding, the IR suite is the last resort. There, radiologists use visually assisted devices to see inside the vessels and attempt to repair them, embolizing the blood vessels that the doctors can't get to with their own hands.

It was in the IR that Vicky Tiase finally found me. Vicky was a nurse at the hospital but also a close friend. I had known her for years, ever since she started coming by the firehouse to meet up with Frank Carino. They had trained together for triathlons long before I got into the sport. Often they would take off from the house for 10- to 12-mile runs in Central Park. As soon as they got back to the firehouse, I would meet them with some water and some wisecracks. Vicky may have had a sweet all-American look to her, but she would give it right back, then say, "Catch you later, Cool Guy," and take off. Later, when I started to run seriously and train for triathlons, Frank and Vicky became two of my regular running and biking partners. She taught me more about nutrition than any diet book could. And after my first year or so of training, she admitted that besides Cool Guy, she had another name for me: Beer Belly Matty, which she stopped using when my runs and rides went longer and my waistline got smaller.

On her way to work that morning, Vicky had gotten a call from Frank alerting her about my accident. When she didn't find me in the OR, she went searching, using a trail of blood that led through the hallway of the third floor to the elevator and then up two floors to the IR. She looked into the room I was in and saw me laying there, from the neck down, my face hidden by a drape. She saw the monitor tracking my blood pressure and heart rate. A few days earlier, the two of us had run a 15-K race in Central Park. I finished in just under one hour and 11 minutes, beating her by 25 seconds. Now she was watching me—and a whole different set of numbers. She put her hands up to her mouth and cried to herself, *This can't be happening. You've got to fight this, Matty, you've got to fight. Oh, fight, please, fight.*

Her pleading, and the radiologists' efforts, only did so much. My vitals started to drop lower and lower. At one point, Vicky had to turn away. She could see my heart rate was struggling to stay at 40 beats per minute, which was well below my resting heart rate of 55.

For close to two hours the radiologists and Dr. Eachempati did the exacting work of detecting and patching holes in my vascular system. They managed to close many of them, enough so that by 10:30 Dr. Eachempati decided to move me to the intensive care unit, where the medical team would continue to try to stanch the bleeding using more traditional methods. By now I had received 21 units of blood, with my body continuing to demand more.

Around 11:30, after working on me for more than four hours, Dr. Eachempati walked out of the ICU and into the waiting area. It's the size of a small conference room, brown-paneled and windowless, just feet from the ICU. My family had been gathering there since Jimmy and my parents first arrived. My brother Chris was the next one there, rushing over from his midtown office where he worked in financial services. Eddie, who was also a firefighter, came in after his overnight shift ended at 8 a.m. The others, Michael, Robert, Frank, Maureen, and Eileen, each made it by 9:30.

But it wasn't just the Longs who filled up the waiting area. A bunch of the Cronies had come in, as well as dozens of other FDNY officials and firefighters. There were priests and nuns my parents knew. Some 50 to 60 people from my assorted worlds crammed into the room waiting to see how I was surviving—*if* I was surviving—and to support my family. For most of the morning, they had received very few updates from the doctors. Mostly what they knew came from the radio and TV, and much of it was inaccurate or scary. One radio station had reported that it was me driving the bus and that I had struck a pedestrian. And during one TV newscast, Mayor Bloomberg came on and asked New Yorkers to pray for me. "He is gravely injured," the mayor said. Maureen burst into tears when she heard that.

The mayor was only speaking the truth. And that's what Dr. Eachempati told my parents when he made his first visit to see them that day.

Dr. Eachempati, who is no more than five foot seven and a lean 150 pounds, was 39 years old at the time. A graduate of Northwestern University, he did his residency in Detroit, where he had plenty of practice with trauma cases. When he came out of the ICU, he saw my parents huddled with my brothers and sisters. They were saying the Lord's Prayer. The rest of the family stood back as the doctor gave my parents the little he could offer. He was consoling but frank. "We're doing everything we can, but your son is in very bad shape," the doctor said, then paused a second. "We just can't seem to stop the bleeding. Understand, it's very likely he's not going to make it, and I want you to be prepared for that."

Understandably, Mom wasn't. After waiting for hours for some good news, this was all he had to give her?

"Does he have any chance, Doctor?"

Dr. Eachempati gave it to her straight. "Mrs. Long, in cases like this, where the injuries are so extensive and the bleeding so massive, he has less than a 5 percent chance. We'll do all we can, but I want you to know the truth."

Mom just looked at Dad, and then at the doctor. She had raised nine kids, and she knew us all pretty well. What made us tick. Before Dr. Eachempati left them, she told him, "Doctor, I just want you to know that is my boy, and if he has a chance, he will take it. He did the Ironman. He just did the New York City Marathon. He's doing the Boston Marathon next spring. He's strong, very strong."

Dr. Eachempati did a bit of a double take when he heard Mom mention the marathons. It just so happened that he had run the New York City Marathon the same day I did. He understood the training involved, the endurance required, and, well, the effort the race places on your heart. He suddenly had a better sense of who I was and why my heart had been able to last this long.

My love for endurance sports came out of the blue, in the fall of 2003.
One night I got a call from Noel Flynn. At that point Noel and I had
known each other only a few years. He worked in banking, but we
had mutual friends in the fire department, and he was also a Third &
Long regular. He told me that he had just signed up, on a lark, to do
the St. Anthony's Triathlon—a race involving a 1.5-kilometer swim,
40-kilometer bike, and 10-kilometer run—the following spring in
St. Petersburg, Florida. He was going to use the event as a way to
raise money for a cancer charity, and now he needed to enlist friends
to do it with him. I was his first call.

"Matty, we'll train together, raise some money, have a few
laughs," he told me.

"Noel, sounds promising, don't get me wrong. Thing is, I
haven't been on a bike in years."

"Neither have I, Matty. The race organizers say they have
coaches who will work with us."

"But it's my back, too. It's been acting up lately. Pretty sore
from the weights I've been lifting."

"Matt, you need to mix up your workouts. Cross-training in
these other sports will help your back, you'll see."

"Sure, but here's the deal, and don't let this out, got it?"

"What's up, Matt?"

"I sink when I swim, Noel. My arms move like windmills, but I
don't go anywhere. I just sink. It's been that way since I was a kid.
I never learned how to do it right." The phone went silent for a second. "Noel, there's no way I'd be able to handle the swim."

"Matt, I told you. They work with you on everything—the
running, the biking, and especially the swim." Then he paused. "I

don't know, seems like you have a lot of excuses. I'm just wondering, are you scared to try this or something?"

Scared? He didn't want to go there.

"Noel, you calling me scared? Okay, you got me. Where do I sign up?"

Jimmy used to say that I brought 1,000 milligrams of Matty Long to everything I did. Once I told Noel I was in for the triathlon, those 1,000 milligrams raged. I signed up for swimming lessons, then I bought my first bike in 20 years, the Trek 2200, for $1,400. When Tommy Corrigan, one of the Cronies who Noel and I had recruited to do the triathlon with us, saw my Trek for the first time, he laughed out loud. "Matty, a $1,400 bike? What are you thinking? You're going to be one-and-done when we finish this."

Tommy had some history to back up that prediction. You see, I wasn't a complete novice to endurance sports. I ran the New York City Marathon for the first time in 1996, but I did it then not to lose weight or to qualify for the Boston Marathon or even for the free T-shirt. No, I did it to impress a woman. Her name was Maggie, and we knew each other from Breezy Point, a beach town out in the Rockaways in Queens, where both our families had small summer houses. She also used to come into Third & Long now and then with her friends. We started seeing each other that July, and on one of our first dates she told me that she planned to do the marathon that fall with her friend Kat—and she wanted to go pretty fast, maybe break four hours. I told her that I could get into the race through the fire department.

"I'll run it with you, Maggie," I said. "It'll be fun." Then I wished I had kept my mouth shut.

I had just 12 weeks to get ready; most recreational runners need at least 16 weeks of slow and gradual buildup of mileage before attempting the 26.2-mile distance. I had no business doing what I was trying to do, and it showed. After one long training run, an 18-miler, Maggie's mother caught a glimpse of me. I was doubled over and barely breathing. "You're going to kill that boy," she told Maggie later.

On Marathon Sunday, Maggie, Kat, and I managed to stay together through 24 miles; for a while I was feeling so good that I was actually sprinting to the aid stations to pick up cups of water for the girls so they didn't need to stop. But then, as we made our way through Central Park, my stomach began to wrench and my head got woozy. I started to slow down, and I told the girls to go on without me. They had a time to beat, which they did: Maggie and Kat finished in 3:55. I came in seven minutes later, dazed and hunched over.

The next day, at the firehouse, Tommy kept reminding me, "Matty, in case you didn't know, you lost to your girlfriend yesterday."

That's not all I lost. A few weeks later Maggie and I broke up. And it would be a long time before I had a reason to run that far for that long.

The St. Anthony's Triathlon provided it. I finished the race in 2 hours and 42 minutes, and I felt strong the whole way. I even did well in the swim leg, once I figured out how to stay away from all the other competitors' kicking feet and flailing arms. That summer and fall I signed up for a dozen more triathlons. The sport hooked me, hard, as if it were my latest girlfriend. The training, the competing, and even the parties these triathletes threw afterward all offered something fresh and intense. I hired coaches to make me a better runner and, yes, an adequate swimmer. I went to Lake Placid that summer to watch Frank and Vicky compete in the Ironman and started planning on how I could ramp up to race in that event, too.

In a short amount of time I got fitter and faster, and kept looking for the next challenge.

———

After spending those brief minutes with my parents, Dr. Eachempati returned to the ICU, and for the next seven hours, he, Dr. Lorich, and the other medical professionals continued to work on me. When Dr. Lorich first met my parents later that day, he told them, "As long as he's breathing, then we're going to keep working on him." And then he gave Mom and Dad a small smile.

Those hours featured a cascade of overlapping maneuvers and push-and-pull dynamics. Dr. Eachempati barking orders, and everyone following: "You, hang this IV. You, run to the blood bank and get the next four units of blood. You, order these meds. You, call x-ray and get them over here. You, pull up the last set of blood draws. Is that blood count that I asked for back yet? Have the factors gone in, do we need more IV access for more meds? Is that catheter in place?"

But for all the energy expended, the results were frustratingly minute. At 6 p.m., 12 hours after my accident, my blood pressure still hovered around 70 over 40, and that was with more than 35 units of blood having been pumped into me. The typical human circulates about one and a half gallons of blood throughout the body. By this point, four times that amount had left my system. Dr. Eachempati, Dr. Lorich, and the other attending doctors were stumped. They thought they had found every wound that could be causing the bleeding. But I still wouldn't stop bleeding.

Finally, Dr. Eachempati made the decision to return me to the OR where he and his residents found multiple bleeding blood vessels. They also repacked my pelvis and then had to decide about the colostomy. Throughout the day Dr. Eachempati and Dr. Lorich, using just their hands, kept cleaning my pelvis. It had been hours since my last big meal—dinner the night before at Debo's—but it didn't matter. Regardless of when or what someone eats, the intestines continually turn over their linings, producing waste that must be eliminated. The waste contains contaminants, and if they are not released from the body properly, they can poison the system. As much as the doctors tried, they couldn't keep this poison from collecting in my pelvic area. It presented Dr. Eachempati with a dilemma: He needed to stop the waste from seeping into my pelvis, otherwise it could kill me. But to do so, he would have to perform a colostomy, diverting my bowel movements from the natural way of egress and instead through a new hole he would open on the left side of my abdominal wall where the waste would collect in an IV bag. The inherent complication with the latter was that there were no guarantees that a colostomy could be reversed— if I lived, that is. Ultimately, with the possibility of toxic shock looming, Dr. Eachempati performed the colostomy. Then I went back to IR, where the doctors spent another hour looking for more microscopic tears that might be sources of the continual bleeding.

By close to 11 p.m. the bleeding was, finally and for the most part, under control. I had received 48 units of blood in a 17-hour span. An extraordinary amount. I returned to the ICU in critical but stable condition.

Just before midnight, a nurse brought my parents and then pairs of my siblings in to see me. I was unconscious, my chest sliced open, my sheets stained in red. I was alive, barely.

And I looked nothing like an Ironman.

# 5

# BAR NONE

Throughout the city on Thursday, December 22, 2005, New Yorkers faced the consequences of the ongoing transit strike. A Brooklyn musician was forced to walk seven miles to a performance in Manhattan, with a 65-pound tuba saddled to his back. A mother and daughter got fleeced by a cab driver who charged them $50, twice the normal fare, for a ride from Lincoln Center to their home in Brooklyn Heights. And a baker in lower Manhattan lost $1,200 in business when he couldn't deliver his doughnuts and crullers to customers because more cars than normal choked the city's streets.

All those people, obviously, endured a frustrating, draining day. But sadly, I had them all beat. I got run over by a 20-ton bus. And at the end of that day, I lay flat on my back in room 413 in the intensive care unit at New York–Presbyterian Hospital, my eyes closed, so sedated that I might as well have been in a coma. My midsection was spread open, dissected like a frog in a high school science experiment, with my abdomen filleted and pinned to my sides so that the next day doctors could continue digging in and maneuvering through my exploded perineum. And now, instead of the bicycle seatpost that had gored me at the start of this day, a metal rod the length of a coat hanger protruded from the hole between my sternum and where my belly button used to be. It was an external fixator, there to keep my shattered pelvis intact as it began the long process of healing. I had two similar fixators attached to my left leg, one to my broken tibia and one to my broken femur. Medically treated bandages and adhesives covered a swatch of my right hip, where a six-inch-by-six-inch piece of skin had been shorn away. A ventilator tube was inserted down my throat, IV tubes pierced my arms, a colostomy bag hung from my left side, and two catheters drew urine from me. It was undetermined at that time if the damage done to my penis, rectum, and other below-the-waist organs would ever allow them to function as they once did.

Yes, I had had quite a day.

And it was all because 35,000 transit workers decided to go on strike five days before Christmas—and made me and millions of other New Yorkers change the way we went about our lives. Then, as if to pour salt on my wounds, a little over five hours after the bus had crushed me, the strikers announced an end to their job action.

Publicly, negotiators for the Metropolitan Transportation Authority, the state agency that oversees the buses and subways, and the Transport Workers Union, which represented the striking workers, said they had been negotiating throughout the previous night and into the morning. Finally, just around 11 a.m., they agreed to a return-to-work settlement that would allow the two sides to continue talking about a new contract while the workers returned to their jobs. On the surface, a real kumbaya moment. But my family and friends, waiting and pacing just outside the ICU, and wondering if I would survive, grumbled that the settlement was purely a face-saving attempt in light of my situation and the horrific mess ensnarling the city. For days, many New Yorkers, politicians, and those in the media had derided the transit union for its actions and the grandstanding of its president, Roger Toussaint. The strike, first of all, was illegal. Toussaint and the strikers broke a long-standing state statute, called the Taylor Law, that prohibits public employees like police officers, teachers, and, yes, firefighters, from calling a job action. The Taylor Law can be a numbing impediment to labor negotiations, preventing unions from playing the ultimate trump card—not showing up for work—when bargaining for a new deal. Those of us in the FDNY knew that all too well. Less than a year after 9/11, with firefighters still enjoying a big bear hug from the people of New York and around the world because of our losses at the World Trade Center, the city and the firefighters union began to negotiate a new contract to replace a deal set to expire on June 30, 2002. That date came and went with no new agreement; it would be nearly four years before both sides reached a new contract, a period during which we lived with the same pay scale negotiated years earlier. For many of the nearly 9,000 firefighters in the department, that delay hit their wallets hard. But as tempting as the notion of calling a strike was, we never even considered it.

We didn't break the law.

Roger Toussaint must have read some other version of the Taylor Law—one that exempted transit workers from the no-strike mandate. Or maybe he was just plain arrogant. Whatever his motives, when his members went on strike, the consequences left the city reeling. First off, a judge immediately fined the union $1 million for each day members remained on strike. These people, of course, were striking over money; they wanted a pay raise, and they didn't want policies regarding their pension changed. Instead, they ended up forfeiting $2.5 million in fines. And the strike drew Mayor Bloomberg into a war of words with Toussaint and his members. During one press conference the mayor said the union leadership had acted "thuggishly." That remark only riled Toussaint and his followers more, with some suggesting that Bloomberg's rhetoric was racially motivated because minorities overwhelmingly constituted the union's membership. Toussaint fired back by comparing his fight with that of Rosa Parks and Dr. Martin Luther King Jr. At one point he said, "There is a higher calling than the law. That is justice and equality." Some justice. During the 60 hours of the strike, city businesses lost approximately $100 million. Kids missed school. Supplies of blood ran dangerously low because donors couldn't get to the blood banks.

And I was left to tap heavily into those depleted blood storages, the recurring transfusions keeping me alive in spite of my 5 percent odds.

From the point of my accident, local TV reporters covered my story and its life-or-death plot line right from the hospital. And the next day, the city newspapers weighed in. "Biking Bravest Struck Down by Bus" shouted the headline from the *New York Post*. The *New York Times*, with its story "Firefighter on Bicycle Hurt in Crash with Charter Bus," ran a photo of me from just before the start of the marathon, six weeks earlier. It showed me hamming it up for the camera, posing like a bodybuilder, flexing my left biceps, a goofy smile creasing my face.

All the stories wrote of my condition ("critical but stable," "grave"), the amount of blood I had already been given, and why I was on a bike that day. Jimmy was the family member most often quoted. When asked why I was biking to work that day, he told a reporter from the *Post*, "It was the easiest way for Matt to get around the city with the strike happening. Everyone was told to find other means to get to work, so he did." In one way, Jimmy was just doing his job as a spokesman for the FDNY and on behalf of a fallen firefighter. But his words spoke to how well he knew this particular firefighter. The Long Twins—that's what people used to call us. Or Hurricane Matty and Serious Jim. Or Oscar and Felix. We didn't care what people called us; we knew who we were: brothers and best friends, always.

Suddenly, though, with me lying in a hospital bed, barely alive, *always* didn't ring with as much certainty. But Jimmy didn't let on. "He's a fighter," Jimmy told one reporter. "He always has been."

If anyone knew that, it was Jimmy.

═══════════

"Matty! Matty! Matty!"

On a winter night in 1989, the 20 or so friends among the basketball crowd at Iona College kept chanting my name. They were college buddies and friends from Brooklyn, and Jimmy was there, too. I pretended not to hear them. I rarely played that one season I made the varsity team at Iona, a small Division I school just north of the city. I was known as a 20-20 guy. If we were up by 20 points or down by 20, I had a chance to see some action. Otherwise I just sat on the bench. But that night I decided to juice up the crowd some. So I jumped up from the bench and started to take off my maroon and gold warm-ups, as if the coach had actually called my number and wanted me in the game. My buddies went ballistic.

"Matty! Matty! Matty!"

But then I sat back down, and you could hear the fellows groan. I smiled to myself. *Got 'em.* I turned and found Jimmy and gave him the look. Left eyebrow tilted up. Head cocked to the right. The left side of the smile nudged upward, slightly creased. He'd seen it millions of times, the look that said, "Got to have fun, bro." And he cracked up.

Basketball and Jimmy. They were my two constant companions as a kid. Growing up, Jimmy and I played hoops all the time, no matter the season, no matter the setting. When we lived in Cypress Hills our backyard had no basket, but that didn't stop us. We would play in front of the house, just Jimmy and me, until late at night, dribbling under the streetlights, trying to drive by the other one, winning a point by getting a foot on the curb. We'd elbow each other, shove each other, and call each other for fouls. The games usually ended when a foul got too hard and a fight broke out. Once we moved to Bay Ridge, and we had a hoop right outside the back door, the games got even longer and the action more intense. One time things got pretty chippy, and we started hurling the ball back and forth at each other. Finally, Jimmy became so annoyed that he kicked it at me, but he ended up punting it over my head and the ball crashed through the window of the house next door. He looked at me, I looked at him, and we both knew what to do: scram. Eventually we owned up to breaking the neighbor's window—and then got back to the game because we never let the fights last too long. There was too much playing to be done.

In grade school we joined church teams around Cypress Hills, and in the summer we went to basketball camps. I was the scrappy, jabbering point guard, Jimmy the dependable low-post threat. We used to go everywhere together with our basketballs, and usually we had our best friend, Ray Paprocky, a kid who lived down the block, with us. We became the Three Amigos. At lunch, at recess, you name it, we were dribbling basketballs, and after school we ran home, got changed, and played hoops until it was too dark to see.

Not much could stop the Amigos. The one time when the gears shifted was Friday night. That's when we all met at the Haven Theatre, an old, run-down single-movie house a couple of miles from home. But for two bucks, the price was right. We must have seen *Star Wars* half a dozen times at the Haven. Then, when we got home, Jimmy and I would head to the bedroom we shared with Michael and Robert—yes, four boys in a single room; it was so tight it felt like we were sleeping in an Apollo space capsule—and stayed up talking about the movie we just saw or some story Ray had told us earlier in the night or, of course, basketball. The conversations never went too deep. Occasionally, we might talk about what we wanted to do when we grew up. Jimmy had an inkling he wanted to be a cop or a firefighter; I wanted a job in Manhattan, maybe something on Wall Street. It didn't matter really what it was. I just wanted to be in the city. Even as a kid I knew Manhattan offered something no place else, even neighboring Brooklyn, could. Sometimes Dad would take us into Manhattan for dinner, and once we crossed over the Brooklyn Bridge and started maneuvering around the traffic and racing other cars to grab a parking space on a crowded street, and then walking into a restaurant with maître d's and with waiters rushing around taking orders, and then hearing all the talk over the clanging plates and glasses—the excitement just sparked an appetite for more.

But again, Jimmy and I didn't think too far ahead; we thought about tomorrow and what was in store. We were always that close. Even though 14 months separated us, they might as well have been 14 minutes. I can remember coming home from kindergarten one day in 1971, and there was Jimmy waiting for me, his nose poking through the metal fence in front of our red brick house, where we had moved when the apartment above the ice cream parlor got too tight for the ever-expanding Long family. He wasn't allowed to go outside the fence, so he would just look down the block searching for me to turn the corner for home. By 1977, all he had to do was poke his head into the other fifth-grade class to find me. I had been kept back because of my poor reading. At first my ego took a bruising. But when I realized Jimmy and I would be classmates together from that point forward, the situation took on a whole new look. We were now officially the Long Twins. Me, the hyperactive, fast-talking kid with a mop of black hair pushing the pedal. Jimmy, a little more reserved, a little slower to show his cards, but ready and willing to do anything, anytime.

One such occasion came early in high school. Just before we

were to start our freshman year at Christ the King, a Catholic school with a strong basketball reputation, the teachers went on strike. The longer the strike lasted, the later the school year would go, and the more it would cut into summer vacation, an unappealing option for two guys who lived to be outdoors. So Mom and Dad pulled us from Christ the King and enrolled us in the local public high school, Franklin K. Lane, which was known for being a bit rough-edged and cliquish. If you wanted to be with the in crowd, for instance, you dressed a certain way—in the right jeans or the coolest sneakers. On our first day Jimmy and I wore our Christ the King uniforms: corduroy pants, collared shirts, and black leather shoes. "We bought those clothes for school," Mom had said the night before classes started, "so you're wearing them to school." Jimmy and I followed Mom's orders, then got taunted by the thugs at school who threatened to beat us up if we continued wearing those kinds of clothes.

When we got home that night, I told Jimmy, "That's never happening again." The next day, we dressed in our Catholic school clothes, said good-bye to Mom, and got on the bus to school. But this time, we jumped off one stop early. We ducked into a pizzeria and changed into the jeans and sneakers we had stashed in our book bags. No one at Franklin K. Lane High School ever bugged us again about our clothes.

A year later Jimmy and I transferred to Bishop Ford High School, another Catholic school, but this one was an easier commute to and from our new home in Bay Ridge. We made the junior varsity basketball team our first year at Ford, which helped ease our way into a new circle of friends, although I also made sure to socialize with kids from all over the school—musicians in the band, kids who performed in the school plays, the smart eggs in the honor society, and, of course, the cheerleaders. Some of the jocks wondered why I hung out with such a mix of people. "Guys,"

I told them, "everyone has a story, and I like hearing them."

Unfortunately, my basketball story—at least the one I had created in my head—never materialized. I had fantasized that Jimmy and I would be hoop heroes, leading Bishop Ford to city titles with our pestering defense and clutch shooting. That college powerhouses from around the East would hear about Matty Long, the slick guard with the quick-release jumper, and Jimmy Long, the beefy forward who could grab every rebound in his zip code, and offer us four-year scholarships. As it turned out, only part of the story came true.

Jimmy, who had sprouted a couple of inches over me—he was up to six foot three—earned a spot on his college team at the City University of New York. But no schools showed interest in me, so for the first three years of college, I watched games enviously from the stands as just a fan. Growing up, I had dreamed of playing college basketball, of playing in big arenas like Madison Square Garden, of being in the team photos that line the walls of most college gyms. Through my first three years of college, though, it seemed like that dream had no chance of coming true.

Then, the summer before my senior year at Iona, I worked on my game every day. I practiced my jump shot in the backyard, ran sprints up and down our block in Bay Ridge, and got into the best shape I could. I worked as hard as anyone ever did to get something he always wanted: the chance to someday tell my kids that their dad had played college ball. Through the first four days of tryouts, I showed up earlier than anyone else, then hustled more than anyone on the court. The effort paid off. On the last day of tryouts, the coach, Gary Brokaw, pulled me aside and told me I had earned my spot. I wouldn't see much playing time, I wouldn't travel to many road games. But I had a jersey—number 20—and the chance to give my buddies something to root for, and Jimmy something to laugh about.

When Jimmy and I went to different colleges, it meant that for the first time the Long Twins were going their separate ways. But we never lost touch.

We called each other almost every night. Whenever I could I would drive down to Staten Island and watch his games, and he would introduce me to his new friends—a lot of city kids who were the sons of firemen and cops. Then, when he came to visit me at Iona, in a tony part of Westchester County, I took him to the bars where I was starting to get regular bartending work—like Striders and Gary's and Bumpers—and had him meet my new buddies, mostly guys with ambitions of making it big in the city. For all the differences among our friends, whenever we all got together, everyone got along. Future cops and firefighters mixing easily with would-be Wall Street hotshots and city slickers. The formula worked; in fact, it worked so well that when Jimmy and I opened Third & Long, it became the secret of our early success.

We launched the bar on a Wednesday night, about 10 days before Christmas, in 1991. Third & Long satisfied to a T my idea of the quintessential bar: a place, right in midtown Manhattan, where young professionals and folks just out of college could kick back without any pretension. Where guys coming in after a softball game could comfortably hang out with midtown lawyers and advertising executives and media types enjoying a drink before everyone headed home or out to dinner.

It wouldn't be a fancy nightclub with techno music and strobe lights and $20 cover charges. No, I wanted it to feel like a neighborhood hangout, the Irish pub of everyone's college days. It was maybe the length and width of a basketball court, just enough room for 80 people, tops. When you entered through the swinging front doors, you stepped right up to the bar—26 feet of mahogany with three brass towers pouring 18 different types of beer, from stout to lager. A half dozen TVs rimmed the walls so you could watch games from all around the country. Or you could sit near the jukebox in the tiny lounge in the back and just sing along to the tunes.

Mostly, I wanted Third & Long to be a friendly spot, a place you felt comfortable walking into by yourself, a place that people called their home base. Jimmy and I certainly felt that way. A couple of years after we had opened the place and had gone on to join the FDNY, we put up two black-glass mirrors behind the bar. Each had a Celtic cross and a fire helmet etched into the glass, one for Jimmy's company, Ladder 16, and one for mine, Ladder 43. And next to them we hung a vintage poster from Rockaway Playland, the old-time amusement park where we used to go as kids. The helmets and the poster told our story: two Irish firefighters, two brothers, from New York City.

On opening night I didn't know what kind of crowd, if any, to expect. Afraid it might turn into a bust, I called a friend from Deloitte & Touche. I had worked at the accounting firm right out of college, and failed so miserably at deciphering balance sheets and financial statements that I was canned after 18 months. But I stayed in touch with a number of people there, so when I looked to drum up business for the first night, I lobbed a call into one of my friends. It just so happened his department's Christmas party was that night. "Matty," my friend said, "no worries. A crew will be there before our party. See you at 6 p.m." Sure enough, we opened to a near-capacity house, and when I finally closed up, on a high from an exceptional night, I remember thinking, *This bar business is like a bank. People come in and hand over their cash.*

If it had only continued to be that easy. A few nights later was Christmas Eve, and I was alone behind the bar, serving beers to an old man who had no place to go. I kept peeking at the front door hoping someone would join Gramps and me. No one did. Finally, around 10 p.m., I told the old man last call. Then I headed to Brooklyn to spend Christmas Eve with my family.

When I walked in, Dad said, "What are you doing here? I thought you'd be working the bar?"

"Slow night, Dad. I shut her down early. I'd rather be home with you guys tonight."

It may have been Christmas Eve, but Dad was in no holiday mood. He gave it to me straight, straight from a man who had babysat small shops all his life. "Matt, you wanted to be in the bar business, so let me remind you: Bars don't make money when they're closed. Get used to the long nights, kid, otherwise you'll be out of business by Saint Paddy's Day."

Jimmy and I quickly put our heads together. We knew, at least from the outset, that we couldn't depend on a walk-in crowd. We needed to spread the word to our different circles. So we contacted old friends from Cypress Hills and from Bishop Ford. Jimmy reached out to his buddies from college, and I did the same with the Iona crowd. We figured if we could bring in a dozen folks most nights from each of these groups, the bar would be at least half filled. And a bar with a little life can tease outsiders off the street.

Well, our pals came in and they kept coming back, bringing new friends. They came on weekends, when the jukebox cranked the loudest; Jimmy was in charge of filling it early in the night and never letting it go quiet. They came midweek, a time when bars can struggle. Then we started attracting a whole set of new faces by trying every promotion we could think of. One night we walked around Madison Square Garden during a college basketball game passing out fliers; after the game, more than 100 fans crowded into the bar. Then we turned Tuesdays into Dollar Bud Night and watched a bunch of young (and frugal) customers make us their regular hangout.

But our big break came one night in 1992, when we had been open maybe two months. Joe O'Laughlin, a friend I had working behind the bar with me a couple of nights a week, told me about a fellow named Terry Brennan. Joe talked about Terry as if he were Paul Bunyan: a big redhead—five foot ten, 220 pounds, with a six-foot smile. T-Red, as he went by, told funny stories to customers and, just as important, listened to all of theirs. The way Joe put it: "You put T-Red behind the stick, his fans are sure to follow." He sounded too good to be true, but too tantalizing not to try out. So on a Saturday night, I put Terry behind the bar with Joe and Mike Lang, another regular tender. Then I froze. From 7 p.m. to well past midnight, 400 people spilled in and out of the bar. Jimmy and I weren't prepared; by 10:30 our kegs were running dry. I shot uptown and raced into a friend's bar, shouting, "I need beer!" Within minutes I had five kegs loaded into a cab and raced back downtown. We tapped them seconds after I got back into the bar. Then for the rest of the night I watched as T-Red refilled beer mugs and cocktail glasses faster than a short-order cook flipping burgers.

Around 2 a.m. I looked over at Jimmy and simply mouthed, "He stays." Jimmy nodded back. Third & Long was off and running.

Jimmy and I made good partners. We had worked in Dad's ice cream parlor during high school, so we had a sense for business. We also played off each other's personalities: Jimmy, the two-feet-on-the-ground guy, made sure we managed the place with some degree of professionalism; I, the P.T. Barnum, drew the buzz, devising the next promotion and making sure everyone who came in had a good time. It wasn't always perfect. Some months making the rent could get dicey. And more than once the two of us argued about how best to run the joint. We could get loud and intense. But like the days when we were playing basketball as kids, and the games got chippier and the fouls got harder, Jimmy and I always seemed to find a way to recover, and recover quickly.

Nothing could break up the Long Twins.

———

Jimmy couldn't help it when he first saw me in the ICU that night. No matter how much the doctors had warned him, he teared up the moment he stepped into my room, monitors beeping, doctors and nurses rushing around. I didn't look myself. With the amount of fluid displacement I had suffered, my face and head had blown up to the size of a basketball, and my eyes, even if I had been awake and could open them, were swollen shut. My bike helmet had apparently protected my head from any trauma, but it was unknown whether the blood loss had created any permanent brain damage.

Jimmy had come into the room with Eddie, my youngest brother and the third firefighter in the family. Eddie stood by my bed wondering how, after so many hours, my sheets could still be so bloody. He whispered, "Be tough, Matty. You're going to get through all this. Everyone's pulling for you."

The two kept their visit short, a couple of minutes at most, and then rotated out so all the other siblings could take a turn. Each brother and sister said something to me, not knowing if they might be the last words they shared. Eileen, the elder of my two sisters, came in with her husband, Joe. She was three months pregnant with her first child, and it was the end of a long day. Still, as was typical of Eileen's upbeat, rat-a-tat manner, she gave me a short recap of the world at that moment.

"Mom and Dad are doing fine," she said, staring over me. "You have a couple of injuries; the doctors are taking great care of you. You're strong, Matty; you'll get better, just wait. You're going to get through this." And then she gave me a kiss on my forehead.

Moments later, as Eileen left the hospital for the night, she said to herself, *Oh, God, Matty's gonna die*, and said another prayer.

━━━━━━━━

I made it through that first night, but there was no guarantee I would make it through the next.

The bleeding, so profuse on the day of the accident, remained under control until the next morning, when Dr. Eachempati changed the dressings around my stomach. Then, like a scab that starts to bleed once a bandage is peeled away, my midsection commenced hemorrhaging. Through the morning I received several more units of blood, pushing my two-day total to 69. But remarkably, once Dr. Eachempati completed the repacking of the abdomen, that was the end of the transfusions. There would be no repeat of the previous day's bloodbath.

I also did not return to the OR that day. Dr. Eachempati and Dr. Lorich had determined that after all I had been through, my body needed some rest. My blood pressure had improved considerably. Still, the threat of infection concerned the doctors. At any moment sepsis or pneumonia could take charge of my system, potentially muting the lifesaving work of the day before.

The next day, Christmas Eve, was a different story. The fractures I had sustained to my legs and shoulder had initially been treated with temporary fixtures; those injuries took a backseat to the more excessive and critical ones, my shattered pelvis and battered soft-tissue organs. Prior to my accident Dr. Lorich had planned to leave the city with his family for the holidays. Instead, he stayed in town, scheduling surgery for December 24. Dr. Lorich was an acclaimed orthopedic specialist, a graduate of the University of

Pennsylvania whose career had sent him to some of the most intense trauma centers in the world. He had even spent time at Landstuhl Regional Medical Center in Germany, the hospital where many critically wounded American soldiers pass through on their way home from Iraq and Afghanistan. As such, he had a baseline for how severe my injuries were. He compared mine to what a soldier might suffer if struck by a mortar shell. On the day of the accident, he worked mostly on my pelvis, stabilizing it to help control blood loss as best as the emergency conditions allowed. Only time would tell if my pelvis would heal close to normal. On Christmas Eve Dr. Lorich operated on my left leg. I had used that leg to run races as long as 26.2 miles, to do triathlons of 11 hours, and to climb narrow ladders to the roofs of burning buildings. Now, with compound fractures to the tibia and femur, it was in pieces.

By 3 p.m., the surgery completed, I was wheeled back to my room in the ICU. I spent Christmas Eve on a ventilator, asleep and sedated.

# 6

# LETTERS FROM HOME

*Christmas Eve*

*Dear Uncle Matt,*
*I just went in to see you. Everyone says you are looking so much*
*better. It's been three days and, boy, has it been hard. Stay strong;*
*you're a fighter. I miss you and love you so much. Get better soon.*
*I'll still be here waiting for you.*
*Love always, Meghan*

*Matt,*
*Sitting here with Mom, Dad, Frank, Pam, Jim, Ed, and two young*
*guys from 43. I was just in to see you. You're looking great. It's a little*
*quiet right now, but you have had so many people up here to see you all*
*day long. Terry ("T-Red") and I were just talking and he said he was*
*going to ask you to train him when you get better. That should be*
*something. Hold him to his word! You are loved by a lot of people. I'm*
*proud and lucky to have a brother like you.*
*Talk to you later, Robert*

*Matt,*
*Just have to tell you—you have a male nurse tonight. We're gonna make*
*some calls and make sure that doesn't happen again. A cutie R.N. will be*
*back ASAP.*
*Love, Pam (your favorite sister-in-law)*

Those were just a few of the messages written inside the black-covered diaries left in the waiting area of the ICU and available to anyone who wanted to scribble a note to me, in the hope that I would have a chance to read them someday. The guys from the firehouse had the idea to start the Black Books, as they came to be known. A few years earlier, Mike Foley, a firefighter from our house, ended up in New York–Presbyterian for several weeks recovering from extensive burns he had suffered during a flashover fire. Back then we picked up a ruled ledger so Mike's family and friends could leave messages for him, chronicling what he was missing as he convalesced. As you flipped through the pages, though, it seemed each message told of what the writer was missing—namely, Mike.

The Black Books gave my family something to do when, really, there was so little for them to do. Except wait. And they were just one of many gestures the FDNY, and particularly the guys from Engine 53/Ladder 43, provided my family. Each day off-duty firefighters took turns driving Mom and Dad back and forth from the hospital. In all five boroughs of New York, firehouses staged blood drives in my name to help replenish the shortage caused by the transit strike. Then there were the meals. Firefighters kept my family and anyone who came to visit them plenty fed; each day while I was in the hospital, a house delivered lunch and dinner to my family. Kevin Torrey, one of my closest friends, became the Ladder 43 liaison for my care. He coordinated all these efforts, including scheduling a firefighter to stay outside my door at all times, serving as a personal assistant to my family and a bodyguard of sorts for me. It was as if I were Don Vito Corleone in *The Godfather*.

During the first couple of days, Kevin and the other Cronies never left the hospital except to go home for a shower and to get their shifts covered. They did what friends do, but also what firefighters understand is their responsibility when one of their own goes down. They rallied around a brother, a tradition within the department as old and continuous as the shield on our helmets.

———

I'll never forget my first day as a firefighter—not because I made some lifesaving rescue or helped put out a raging high-rise fire. If it had only been so routine.

I reported to Ladder 43, on Third Avenue and 102nd Street, at 3 p.m. sharp, just an hour or so after graduating from the academy and in full uniform: navy blue polyester suit with the 43 company patch on the right side; light blue, military-style dress shirt and navy polyester tie; black patent-leather shoes. As I walked in I could feel every eyeball in the house on me. The crew on duty wore their simple, department-issued daily fatigues: navy blue T-shirt and shorts. Meanwhile, I looked like some lost guard from the Tomb of the Unknown Soldier. After a few introductions, a couple of guys gave me a quick tour of the house, then told me to head upstairs to see the lieutenant.

When I got to his office, the door was open. I looked in and saw a guy with fire hydrants for forearms sitting behind the desk. I knocked on the side of the door. All I heard back was "Yeah."

"Lieutenant, it's probationary firefighter Matthew Long reporting for assignment," I said. And I offered a hand salute.

Fire Hydrant Arms didn't look up; he just motioned me into his office, then simply said, "Sit down." Which I did on the double. For what seemed like an hour but probably was less than 60 seconds, I sat there dead silent while he did paperwork. Finally, and still without looking up, he started firing questions at me. "Where you from, Long? Where did you go to school, Long? Why did you want to be a firefighter, Long? How did you get assigned here, Long?" I could feel my knees shaking as I tried to keep up with the barrage. Fire

Hydrant Arms kept scribbling, his eyes locked on the paper, not once glancing up.

The inquisition went on for another couple of minutes, when suddenly the lieutenant pushed his chair back, stood up, and walked from behind his desk. My eyes popped out like ping-pong balls. I couldn't believe it. The man had nothing on below the belt but boxer shorts. My head stayed still but my eyes followed him. He shut the office door.

*Uh-oh*, I thought. *What the hell is going on here?*

Then he sat back down and began to pepper me again. I answered his questions as best as I could, but I couldn't stop thinking of what I had just seen: this lieutenant in his Joe Boxers.

Finally, after a few more minutes, he told me to go back downstairs and get to work. No handshake, no nothing. I bolted out of there faster than the Road Runner.

Moments later, my head still spinning while some of the guys showed me another part of the house, I felt a tap on my shoulder. I turned. It was Fire Hydrant Arms—and he had pants on. "Hey, Long," he said, kind of casually, "I'm Greg Forsyth, nice to meet you. By the way, I ain't no lieutenant. Just a firefighter, like you." Then he smiled. "Welcome to 43!" And then the rest of the guys broke out laughing.

Yes, welcome to 43 and to life in the firehouse. A life of pranks and put-ons and ball breaking, of water bucket tricks and fake phone calls and grown men acting like seventh graders. And while it's a world that forces you to always have your guard up, the antics serve a purpose: to test just how thick your skin really is. To see if you will crack, lose your temper, demand revenge. And that's not acceptable. Because if you break under the silliness of the firehouse, then you're likely going to break when you're needed most: on a call or at a fire. And that's not acceptable, either.

As firefighters, we know that at any minute we could be risking our lives for complete strangers or for one of our own. So we need that bond among all 60 guys in the house. It doesn't matter if you are on the engine (the crew pumping the water and running the hoses) or on the ladder (the guys, like me, doing search, rescue, and ventilation). When we go out on a run, we must be a team. An engine man must know that the ladder will vent a building so that the heat will rise and not fry his ears while he's hosing down the flames. A ladder guy must know that someone is on the nozzle, dousing the fire, as he's crawling down a hallway or searching a bedroom. The fraternal connection evolves over the hours we spend together, eating meals together, cleaning toilets together, swabbing the bay area together, and yes, busting each other's chops together.

Those expectations become ingrained, along with the shared commitment that on any call, *We all come out alive.*

I knew little about this brotherhood or these traditions when I joined the department in 1993. Jimmy and I had taken the FDNY entrance exams years earlier, when we were still in college, simply to get Dad off our backs. For all his small government talk, Dad knew a civil service job could provide something that he never enjoyed as a small-business owner: a degree of job security and a steady income. "Just take the tests," he badgered us. "Who knows where the future will take you?" So we did and we did well. But because of a backlog of applicants, the FDNY didn't contact us for seven years. And when the call finally came, I wondered if the time was right for such a move.

At that point Third & Long had staked itself as a pretty popular midtown spot, and Jimmy and I had started thinking about opening another place. We were hitting our monthly numbers, and then some. But as I knew, and as Dad kept reminding me, the business could tank in a blink. Bars are prisoners to the whims of the city—customers relocate, rents get raised, trendier spots open—making them a here-today, shuttered-tomorrow proposition. Also, I was 27, with no retirement plan, no health insurance, and no safety net. I needed a career. The FDNY offered Jimmy and me just that—plus, we had learned, it didn't prohibit guys from owning bars on the side.

So one night I asked Jimmy, "Bro, are we in or out?"

He simply said, "Let's do it."

A few weeks later I was off to the academy—the Rock—for a three-month stint of basic training.

And the Rock was just that, basic. An off-off Broadway simulation of what might happen at a fire. The layout of the academy is like that of a Hollywood back lot, with most of the dozen or so structures just hollowed-out imitations of office buildings and brownstone apartments. Probies run hoses in and out of these fake complexes, rushing around with 100 pounds of equipment on their backs and 100 little details in their heads. But while it's instructional, the Rock can't duplicate the danger of an actual fire. That's why, as most firefighters will tell you, the real education comes when you are assigned to a house and are surrounded by the "senior men"—those firefighters with 15, 20, 25 years of experience. Men who have shaken hands with the Red Devil more times than they can count. And as dictated by the traditions of the department, the senior men make sure that no matter how long you have been on the force, 10 minutes or 10 years, you get continual on-the-job training so that when we go on a run, *We all come out alive.*

At Ladder 43, I fell under the tutelage of veterans like George Hear, Jim Sears, Johnny Colon, Kirk Lester, and Greg Forsyth, guys with decades in the department who knew more about fire than Lucifer. They could detect the cause of a blaze, whether it be rotting wood or oily rags, with a sniff of their nose. After lunch or after a call, and with no big pronouncement, they pulled us aside and tutored us. They corrected what we had done wrong on the last call or drilled into our heads what could happen on the next one. Teaching did not come under their formal job descriptions; it was just part of the tradition. They were the senior men, so they knew they were our guardians.

We needed vets like these guys in our house because we were a busy one. During a typical 24-hour shift, we might respond to 15 or 20 calls. Of course, not every one was an inferno; it could be a grandmother stuck in an elevator or kids fooling around with a call box. But you just never knew what might be at play when the ticket came in. Or what might happen once you're on the scene, especially when you're just a rookie.

Early in my first year, on a cold morning in February, we got a call about 5:30 a.m.: "Fire on the top floor of an apartment, people trapped." By the time we came within two blocks of the fire, we could smell the smoke and see the orange glow in the early morning darkness. That day I was working with the inside team as the can man—the man with the fire extinguisher—along with Bill Duffy and Captain Al Hagan, our boss. Our job: Get to the fire floor and search the adjoining apartments. When we reached the floor, Captain Al ordered Duffy and me to force open the door to apartment 6C. He would search that apartment for residents while Duffy and I moved down the hall to the next apartment. It was hot and the smoke made it hard to see. After Duffy and I searched 6B, we made our way back to the apartment where we had left Captain Al. Lying low on the floor, I said to Duffy, "He should be out by now, right?"

Duffy said, "Yeah, let's go in and check it out."

I crawled in on my belly, making a left turn along the wall before coming to a door. The smoke billowed down from the ceiling to within three feet of the floor. I opened the door—and found Captain Al in a bathroom. "Hey, shut the door!" he yelled. "I'm taking a piss in here!"

I slammed the door, and for a second, while waiting outside the bathroom door and fighting the adrenaline rush of the fire, I wondered how Captain Al could so calmly take his morning leak at a moment like this. Duffy knew the answer. "Matty, the captain's got 20 years on the job. He knows what has to be done." Then he paused. "And when you got to go, you got to go." We laughed for a second and then got back to the job.

Unfortunately, one of my next fires didn't end with a punch line. It was another top-floor fire in a housing project. I got my orders from Lieutenant Dan Thompson to head up to the fire floor and do a search and rescue. But as I moved down the smoky hallway, another firefighter forced open a door. With a swing of his ax, he accidentally broke the high-pressure hose that fed air into my mask. Suddenly I had no air coming in, and I was suffocating behind the mask. I panicked, threw off my helmet, and ripped off my mask. I needed fresh air badly, so I started backing out of the burning apartment.

But then Lieutenant Dan saw me. "What's up, Long? Where are you going?" he shouted at me.

"The hose, it broke. I'm having a hard time breathing."

"Bro, shit happens," he said. "You got to get back in there. Let's go."

I followed his order and worked without a mask for 30 minutes, with smoke burning my eyes and choking my lungs. But from experience, Lieutenant Dan knew I wasn't in danger. The stinging eyes and the grumpy lungs would be temporary. The bigger concern was the fire and the job we had to do.

In just a few months, by going to fires and listening to the senior men, I became more acclimated to this new world, and career. The days and nights of pouring beers at a corner pub seemed like a century ago. Every day I was learning how to be a fireman, and the lessons didn't have to come from a top-floor fire with Captain Al at my side. When I first got to the firehouse, I barely knew how to make a peanut-butter-and-jelly sandwich. Pretty soon I was helping to cook dinner for the entire company, preparing everything from chicken Parmesan to New England clam chowder. And I became one of the better pranksters at 43. You name it, I did it. I'd snag a new guy's shoes and rubber-cement the soles to the bottom of his locker. I'd have some fellow talking in circles with one of my crank phone calls. But my favorite was "the Bucket." I would take a pail of water, climb to the roof of the house, lean over the edge, and, when an unsuspecting firefighter approached the front of the house, let the water tumble. Splat! I did it once to Joe Torregrossa—Joe T., as everyone called him—as he was flirting with a very pretty young lady outside the house. He had just gotten her phone number and was looking smug. Then, bam! He was drenched. You could hear him yell "Long!" all throughout East Harlem. Sure, it was silly, sophomoric stuff, but it kept the guys loose and the bonds tight.

You take those relationships with you on each call, and from the wisdom of the senior men, you assemble a portfolio of best practices that you can instantly, unconsciously, riffle through when the Red Devil does get too close. Your confidence heightens, but not your cockiness. You're a basketball player who knows when it's smarter to drive to the hoop against an opponent than to pull up for a long jumper. You become instinctive, not reactive. And then, when that happens, you know you are closer to what you want to be, a senior man, ready to pass down the traditions and not just absorb them.

Maybe for me, the moment when that vision first took shape was on Christmas Eve in 2000. Around 6:30 p.m., we got called to a fire on the third floor of a project building on 104th Street. I was on the inside team, the irons man. That meant I carried the Halligan and ax, tools that will open any locked door in the city. I was with Lieutenant Greg Prial and a kid assigned to the ladder company from the engine for the night's shift. When the three of us got to the third floor and to the apartment where the fire apparently had started, we put on our masks. Then the lieutenant ordered, "We're going to the right. Matty, you stay at the door until the engine crew gets here. I got to have you by the door in case something goes wrong." While I waited, I heard someone who lived in the building yell, "No one lives there! It's vacant, it's vacant!" That was good information to have, but we still needed to check the apartment to make sure.

Finally, when the engine guys arrived, I started to make my way into the apartment. I got down on my stomach and began to crawl through the foyer. Suddenly I saw a stack of mail and newspapers on the floor. *What's that doing here?* I said to myself. *It's a vacant apartment. How did that get there?*

Instinct took over. I crawled deeper into the apartment, my chest hugging the floor to avoid the heat of the fire. Heat rises, but if it has nowhere to go, it starts coming down. This apartment was sealed tight. I made my way into the bedroom and found a guy lying on the floor. He looked to be in his seventies and was unconscious. He must have tried to put the fire out himself, then ran into the bedroom and passed out. Immediately, I radioed what I had found. "Forty-three Irons. I have a 10-45, a 10-45; man down in the back bedroom. I'm going to start dragging him out." He was big, maybe 250 pounds, and all dead weight. I pulled him from under his arms, just dragging and dragging, to the front of the apartment. He was almost at the door when Lieutenant Prial showed up. We scooped him up and got him out of the apartment and to the stairwell, where a team of firefighters helped to carry him down and out of the building to a waiting ambulance.

I visited the man two days later in the hospital. His room was filled with relatives standing around his bed. I spent only a couple of minutes with the man. His name was Rodriguez, and his family said he was doing better. "Okay, thank you," I said. Before I left, I wished everyone a Merry Christmas but never told the man that I was the fireman who had pulled him from his burning apartment.

A few weeks later I received a medal and citation for the save. It was the first of my career. When I got my award, the division chief said, "We'd like to congratulate Matt Long for a great job on this rescue. Thank you very much for keeping the traditions of the FDNY alive."

And then he placed a little pin on my jacket.

———

*Christmas Eve*

*Dear Matt,*
*There is a tremendous amount of love out here! All this love and the prayers are for you, brother. Come out and join us.*
*Love, Michael*

*Duke,*
*Just went to see you. You look damn good, my man. Tough, just like the Duke, your celluloid hero. Keep running to that finish line. You're an inspiration to us all. I saw John Andariese last night when I stopped off at Smith & Wolly's. He said, "Matty will be the inspiration for tens of thousands when he gets through this and competes again." By the way, the entire gang, including all the waiters and busboys, are asking for you.*
*Happy Christmas, T-Red*

*Matt,*
*My brother, friend, and godfather. You have taught me so much about life. You are a man who puts his all into everything he does—with work,*

*your fitness, and most of all your family. Knowing this about you, I have no doubt that you are putting your mind to the fight you have ahead, and you will win this one. The 2006 Marathon is roughly 11 months away; I hope you will be at my side at the start. Three hours and 13 minutes is a high bar that you set, and I hope to get there. I love you, and Christmas will not be the same without you and the laughs that you bring.*
*Love, Eddie*

Every family has its holiday traditions, and the Longs of Bay Ridge, Brooklyn, had ours. Every December 25, Dad pulled out his favorite red sweater. Mom assembled more Nativity scenes in her living room than there were stables in all of Bethlehem. And Jim Gay—or Uncle Jim as we called him even though he wasn't related to us; he had gained honorary family status by being one of Dad's best friends for 40 years—arrived for dinner with a container of shrimp from Costco big enough to feed Dad's old Marine battalion.

I also had my own holiday rituals. I would arrive back at home on Christmas Eve in time for a late dinner with the folks, then join them for midnight Mass. After church we'd sit around the living room with a glass of wine and carols on in the background, before wrapping the last gifts for the nephews and nieces. By 3 a.m. or so I would head up to the third floor and to my old bedroom, the one I had shared years earlier with Michael, Jimmy, and Robert. It might seem kind of strange, a firefighter in his late thirties, back home in the bed he grew up in. But that was just it. I was home.

Funny, but years earlier, after graduating from college and coming back to Brooklyn, I couldn't wait to bust out of this place. Don't misunderstand. You couldn't beat Cypress Hills and Bay Ridge as backdrops when you were a kid. How could you go wrong with endless hours of basketball and an ice cream parlor as your clubhouse? But four years of college had introduced me to so many different types of people, so many more than Brooklyn ever had. I loved meeting them and hearing their stories and learning what they knew. Maybe my fascination with their stories went back to fifth grade, when I was told I wasn't a good reader. Well, I never became one, but I did become an excellent listener. I discovered so much about the world from hearing people tell me what life was like where they came from. And Manhattan offered the opportunity to meet even more people with more stories, a place where I could broaden my circles of friends—my Olympic rings, as I called them. In Manhattan, at any bar or restaurant, you could be talking to someone from Boston one minute, then turn around and talk to a girl from Queens, or a guy from Connecticut, or someone from Dublin or Paris. So many people feel anxious around strangers; I felt energized, confident that they would be as glad to meet me as I was them.

One night, for instance, I was in Smith & Wolly's enjoying a drink by myself at the bar. All of a sudden this fellow sat down beside me. He had a big, round face and a gleaming, shaved head; I had seen him somewhere before, but I couldn't place him. Then I heard him order a Cabernet with this distinctive Irish brogue. Immediately, I knew: It was Ronan Tynan, the Irish tenor who recently had lent his singing talent to countless 9/11 memorials for fallen firefighters. I quickly introduced myself to him, and for the rest of the night, we traded stories about Ireland and music and firefighting. It was as if we had been friends for years. Finally, with the bar closing, I told Ronan that my mother was a big fan. Would he mind giving her a call?

"Matty, it's two in the morning! Don't you think we'll wake her?" he said.

Sure, but when Mom discovered who her late-night caller was, she smiled for weeks—and so did I.

It was that kind of serendipity that had pulled me to the city and for nearly 20 years had kept me there. I loved my life in Manhattan, the nights out with friends, the excitement of my job in the firehouse, the bopping around to races and triathlons with an energetic tribe of athletes. Sure, I envied my married friends, the guys I used to spend all hours of the night out with. Frank Carino now had a wife and a dog on Long Island. And it seemed as if all the Cronies—Pat Ginty and Tommy Corrigan and John Kelly— had migrated with their young families to the suburbs, too. Even Jimmy had settled down with a terrific wife, Pam, and they were looking to start a family soon. And me, the one who thought he wanted a wife and kids more than anyone, I was still a bachelor living in a one-bedroom apartment in Manhattan. But until the right girl came along, I would make my bachelor life as fun and memorable as I could. And when I needed a break—well, I could play the role of the prodigal son and come on home.

The first thing I would do on Christmas morning was put on this ratty red and gray sweater that had been my Christmas uniform for years. Then I would head downstairs for Dad's once-a-year attempt at making breakfast: slightly burned bacon and made-to-order eggs. Then we waited for the avalanche of relatives: the brothers and sisters, their kids, two sets of aunts and uncles, the grandparents. Thirty or more people crowding into Mom and Dad's narrow little house on 76th Street. Once they arrived, the day became a blur of eating, watching old Christmas movies on TV, playing some basketball in the backyard, drinking, and lots of laughing over old-time stories. It was a bit surreal, but even as we had gotten older, whenever we came back to Mom and Dad's house and sat around the long, oval dining-room table, all nine brothers and sisters reverted to the silliness and good-natured teasing that we had done as kids. I'd say something to Eileen about her hair, and she would say something about mine—or the lack of it. Or Robert would egg Mom on about dinner, and she would threaten to get out the wooden spoon, the one she used to rap our rear ends with when we misbehaved as kids. And when we sat down to do the Secret Santa present exchange, we would wait to see whom the lucky person was that Frank had to shop for. "That poor sucker," someone would say, and we all would break out laughing. Frank had earned the title of family cheapskate one night when the nine of us put it to a mock vote. "Hey," Frank said with a smirk when the votes were counted, "I thought you all liked those baseball caps I got at Wal-Mart." So when it was time for Frank to hand out his gift, 30 voices went silent—all waiting to erupt in hoots.

It was Christmas at the Longs, Bay Ridge, Brooklyn.

Obviously, my accident threw a sharp curve into that year's Christmas festivities. My family had been on a round-the-clock vigil since I had been admitted to the hospital, with Mom and Dad arriving each day around 8 a.m. and staying until they could be convinced to go home and get some sleep. Meanwhile, after it had become clear that I would be in the ICU for an extended stretch, my brothers set up a schedule on which one or two of them planned to stay over each night. The waiting room had become Long Central, and as Christmas Day arrived, with me still comatose and hooked up to a battery of contraptions, it easily could have turned into a Scrooge-like holiday.

It was anything but.

The family, as well as the dozens of friends who came to the hospital that day, tried to keep it as festive as possible under the circumstances. Mom and Dad went to Mass in the hospital chapel,

Dad, of course, in his red sweater. Later in the day a group of fire-fighters from Jimmy's house arrived with dinner for everyone: filet mignon, turkey, potatoes, yams, string beans, and apple pie. The guys had picked up the food Mom and my sisters had bought for the family dinner and prepared it in the firehouse kitchen. There was shrimp, too. Uncle Jim brought his traditional bucket from Costco, although when he discovered they were still frozen, he ended up defrosting them in the sink of the hospital restroom. After dinner, another visitor made it to the waiting room: Santa Claus. It was actually a firefighter dressed in red who had been visiting sick kids throughout the hospital. But he stopped off in the waiting area, which gave Maureen's kids, Matthew and Kate, a thrill. They were only three and one, the youngest of the next generation, and making their first visit to the hospital. Thankfully, they couldn't grasp what all the commotion over me was about. But they understood Santa Claus, especially when he gave them each a gift.

The present, though, that everyone kept talking about had come earlier in the day, when Mom and Dad made a visit to my room. The swelling in my face and head had gone down some, but my eyes were shut tight as they approached my bedside. Mom wished me a Merry Christmas and then gave me a kiss on the cheek. Suddenly, my head started to lift ever so slightly and my eyes opened. Not for long. Maybe a second or two, but long enough for Mom to let out a cry, "Mike, did you see that? He opened his eyes. Oh, my God."

Dad had seen them flutter, too. He told a nurse, who smiled at my folks. She explained that Dr. Eachempati had lessened the sedation in order to gauge what effect, if any, the blood loss had had on my brain.

It was still too early to tell, but for the time being, on this Christmas day, I had given my family something: a little bit of hope.

═══════════

*Christmas Day*

*Merry Christmas, Uncle Matt,*
*Today is the first day I have come to see you. At first I didn't want to come,*
*but then my dad said something that made sense. At races I only see you at*
*the finish line. My dad told me, though, that I would still need to be at the*
*race in order to see the finish line. I know you can win this race because you*
*are my Ironman. Get better, and don't think for one second that I am*
*going to hold anything back in the Ironman we do together. It would be an*
*honor to run it with you. Side by side, my hero, my godfather, my inspira-*
*tion. I love you.*
*Your protégé, Michael*

*Matt,*
*It has been a great day for you and all of us. You should be so proud of the*
*impact you have had on so many lives. It shows by the outpouring of people,*
*calls, cards, and tears. You have been a very good person, and I am so proud*
*of you. Never change, keep strong. You are loved by so many, and I now*
*understand how much courage you have.*
*I love you, Dad*

*Dearest Matthew,*
*Today you opened your eyes and tried to reach us. What a wonderful*
*Christmas present for Daddy and me, and for you. On his birthday, Jesus*
*and the Blessed Mother are celebrating with you, giving you their love and*
*holding you in their arms, protecting you and giving you the will to fight*
*and win.*
*Love you, Mom XOX*

# 7

## CHEESEBURGER, FRIES, AND LONGNECKS

A few years earlier, during another Christmas season, Jimmy and I had come up with what we thought was the perfect present for Mom. By this point the nine Long kids were pretty much grown and out in the world, so we figured Mom deserved something special, something a little extravagant. She had, after all, spent 30 years cooking for us, shopping for us, and taking us to every kind of practice under the Brooklyn sky. So Jimmy and I bought her a mink coat—a mahogany-colored, shoulder-to-knee, soft-as-silk mink—that she could wear to the big-deal political dinners she and Dad were often invited to.

When we gave Mom the present, we told her it was something from all the kids. A big thank-you from nine lucky people. As she opened it, her eyes widened. "Oh, my. This is . . . this is gorgeous," she stammered. "But it's . . . it's too much. You . . . you shouldn't have."

Mom had never wanted a career. She was content to help Dad with the ice cream parlor and his political activities. Mostly she just wanted to raise a happy family with kids who worked hard, didn't get into trouble (or at least not too much), went to church every Sunday, and were there for each other. For the most part we delivered, though we were hardly a choir of angels. Over the years the nine of us had some loud and legendary showdowns—Robert and I had had run-ins that rivaled the Ali-Frazier matchups—that sent Mom first to her rosary beads and then to the wine rack. But if any one of us needed a hand with something, whether it was help finding a job or a pick-me-up chat after a rough breakup, eight ready and willing people were always just a subway ride away to give it.

That simple, that easy, just the way Mom showed us.

This Christmas I gave Mom something perfectly suited to those sensibilities. Just seeing me open my eyes kept her humming all day long, and the days after. As people arrived at the hospital to visit and asked her how I was doing, Mom had a ready answer: "Matthew opened his eyes today!" And for her that said it all. I may have been a 39-year-old man living on my own in Manhattan, but I was still her son.

The next day I pulled the trick again, this time for Eileen and Maureen, as well as my niece Meghan. And, like Mom, they ran back into the waiting room and told everyone. I'm glad I could make them smile a bit, especially after the torturous days I had put my family and friends through. But I have no recollection of any of this. With the sedatives and pain medication floating through my system, I remained virtually unconscious, alone in some gray world that I had been living in since the accident. Familiar voices, those of Jimmy, T-Red, Robert, one Crony or another, Dad, Mom, or whoever came to my bedside, might whisper something to me—"You're looking good, Matty"; "Hey, bro, hang in there, I love you"; "This is just one more race to run, be strong"—but the message would tiptoe into my subconscious and die. Only with the sedation lowered did I react to these whispers and, with a mere wave of my eyelids, let someone know that I at least heard them. It was a mild gesture, but the doctors took it as a sign that maybe my brain hadn't turned to whipped cream from all the blood I had lost.

Still, they remained cautious. Dr. Eachempati and Dr. Lorich told my parents that I was due for upwards of 10 operations over the next two to three weeks as they continued to reconstruct my body. Dr. Eachempati also needed to regularly change the packs in place around my midsection. My abdominal wall had been so shredded and scarred that no one surgery would be enough to determine if the affected muscles and nerves could return to full functionality. And, of course, I remained susceptible to the unknown. "When you have so many blood transfusions, your biggest risk is some overwhelming infection," Dr. Eachempati told my parents early on. "And that's what most people die of." A couple of days after Christmas, in fact, I came down with pneumonia.

And yet, even with all my impairments, the doctors couldn't get over how well I was actually doing. They took the mere fact that I was breathing—even with the help of a ventilator and tracheostomy tube—as a victory. So far I had beaten the 5 percent odds they first gave my parents. I should have died the morning they carted me into the emergency room. I didn't, Dr. Eachempati later said, because, for one thing, I came to the right place, a hospital renowned for its trauma care. The surgeons who worked on me during the first 17 hours, when the bleeding refused to stop, ranked among the best in the country. Mom would tell people later that it was God who pointed the ambulance in the direction of New York–Presbyterian and not toward another hospital where the care may have been inferior. But Dr. Eachempati also told Mom and Dad that something more intrinsic to my case had kept me from dying at the outset: my

overall fitness. "His body was conditioned to withstand a huge meta-
bolic insult," the doctor explained. "Even though his blood pressure
is low and he's having very low amounts of organ perfusion for
extended amounts of time, those organs aren't suffering because
they've been conditioned to deal with plenty."

In one day I lost the equivalent of five times my body's blood
supply, but my heart never stopped pumping. You could compare it
to a car engine that doesn't stall even though it's being fed with just
an eyedropper full of gasoline every few minutes. The muscle worked
overtime that day, as it had been doing for months, ever since I had
made it my goal to finish, in a four-month span, an Ironman and a
very fast marathon.

I survived because I had trained my heart to do the same: survive. Becoming an Ironman had kept me from becoming a dead man.

For the better part of a year, I had spent hundreds of hours and had
completed thousands of miles preparing for the Ironman in Lake
Placid and the New York City Marathon. Through May, June, and
July, with my teammates from the Asphalt Green Triathlon Club, I
followed a regimented schedule whose only variable was my own
inclination to add more mileage than my coach, Anthony Carillo, a
20-time Ironman finisher, dictated. My week went something like
this: Tuesday at 5:30 a.m., three times around the six-mile loop of
Central Park on our bikes, which included the demanding Harlem
Hill, a one-third-mile stretch that climbed 84 vertical feet at a ridic-
ulous grade of 4.4 percent; Tuesday evening, back in the park for
speedwork, where we ran as many as six miles at sub-eight-minute
pace; Wednesday morning, the insane Brick Workout, where we
again biked the park's loops three times, immediately followed by an

up-tempo 20-minute run; Wednesday evening, a 3,000-yard swim; Thursday morning, a 40-mile bike; that evening, another 3,000-yard swim; Friday, an eight-mile run. All that was just the tune-up for the weekend: Saturday, a long bike ride that took us through Manhattan, over into New Jersey, and up to Bear Mountain Park in southern New York, then back—a five-hour, 90-mile round-trip that tested stamina, strength, and our stomachs; Sunday, your basic 12- to 16-mile run, followed by a massage and a couple of beers.

On paper, Anthony told me, this weekly routine would be enough to get me in shape for the Ironman in July. But I wanted to do more. Many days I started tacking on a second workout before, after, or in between sessions with my teammates. I ran with the guys from the Rock, runs that never went less than five miles and often went much more. Tommy Grimshaw wouldn't hear of anything less. If some firefighter ever came into our locker room at the fire academy boasting of finishing a hard three-miler, Tommy would slay him. "Three miles? That ain't a run; that's a jog. Get out of here!" But when Anthony found out about my two-timing, he called me and laid into me good, in a tone I had never heard from a guy who's usually as mellow as a yoga instructor.

"Why am I coaching you if you're not listening to what I say? Maybe you know better than me, I don't know," he ranted seconds after I had picked up the phone. "I'm mapping out a plan that's going to get you to the finish line, if you listen to me. And if you listen to me, then I can say we got there together. If you don't listen and you don't get there, you can't blame me, because you're not doing my workouts!"

He was right, of course, and I got in line after that—although I still craved more. I had fallen hard for the physical exertion of the training, especially when it came to running. That sport was so simple and yet so fierce. All I needed was a pair of running shoes and shorts, and I could go hard, go long, and go anytime, for hours.

Any chance I had to run, I did. Once, on Thanksgiving, I ran the 13 miles from my apartment in Manhattan to my folks' place in Brooklyn, just in time to carve the turkey. ("Eww, take a shower first!" Eileen screeched.) Another time, Noel and I were due to run a 5-K race in Brooklyn. Instead of taking the subway out to Prospect Park for the race, we ran to it—and then back afterward—for a total of 17 miles. My home course, though, was Central Park, in the heart of Manhattan, a sanctuary I shared with hundreds of like-minded athletes. Its topography provided the perfect mix of uphills, downhills, and flats, and a glance at the panorama of the Manhattan skyline reenergized depleted spirits if not exhausted quads. Often, I would run in the park with Frank or Noel or Vicky, or maybe some of the guys from the firehouse, and we'd catch up on life while still pushing the pace. But I also loved going on my own and getting into a cat-and-mouse race with some total stranger. If I was churning at an eight-minute pace but then got passed by someone, my antennae went up. *Whoa, what's going on here?* I'd say to myself. Then I'd pick it up, accelerate to 7:30, and pass him. Then he'd rip by me, and I would have to crank it up again. No words were ever spoken, but a conversation was taking place, at least in my head.

*Harder, Matty, harder!*

*Gotcha, okay! Okay!*

Friends who didn't understand often questioned my sanity when I told them the amount of running I was doing—40, 50, 60 miles a week. "Don't you get bored?" they wanted to know. Never. I could run all day. I was having that much fun and getting so much out of it. I kept getting faster, I was staying in shape, and I was meeting new people at every race I ran. I never seemed to get hurt, either. Common running ailments like shin splints, runner's knee, plantar fasciitis—for some reason, I avoided them all. Maybe it was Anthony's coaching (when I followed it) or the stretching I did before or after a workout. Or maybe I was just lucky: My body and my mind meshed with running like no sport I had ever done, even basketball. We had the perfect marriage going.

And to think, if it weren't for a bad back and a bruised ego, I may never have come to realize running's seductive powers.

———

One day in the summer of 2003, I walked into the firehouse and noticed some of the newer, and younger, guys in the company lifting weights in our gym. I couldn't get over what I was seeing: These 22- and 23-year-olds hoisting 300-pound weights as if they were grabbing groceries out of a shopping cart. I said to myself, *Damn, they're strong. A lot stronger than me.*

And then I got nervous.

By now I had been with Ladder 43 going on 10 years, but the personality of the house was quickly changing. The fallout from 9/11, when 343 firefighters died at the World Trade Center, prompted many of the senior men in the FDNY to retire, men whose experience and personality could never be replaced with new recruits or even transfers from other houses. You see, *senior man* is not an official FDNY rank like lieutenant or captain that you qualify for by passing an exam or by getting promoted up the department ranks. No, you earn senior-man status by putting in your time at one particular firehouse. Every house has a wall with head shots of its members, and the photos line up according to service time. As one guy moves out, your mug moves up—and the closer you get to the front of the line, the closer you are to senior-man status. But there's more to the title than longevity: The generation behind you better respect you. Some senior men in Ladder 43 earned their standing by showing younger firefighters the tricks of fighting the Red Devil. Other guys did it in the way they conducted themselves around the house. No task, be it window washing or toilet scrubbing, was beneath them, even after 15 or 20 years on the job. By putting the house and those who worked there ahead of everything, these men elevated themselves to an elite level in our little world.

Some of the Cronies I grew up with in Ladder 43, like Pat Ginty, John Duffy, and Pat Cleary, had higher aspirations than I did. They were willing to spend their free time studying to become a lieutenant or captain, jobs with a loftier rank and a better paycheck. But I wanted no part of that career path. I liked chasing fires and the responsibilities and excitement that came with the job. My goal was to be a 20-20 man: 20 years on the job, 20 years with the same house. Simple but satisfying. But I wasn't sitting back, either. As my years of service in Ladder 43 piled up, I expected my stature to do the same. I wanted to be looked upon as a rising senior man, respected by new members for my skill and experience—and my willingness to share both.

But for some reason I got it in my head that I also needed to look the part, and that's what scared me that day when I watched those younger men pumping 300-pound irons. I thought if they didn't see me matching those numbers, they wouldn't place much credibility in me. On my best lifting day, though, I topped out at 200 pounds, maybe 210, and I knew better than to go more than that. Plus, I didn't think I needed that much bulk to do my job. Still, whether it was my competitive nature or just plain stupidity, I started lifting beyond my norm. As I hit 225 pounds, my biceps bulged like never before. As I got up to 240, my pecs became more defined. And as I reached 265, my lower back began to . . . *ache as if some mutant porcupine had wedged its way into my spine*. It was a pain like no other I had ever felt in my life.

I had overdone it and was about to pay the price.

Days after I hit that mark, I couldn't get out of bed without wailing. I gave up the weekly basketball league I had played in since college because I couldn't race after a loose ball without feeling it in my back. I walked around crooked, even after I saw a chiropractor. The doctor gave it to me straight: My body was out of balance. I had this strong, firm upper body and a flabby, do-nothing core. I weighed 212 pounds, 35 more than my college days. All the long-necks of Budweiser and pints of Guinness that I had tossed back over the years at Third & Long and Turtle Bay and other watering holes around the city were now starting to comfortably settle in around my midsection. The firefighter's diet didn't help matters, either. In the firehouse, we usually ate at 9 p.m., and if you had a 10-inch plate, you put 11 inches of food on it. You didn't ladle one portion of pasta on your plate, you ladled three. You didn't eat a couple of chicken wings, you ate half a bucket.

For a long time playing basketball and going for the occasional three-mile run had been enough to keep me in shape. But now, at 37, nature was getting the better of me. My burning back made me realize that I needed to bring some balance to my body and in how I ran my life. Fortunately, just about this time Noel called to suggest training for the Olympic-distance triathlon in Florida in the spring of 2004. Any early hesitation to take it on—especially my worries about the swim portion—evaporated when I saw what the multiple days and weeks of cross-training were doing to my body. We started working out in October, and by the time we arrived in Florida for the race, I had lost 37 pounds. And then I kept it off. Training and competing in endurance sports was not only exhilarating, it was the best weight-loss program I could ever find. I felt better. The pain in my back disappeared. My core got ripped. And Vicky Tiase stopped calling me Beer Belly Matty behind my back.

I also wouldn't let myself go backward. While I still enjoyed going out with the guys after work, I started nursing a beer instead of knocking back a six-pack. I began ordering spinach salad instead of cheeseburgers and fries. My buddies got on me for my crunchy ways. "We want the old Matty back," John Kelly razzed me one day. But I liked the new one. I was closing in on 40 but feeling like 15. I had more energy and stamina, and I didn't need to bench 300 pounds to prove to anyone, especially a bunch of kid firefighters, that I was in shape.

To remind me of the weight I had lost, I kept a photo of myself—a photo where my cheeks are the size of apples—taped to the inside cover of *Going Long*, a training book that a lot of triathletes refer to as their bible. I labeled the photo "37 Reasons to Keep Training." When I went up to Lake Placid for my Ironman, I left the book on the living room table of the condo where Frank, Vicky, and I were staying. One night, Vicky picked it up and saw the photo. She screamed, "Ah, that's where Beer Belly Matty went!" I gave her a wink and a smile.

The next day, I finished my first Ironman and celebrated afterward. With a cheeseburger, fries, and a couple of longnecks.

My conditioning may have helped me withstand a collision with a bus, but within days of the accident, my appearance began to drastically change as my body went into catabolic state. While my heart pumped as hard as ever, other muscles started to shrivel, their strength sapped by the demand on my system to fight off infections. My weight began to drop and drop. By New Year's Eve, eight days after the accident, I had lost nearly 20 pounds. I had a feeding tube and IV inserted in me, but the nutrients were hardly enough to keep up with my declining weight. The doctors assured my family that this was all expected and temporary, and when I was conscious again—whenever that might be—and eating normally, the weight would return. Regaining my muscle tone would be another story.

But as I was shrinking a little each day, the number of people who kept coming to see me or visit my family continued to grow. Some days as many as 60 people were in the waiting area at once, crowding out those visiting other patients in the ICU. The numbers became so overwhelming that the day after Christmas, the hospital decided to move my family up to the eighth floor, where the burn unit was located and where a special waiting area had been set aside for families of injured firefighters. Considering our line of work, firefighters often became patients on the floor.

Over time the cast of people who came to the hospital ranged from the high profile to the lowbrow. As an injured fireman, as well as the son of the New York State Conservative Party chairman, I drew a number of politicians. Mayor Bloomberg checked in on me several times over the first two weeks, as did his predecessor, Rudy Giuliani. New York Governor George Pataki stopped by, too. Another local politician, former New York Congressman Floyd Flake, made an appearance as well, which must have been a bit awkward because he was also affiliated with the company whose bus was involved in my accident. These politicians easily mixed with a wide assortment of other visitors, a virtual "Matt Long, This Is Your Life" production, even with me out cold in the ICU. There was Ray Paprocky, my boyhood buddy from Cypress Hills; Terry "T-Red" Brennan, who became not only a top-drawer bartender at Third & Long but also a partner in Turtle Bay and one of my closest friends; Mark Desautelle, my college roommate and an experienced triathlete who had been passing on his training secrets to me; Captain Jack Culkun, my first captain with Ladder 43; waiters and bartenders from my favorite hangout, Smith & Wolly's, who had placed notes in the restaurant's menus asking customers to remember me; and even Papi, the pie maker from the pizzeria next door to Third & Long.

The clergy from all faiths came, too. At the end of my first day in the hospital, Joseph Potasnik, a prominent New York rabbi, spent a few minutes talking to my parents, who are as Jewish as the Kennedys. As he was leaving, the rabbi told them that he would keep me in his prayers. That's when Dad let him in on a secret.

"It was really nice of you to come, Rabbi, very nice. We had eight priests here earlier and eight prayers, and your prayers are just as welcome."

When Rabbi Potasnik heard that, he leaned over to Mom and Dad and said, "Mike, that should tell you something. It takes eight priests to do the job of one rabbi." For the first time all day, Mom and Dad smiled.

At times it was one big Irish wake—tears and prayers, and some good-natured ribbing, for the deceased—even though the "deceased" hadn't ceased. Eileen joked that in just a few days I had sprouted more hair on my usually shiny head than I had in a decade. Frank Carino kept telling everyone that Starbucks would go out of business unless I got better. My brother Chris, who was recently married, reminded everyone that I still owed him a wedding present. Nanny, my 85-year-old grandmother, reminisced about how she used to chase me with the wooden spoon, and she threatened to get it out again unless I woke up.

The biggest chuckles came, though, whenever the phone in the waiting area rang. Apparently, a number of my former girlfriends kept calling to check in on me. T-Red answered most of them. Each time he picked up, he kept hearing a variation on "Hi, I used to date Matt . . . " The line was so often repeated that Terry began to keep track of it. So whenever the phone would ring, the room went silent, waiting for Terry, in his best auctioneer voice, to announce, "We're up to 16 girlfriends . . . No, hold on [*phone ringing*] . . . Make it 17!" Mom started blushing as the tally kept rising.

Okay, so I was a bit of a ladies' man. It was an open secret among most of my friends and family—if not, perhaps, with Mom and Dad. I loved meeting new women and seeing if they, at least, enjoyed meeting me. And that meant unless I was in a very steady relationship with someone (which wasn't all that often), I was always on: a bachelor in Manhattan, with a happy-go-lucky smile and a personality to match, ready and very willing to meet a new woman, buy her a drink, make her laugh with a silly story, and then see where the night took us.

You just never knew where, and that's what made it so much fun.

Like the time, one brutally hot July night, when I stopped into Third & Long with my roommate at the time, Mike Lang. It was a Tuesday, and that meant Dollar Bud Night. Now, even though I owned the bar, Jimmy and I had made it a policy that we always paid when we drank; it was one measure to keep us from becoming our best customers. After a couple of pops, I said to Mike, "Look around. There are five girls over there, six girls over there, four girls in the back—and there are only four other guys in here. The odds are too good in our favor." So Mike and I each threw $10 on the bar and said to the bartender, "Deliver a round of Buds and Bud Lights to every girl in the place." It cost us $15, at most. When all the drinks were served, we waited to see what would happen. One group toasted us from afar, and that was it. "Okay, Matty, no luck there," Mike said. Another group didn't even wave. "You're welcome," I mumbled under my breath. But then, from the group of four, one girl came over and said, "Hey, how you doing? Thanks for the drink." She was a really pretty brunette with a smile that could unlock a Brink's truck.

"No problem. I'm Matt, this is Mike—nice to meet you."

Well, the next thing you know the young lady and I are out of Third & Long and running around Manhattan—to shoot some pool at a bar downtown, and for drinks at another. By midnight we had ended up at her apartment, which happened to be right across the street from Third & Long. She lit some candles, and then the next thing I knew, I was passed out on her bed. A little while later I woke up in a bit of a fog, my eyes half shut, and roasting from the heat. I elbowed the girl, "Can you turn on the AC? It's hot in here." She didn't budge. I poked her again. "Hey,

hey, hey. Where's the AC? It's getting hot in here." Again, nothing. So I opened my eyes and saw that the bedroom was on fire.

"Holy shit!" I screamed.

I wrapped the girl up in a sheet and pulled her out of the bedroom. "Wake your roommates," I told her, "and get me the phone."
I called 911 and rushed the girls out of the apartment and into the
hallway. I headed back into the apartment to see if I could put out
the fire, but first I yelled back, "When the firemen come, don't
tell them I'm a fireman. Got it?"

They just nodded.

With a bucket I found under the sink, I started tossing water
on the fire, which had started when the candles ignited a window
drape. I was wearing just a pair of boxer shorts. When the firefighters arrived, the apartment was filled with smoke, and all they
could see were my legs as they crawled along the floor. The lieutenant, Vinny Fowler, whom I had once worked with, grabbed one
of my legs while shouting into his radio, "Ten–forty-five! Ten–
forty-five! We have a victim."

I said, "Vinny, I'm fine. The fire's in here."

"Hey, Matty," Vinny said, "what are you doing here? Great job."

We got outside, and he canceled the 10-45 while the other
guys put out the fire.

Then Vinny radioed again. "Chief, this is awesome! I have an
off-duty member and he made a rescue."

I started shaking my head and waving my arms frantically, and
mouthing, "No, no, no."

Vinny looked stumped. "No?" Vinny said, looking at me.
"Hold a second, Chief. Matty, you live across the street from here,
right?"

I nodded.

"Yeah, Chief, an off-duty who lives . . . "

I started shaking my head again.

"An off-duty who came from another apartment . . . ?"

No, Vinny.

"From another bedroom?"

Uh, no, Vinny.

"Chief, cancel the off-duty member. My mistake."

And that was how the night ended, Vinny shaking his head, and the girl and I wondering how we would top this first date. We saw each other a few more times, but soon realized there wasn't much spark between us, so to speak.

That seemed to be the common theme to a lot of my relationships. They started red hot and ended painfully chilly. I chalked up my fast starts to pure confidence. I never had a problem walking up to a woman—could be at a restaurant, or in line at a movie, or just on the corner—and saying hello. Or, as the owner of a busy bar, I would just take a pretty girl off the line, escort her to a seat, and then start chatting. A lot of my friends felt too clumsy around women they didn't know. Not me. You see, I wasn't given the highest IQ in the world or a head of hair like George Clooney, but confidence—well, I had plenty of that. I used to talk with a friend, Matt DelNegro, about having confidence before we went out at night. To get us focused for the evening, we would tell each other, "Go get your little blue bottle on the dresser with the C on the label. Give yourself two pumps of confidence. You'll be set for the rest of the night." Sounds crazy. Probably was. But it worked.

Once I was out with Terry Brennan, and we noticed a striking woman at the bar. "Matty," Terry whispered, "that's Ashley Montana, the supermodel."

"Really?"

The next thing you know, I went up to Ashley and put my arm around her, and said, "Ashley? Matty Long. How are you? How you been?" She just assumed we knew each other, and for the next couple of hours we chatted as if we did.

Another time, we had the fire truck out and were stopped at a corner when I noticed a couple of young ladies walking down the block. I smiled at one of them, and she smiled right back. Before the light had turned green, we had exchanged numbers. Captain Al just shook his head. "Matty," he yelled from the front of the truck, "if you could only put out the Devil as well as you talk up the ladies, this city would be a lot safer."

The problem was, when it came to women, my confidence had the life span of a bathroom air freshener, and then things got pretty musty. I'd find some fault with her, or I would get jealous if I saw some guy talking to her, or I would get frustrated if she became upset that I would rather go for a long run instead of joining her friends for Sunday brunch. Petty stuff, but enough to tip me off that the relationship wasn't perfect, which was what I was looking for. Something like what Mom and Dad had: 40 years of marriage, lots of happy kids. Or like Dad's parents, Grandpa Mike and Nanny, who were married for 70 years. Or what Jimmy or Michael or Eileen or Maureen had found. I so wanted it, but at the time I was naive or stupid and didn't know that a relationship—even one that lasted 70 years—could not be perfect. So, when things became rocky, I scrammed. I could rush into a burning building or run hard for 26.2 miles, but I couldn't cut a girl some slack when things got a little messy.

I had all the confidence in the world, and then not nearly enough.

---

On New Year's Eve my entire family stayed in the hospital. It had been years since we had all been together on this night. With the nephews and nieces coming along over the past few years, it was harder and harder for all of us to ring in the new year together. For so many New Year's Eves, Jimmy and I would be at Third & Long, watching everyone in the family enjoying themselves, and then the two of us would toast each other and give each other a big hug.

I had been looking forward to the coming rendition. The past year had been a spectacular one. My first Ironman. A great showing in the New York City Marathon. An exciting year at the Rock teaching a strong new class of firefighters. Chris got married. Eileen and Maureen had announced that they were expecting.

Yes, 2005 couldn't have been better, and 2006 promised even more.

Before the accident I had made plans to spend the evening with Shelly, a girl I had been seeing since the summer. She worked in real estate sales, and we had enjoyed our time together. Where was it going? I wasn't sure. She was younger than me by 10 years, and she didn't have much interest in running. But I wasn't ready yet to say, "She's not the one."

I still hadn't introduced her to a lot of my family at the time of the accident. So when she came to the hospital on Christmas Eve to see how I was doing, she got the once-over from Mom and the sisters. Shelly told Jimmy she would stop by on New Year's Eve, so she and I could be together as planned.

That night, Shelly came into my room in the ICU just around midnight. She was wearing an FDNY sweatshirt that I had given her. I lay there quietly, the monitors sounding their beeps every few seconds. She whispered that she was looking forward to spending more time with me in the new year. Then she gave me a kiss.

The clock clicked midnight. Happy New Year.

# 8

## AWAKE

Oddly, or maybe just horribly, my family had gone through a very similar wait-and-see vigil only five years earlier.

On a summer night in July 2000, my younger brother Frank, then 21 and just a few weeks out of college, was with several friends driving home after a party on Long Island. It was early in the morning, around 4 a.m., with the roads slick from a heavy rain. Suddenly, an animal jumped in front of their car. The driver tried to steer out of its way but he lost control of the car, drove up an embankment, and crashed into a tree. Frank, in the front passenger seat, took the brunt of the impact. Even with his seat belt on and with the front air bag releasing, his head blew through the car-door window and slammed against the tree. He was knocked unconscious. Rescuers needed the Jaws of Life to rip open the car and free him. He was medevaced to a nearby hospital.

I had worked late at Turtle Bay the previous night, so when Jimmy called me around 7 a.m. to tell me of the accident, I had been asleep for just a couple of hours. At that point, Jimmy didn't have many details, but he said he would get back to me once he did. I stayed in bed for a few minutes, then couldn't wait any longer.

"Jimmy, this is pretty bad, right?" I asked when I phoned him at his home.

"Yeah, I think so," Jimmy said, and then repeated what he had told me a little earlier. "But I just don't know how bad. I'm leaving now for the Island to see for myself."

I told Jimmy I would meet him there. The two-hour drive from the city to the eastern end of Long Island felt like it took a week. I couldn't stop thinking about Frank and what condition he might be in. Mom, Dad, and the rest of the family were already at the hospital when I arrived. We waited a couple of hours before the doctors came out and talked to us. They said Frank had suffered severe brain trauma, with a fractured skull and three hemorrhages. He also had deep lacerations along his arms and torso from the window glass.

When we could finally see Frank in the ICU, his head and face were swollen to about twice their normal size. He was attached to every piece of equipment possible, with bells alerting the nurses of any changes and with tubes and needles inserted into what seemed to be every inch of his arms. I was afraid to touch him or get too close to the bed, worried that I might make the situation worse.

For the next two weeks I watched him lay in the hospital, nearly lifeless, in a medically induced coma. He was on a respirator and soon developed pneumonia. His bed continuously listed from one side to the other so fluids would not stagnate in his lungs and worsen the pneumonia. Dad had a brain specialist from Manhattan come to examine him and determine Frank's long-term prospects. "Listen, if you're going to get a brain hemorrhage, he has them in the safest places possible," the doctor told us. "But if he doesn't get past this pneumonia, he's not going to make it at all."

During the weeks that Frank was unconscious, the family spent hours at his side. I remember helping a nurse wash his arms and legs and shift his body so he didn't develop bedsores. And we talked to him, even though we had no idea whether or not he could hear us. The doctors warned us that it could take months to determine how badly his brain was injured. Even when Frank became semiconscious, he often behaved like an angry bear, flailing his arms and kicking his legs as if he were reliving the accident in his head. The medical staff tied his arms down to the bed and put soft mitts on his hands so he wouldn't hurt himself or anyone else. One time his antics became so uncontrollable that Jimmy, Robert, and I had to force him back on the bed. I remember saying to myself, *Let's just wake him up. Maybe he'll realize that he's okay.*

About a month or so after the accident, Frank did fully waken, but that's when we realized just how severe his brain injuries were. He spoke as if he were five years old, with limited recall of events past that age. The doctors told us that he needed time to "regrow" his brain. For weeks, as he remained in that Long Island hospital, we watched, some days amazed, others saddened, as our brother—the eighth of the nine Long kids—grew up all over again. He had to be taught how to speak. He needed to learn how to write his name. One day we went in to visit and he kept saying the word *footsie.* We looked around the room at each other and wondered what he meant. We decided to rub the bottom of his feet to calm him, and he loved it.

It was all so maddening to witness, because in many ways I could always see a little bit of myself in Frank, even though I was 12 years older. Early on, the age difference had made me more of an uncle figure than a brother. Like the other older brothers, I tried to make sure Frank and Eddie, who was 14 years younger than me, stayed out of trouble. Frank was a free spirit like me, and had a little of my let-the-chips-fall attitude toward daily life. Of all my brothers and sisters, he was the only one who showed much interest in living in Manhattan and for all the fun the city could offer. Maybe I had something to do with that. As a teenager, Frank would work weekend nights at Third & Long, helping to keep the bar stocked, and would stay overnight in my apartment. The next day we might go out to brunch at one of the better restaurants on the East Side or meet up with some of the Cronies for a steak at Smith & Wolly's. He sat there, enjoying a sirloin and laughing at all the stories the guys would tell. He was 16, going on 26.

Now, in his hospital room, Frank sounded as if he were back in grade school. My siblings and I looked for ways to reignite his old self. Frank always loved music, from pop to techno, so I brought him a big boom box and dozens of CDs. I told him stories about family parties at Breezy Point and of basketball games at Bishop Ford that Jimmy and I had played in and he had watched with Mom and Dad. One day I brought one of the Cronies, John Kelly, to see him. John cut hair on the side. After several weeks in the hospital, Frank's hair had grown out of control, and with his face thinned from the weight he had lost, he looked like a lightbulb with a mop on top. John evened things out nicely.

Amazingly, after about seven weeks of occupational and cognitive therapy, Frank regained most of his old self. Fortunately, he hadn't suffered many physical injuries, except for the cuts. He went home and soon went back to work, hoping to push this latest memory well back in his brain.

Of course, my condition—lying in a hospital bed, semiconscious, with all sorts of machines and equipment attached to me—gave everyone in my family flashbacks to "The Frank Story." Especially Frank. While others might come in and try to talk to me with an upbeat tone, Frank, against his natural instincts, usually stayed low-key. One time after visiting me, he told someone, "It's kind of weird to be on the other side. I've always wondered what it was like to be on this side, looking at someone who has no idea of what's going on. People tell you stories about what you missed, but you don't have a connection—you were sleeping."

I understood what Frank meant, but I wouldn't call the weeks of unconsciousness that we went through sleep. To me, sleep was like halftime of a football game, a momentary pause before the action resumed. Sure, I loved my shut-eye, especially after a day that included a muscle-testing 18-mile run or after pulling a 24-hour shift in the firehouse. But I had learned to get by on four, five, six hours of it, just enough to get me juiced up for tomorrow. Many a time I made it to an early morning game with the FDNY basketball team after closing Third & Long only a couple of hours earlier; I may have been a bit hungover, but I was ready to go full throttle. And the day I ran the New York City Marathon in my best time ever, I did it on four hours of sleep; the night before the race, my brother Chris had gotten married, and I was out dancing and enjoying myself until one in the morning.

No, to me sleep was a bottle of Jamba Juice, a swig of Gatorade, something that refreshed me for whatever was next on the docket. I wouldn't describe those days of lying still in a hospital bed, of being in some lonely world where you don't dream, or at least you don't remember what you dream, as restorative. No, for nearly two weeks, when the sun rose but I didn't, when the days moved forward but I didn't, I was not sleeping. I was frozen in time.

On January 3, 2006, the thaw finally came.

———

Since Christmas Day, when for the first time my eyes briefly opened, I had been showing more signs that I was coming out of the fog. If a doctor or nurse asked me to squeeze a hand, I would. When

Pam told me that she and Jimmy would like me to be the godfather of the baby they were starting to plan for, supposedly I smiled a little. So, as the new year started, and I was under less sedation, Dr. Eachempati told the family that it would just be a matter of days before I became more alert, awake long enough to recognize faces and to start communicating. That moment arrived on a Tuesday afternoon, 12 days after my accident.

At first I didn't notice Jimmy standing at the side of the bed. Instead, as my eyes gradually opened, I just looked skyward, at the translucent cover of the fluorescent ceiling light. *Where am I?* Then I glanced around the room. I could see machines with blinking lights. A TV turned on. A large window that looked outside, to what I hadn't a clue. *Where am I?* I could see wires and more little lights blinking. I could see the bars alongside the bed and a white sheet covering my body. *Where the hell am I?*

Then, finally, I saw Jimmy. I didn't need to turn my head; I merely glanced to my right. A few seconds later, I noticed a woman checking the lines that ran into my left arm.

For the past few days, whenever my eyes had opened and for however long, Mom or Dad or Jimmy or anyone else who had come to visit would talk to me and tell me some news. But I wasn't ready to say anything back. This afternoon my eyes stayed open longer, and maybe they looked just a bit more alert than what Jimmy had seen previously. After a few minutes, when it became clear I wasn't going to nod right back off, Jimmy inched closer to me, as if he sensed something was registering with me.

*Where am I? Jimmy, tell me, where the hell am I?*

He had the look of Serious Jim, the nickname some of the guys who worked in the bars had given him. While I might have managed the crew with a more casual style—"Hey, who turned down the music? Let 'er rip"—Jimmy kept everyone on a short leash. If he saw too many empty beer bottles left on a table, he'd give someone the eye as a sign to go clear them, or, even worse, he picked them up himself. Jimmy played the heavy, the bad cop. That was just his way. He always seemed more mature than his years, at least more mature than me, and that's why people were often shocked when they found out I was the elder of the so-called Long Twins.

When Jimmy saw my eyes get somewhat focused, he looked at me, dead-on. "Matt, you're doing great. The doctors say you're incredible." *Doctors?* "You had an accident. A bus hit you one morning a few days ago. The doctors say you're on track, bro, and in a few days you're going to feel even better."

I listened to him, probably one of the few times when I didn't try to chime in. My eyes just stared at his; for a moment I didn't seem to notice that the woman, a nurse as it turned out, was still checking the lines. Jimmy kept talking. "You've had several surgeries, and the doctors are telling us you'll need a few more. You have one tomorrow for your leg and your shoulder." I looked away from Jimmy for a second, toward the end of the bed. I saw just my left foot, raised slightly off the bed, in a sling.

And then I just looked down, for a second or two. I guess I was thinking about what he was telling me, trying to get all that he was saying to lodge somewhere inside my head, with my mind still woozy from all the medication. *A bus hit me? When? More surgeries? What are you talking about, Jimmy?* And I suddenly got scared. And when I looked up again at Jimmy—and I only know this because he reminded me later—I started to tear up. And so did he.

Two firefighters from Brooklyn, crying.

We stared at each other. Growing up we never used to cry. We never saw Dad, the marine, cry. We had no time for tears, just time for basketball and ice cream and fun. But at this moment, it seemed the only thing to do.

A few minutes passed, and then Mom and Dad walked into the room. Jimmy told them what he had just relayed to me.

"Matthew," Mom said softly. "Oh, it is so good to see you. You look so well today. You're getting a little bit better each day."

"Son, you've been so strong," Dad said. "That's all people are talking about outside. How strong you've been through all of this."

Reflexively, I wanted to say something, anything. Seemed normal, especially after you've just heard that a bus hit you. I couldn't, not with the oxygen mask over my mouth and the trach in my larynx. Jimmy sensed I was getting agitated, and so did the nurse, who noticed my heart rate jump. I tried moving my lips, as both the nurse and Jimmy drew closer. Nothing, of course, came out, but Jimmy read my lips.

"Jimmy," Mom said, "what's he saying? What's he need?"

"He wants to know where he is," Jimmy said, looking at me. "Matty, you're at New York–Presbyterian."

I blinked my eyes a couple of times and tried to turn my head. I was only getting more frustrated. Again, I started to mouth what I wasn't able to say. It took a couple of tries before both Jimmy and the nurse realized what I wanted to know.

"He's saying 'special surgery,'" Jimmy said to Mom and Dad.

"What's he mean by that?" Dad asked. "Special surgery?"

Jimmy just looked at me. He knew exactly what I meant. Firefighters in New York hope that if they get injured on the job, they'll end up at the Hospital for Special Surgery. Over the years Jimmy and I had known plenty of men hurt in catastrophic accidents, like falls from rooftops or missteps off ladders, who somehow managed to return to work after being treated at the Hospital for Special Surgery, which ranks among the best orthopedic hospitals in the country. It was located on the Upper East Side, comfortably close to my firehouse. And one block from New York–Presbyterian.

The nurse smiled at me. "Matt, don't worry," she said. "A number of the doctors who are taking care of you are from the hospital. They rushed over right from across the street. They're doing a wonderful job, and so are you."

"Okay, bro?" Jimmy said, tapping my forearm. "You're here and everything's okay. Everybody's helping you, and you should see the friends outside who are here for you. Everybody's been here. Ray, all the guys from 43, your running club. It's been amazing. So take it slow, Matt. Be positive. Just be positive."

I closed my eyes once I heard that.

———

*Uncle Matty.* Those were two words that go together as well as *Bud* and *Lite.* I loved being the helicopter uncle. Thanks to my flexible schedule in the firehouse—if I did two 24-hour shifts a week, I usually had four full days off—it was easy to make unannounced visits in the middle of the week to all my nephews and nieces: Michael's three kids, Michael Jr., Meghan, and Brian; or Maureen's pair, Matthew and Kate. I'd rile them up with a little horseplay or whisk them away for an afternoon in some Brooklyn park. Or just sit and talk with them. Michael Jr. was a high school runner, and I was getting him into triathlons. Just weeks before my accident I had bought him his first racing bike. And the morning before the accident I had driven over to Brooklyn to see Matthew and Kate. They were with a babysitter, playing in the front yard, when I arrived. For an hour I chased them around trying to tire them out and make them giggle.

I had always hoped to have kids of my own one day. So far, the nephews and nieces had more than adequately substituted. "Want a ride on a real fire truck, Matthew? Come see Uncle Matty." "Hey, Brian and Meghan—here's 20 bucks, now don't tell your folks I just took you out for ice cream." I could spoil them, then rush for cover when the homework came out or the baths needed to be given.

So, of course, once I was awake, I was glad to get updates on the kids and what I had missed while I was in la-la land. Meghan came in and told me that all her girlfriends had seen my picture in the newspaper and were asking for me. "They think you're a hottie, Uncle Matty." I cocked my eyebrows to let her know she had some very sharp friends. Then I nodded for her to come closer, and I took her hand. I had missed her 14th birthday. "Happy birthday!" I mouthed to her through the oxygen mask of the ventilator. Meanwhile, Maureen told me how the guys from Ladder 43 had picked up her family on Christmas Day and given Kate and Matthew a ride on the truck. "Matthew was so excited, Matt," Maureen gushed. "It made his Christmas." Her eyes sparkled as she spoke. Then Eileen came in and couldn't keep a secret. "Matthew, we're having a baby boy!" My eyebrows squeezed together into a V. Without my saying a word, she knew she had hit a nerve. I'm an old-fashioned kind of uncle: I like to know the sex only after the kid's popped out. "Sorry, Matthew," Eileen said, smiling, "but we're still having a boy."

Then again, how could I blame them for spilling secrets and talking up a blue streak? They were like freshly popped bottles of champagne, bubbling with excitement—and they deserved to be happy. It would be weeks before I could grasp how much time my family had spent by my side, and how much anxiety I had caused them. Twelve days ago there was talk that I could be dead at any moment. More than once on that first day they watched as I was wheeled past the ICU waiting area heading toward the OR. They could only see my head, and it didn't feature the face of their brother. They hadn't slept well for days. They spent Christmas in the hospital, eating shrimp served from a restroom sink.

Now they could relax and enjoy the moment.

The Cronies had their fun as well. The phone calls from my former girlfriends continued to be a source of conversation among the fellows and other visitors, to the point where Ginty and Corrigan cooked up a little gotcha on me: They would have a nurse slip a wedding band on my finger while I slept, and then, in the morning, they would shock me with the news that I had gotten married during my hospital stay. When word of the plan reached Mom, though, she squashed it. "I don't need him going back into a coma when he hears that news."

Again, the fellows deserved a break. For two weeks firefighters from my house had provided my family with every comfort possible. Meals. Transportation. Companionship. Most nights at least one of them, and often two or three, stayed with my family just in case anything needed to be done or anything happened. They went beyond the call of duty, way beyond.

As did Terry Brennan. Years earlier I needed a bartender to spark business at my new bar, and T-Red came into my life. He turned out to be more than a clutch man behind the stick. If I didn't already have a half dozen brothers, I would have adopted Red into the fold. He became the sweatshirt that gets more comfortable with each wearing and with each beer stain you get on it. We complemented one another perfectly. Two guys from working-class families—Terry's dad was a plumber—who managed to hustle their way into building a successful bar business in Manhattan. We told good stories, with or without a drink in our hands. We vacationed together at the Jersey shore and, once a week, at least, shared a meal at Smith & Wolly's. Some days, like any good friend, Terry could drive me nutty with his quirks. I'm impulsive, he's methodical. At our monthly partner meetings, he could ask more questions than Dan Rather. And he liked to quote lines from literature—yes, the plumber's son can riff on anything from *Macbeth* to *Moby-Dick*—while I still smarted from the trouble I had reading the Hardy Boys in the fifth grade. But when we got on each other's nerves, we just

took a little break until things got busy again and we couldn't
remember what had annoyed us in the first place.

Terry spent more time in the hospital than some family members. Then, when he arrived home at night, he would e-mail our
friends with updates on my condition. His first e-mail went out to
about 35 people.

As Dickens wrote, "It was the best of times, it was the
worst of times, it was the age of wisdom, it was the age of
foolishness." So goes our holiday season, it seems. For
those of you on this list who have had little information or
have yet to have any at all, Matt was hit by a commuter bus
sometime around 5:50 a.m. on Thursday 12/22/05. Since I
received notice of Matt's accident and bolted to the hospital to be close to him, I have watched as the combination of
family, friends, firefighters, police, doctors, nurses, clergy-
men, politicos, and even people visiting other patients have
pulled together to support him and his family with love,
food, tales, and prayer. His life, as well as his infectious
healing smile, has touched so many others. My cell phone
has been burning up with questions of "What can I do to
help?" And I believe that the answer is a moral to this
tragic story. I do not even know my blood type; I think I
have donated blood once, which was in high school to get a
half day off with my girlfriend. But 60-plus different times
some selfless unknown drained their life's blood from their
veins so Matty could have a chance to survive. Crazy how
we can forget what's important. We have more crops than
we need, more cell phones manufactured than you can
shake a stick at, some of us own more than one car, but we
have staggering blood shortages. It just seems so selfish
and plain stupid. Blood replenishes itself in our bodies
once every eight weeks or so. The age of wisdom and the
age of foolishness ring so true. Matt's family wants all to
know how much they appreciate the outpouring of love

and prayers and only asks that you continue the same and also set up a date to begin a program of donating blood.

Terry may have poured it on thicker than a pint of Guinness, but that e-mail seemed to touch a chord. With each new installment, his e-mail list grew as friends forwarded it on to friends who forwarded it on to friends, who contacted Terry asking to be included on future e-mails. He soon had more than 300 names, and they came in handy when he hatched an idea to hold a blood drive. On a Saturday in early January, he organized two sites for the drive, one in front of Third & Long, the other in front of Turtle Bay. The New York Blood Center called it one of its most successful blood drives ever. More than 200 people came and gave a pint. The outpouring was so strong, Terry scheduled another drive one month later at M.J. Armstrong's, the third bar we owned.

T-Red hadn't lost his touch. He still knew how to draw a crowd.

The familiar faces from my past had collectively managed to make, as Dickens (or T-Red) might say, my worst of times bearable for my family and, in the process, for me. But I was about to be introduced to a whole new circle of people, people who over a matter of days had gotten to know my body as well as I ever knew it: the doctors who saved my life on December 22. Their job, though, was far from over.

As Jimmy had suggested, the surgeries continued through the first week of the new year. I was in and out of the operating room five separate times between New Year's Day and January 10. Dr. Lorich operated on my left leg again, this time inserting permanent titanium rods, one that ran from my hip to my knee, and the other that ran from my knee to my ankle. Dr. Bryan Kelly, another orthopedic surgeon, worked on my right shoulder, inserting four metal screws to keep it in place. And Dr. Eachempati couldn't get enough of me, operating on my abdominal area shortly after the first of the year, and then a few days later on my rectum.

Each new operation challenged me physically, mentally, and emotionally. My body swam with medications that dulled the pain but also my mind. Memories of events that took place in the afternoon—a visit with Mom or catching a football game on TV with Robert—would evaporate or get muddy by the time evening came around. Years earlier, when watching Frank fight to regain his brain in that Long Island hospital, I had wondered how something so crucial to our well-being could be so fragile. And now here I was, unknowingly battling the same challenge.

But if I was having trouble remembering things, somehow I was also becoming more engaged. By the end of the first week of January, I finally got out my first words: "Damn, I'm hungry. Get me something to eat!" Mom and Dad were in the room at the time, and Dad looked at me and said, "Yep, he's going to be all right."

I was also becoming more familiar with my surroundings in the ICU. The nonstop buzzing at the nurses' desk outside my door. The view of the East River that I could just about see if I raised my head high enough off my pillow. The sling where my broken right shoulder rested. The external fixator protruding from my stomach, which had become a place to rest my hands. The feeding tube inserted into my left side. The trach entering my neck. The two catheters, one attached to my penis, the other entering an incision just above it. The colostomy bag extending from my stomach . . .

. . . *the colostomy bag extending from* . . .

. . . *the colostomy bag* . . .

I watched that bag fill throughout the day with the waste from my body. My parents and brothers and sisters, my friends—I worried that somehow they could see it filling when they came to visit.

And smell it, too. *Does every patient have one? Is it standard-issue, like the ID bracelet on my wrist? Or maybe just a precaution because, obviously, I can't get out of bed yet with my broken leg. That's it! It's just a precaution. It will be gone when everything is healed. Of course.*

When I could talk finally, I made it a point to be certain. One of my first conversations was with Dr. Eachempati. For a man who went to work each day not knowing what traumatic event might await him, he had an easygoing manner, with a high-pitched voice and a quick laugh. By virtue of his surgical talent, though, his presence demanded attention. When he walked into my room, the residents who were already there virtually bolted to attention. The morning when we first talked, he told me just how challenging my case had been, with the overwhelming blood loss and the multiple injuries, and he made me feel as good as I could that my training for the Ironman and the marathon had somewhat eased his job. "You're a very good runner, Matt," the doctor said, with a slight smile. "I know how exceptional a 3:13 marathon is because I did a 4:45 that same day." Then he chuckled.

I thanked Dr. Eachempati for everything he had done but told him that I still wasn't totally clear on what had happened to me and what condition I was in. I needed to know a couple of things, starting with when he thought I would be released from the hospital.

"A week? Two?" I asked.

"Matt, you have to be patient. You've got a long way to go," Dr. Eachempati replied, his tone becoming more serious. "You should try to get better every day. It may take a week, it may take several weeks. We have to see when all the orthopedic surgeries are done. But we'll make sure you're healthy when you leave and all the wounds are healed and you're going to a safe place."

"Safe place? What do you mean, Doc? Can't I just go home?"

"Matt, once you're out of ICU, you're still going to need time in the hospital to recover. And then several weeks in therapy. Your body underwent a severe traumatic experience. You have to be patient and get better."

Already our conversation wasn't going well. And I had more to find out.

"Doc, the bag," I said, nodding toward my side. "At least tell me when I will get rid of it."

Dr. Eachempati took some time to answer that question. He tried to explain why he needed to perform the colostomy in the first place. "Matt, we were in a life-or-death situation. You were bleeding uncontrollably and your stool, as it pooled into your pelvis, was impinging on the work of fixing your pelvis and stopping the bleeding. You risked dying of sepsis. We did everything we could to stop the bleeding, but we couldn't without the colostomy."

"I understand, Doc, but now that I'm alive, the bag . . . when's it going away?"

He paused a second. "Matt, I know how you must feel. I've performed colostomies before on young patients like you. But usually it's not an emergency situation, like it was in your case. So they are somewhat prepared for it. But to wake up with it is a devastating emotional blow. Especially for a young person who's as fit and active as you are."

"Doc, you're right, it's emotional, but just tell me, when is it coming off, a few weeks, a month? Give me a time frame to work with."

"Matt, you'll need the colostomy bag a minimum of six months to a year."

"That long! What if I want to get rid of it earlier?"

"Matt, we'll want to do what is called a colostomy reversal, but we can't do it until you are fully healed, and there are a lot of other issues to consider. You still need your orthopedic surgeries, and we don't know how long you'll be in rehab. Like I said, we wouldn't do it before six months or maybe even 12."

I shut my eyes. *A year with this bag? What the hell? How in the world am I going to live with this damn thing for that long? I have to run the Boston Marathon in three months. Do the Ironman this summer. I got the bars, the firehouse. My friends. A year?*

"Matt, Matt," Dr. Eachempati called to me. "I say it may be a year because I hope it won't be longer. But I also have to be honest with you."

"Doc, how much more honest can you be?"

"Matt, this may be hard to hear, but the colostomy may be permanent. It's rare that a young person needs one permanently. Very rare. Still, your injuries were so severe. Your rectal area suffered terrible, terrible trauma. It's unknown right now whether the muscles and nerves in that area will ever recover. So we'll have to wait. But you have to understand, Matt. Performing the colostomy was necessary, absolutely necessary, if we were going to save your life. At that moment, that's what we were worried about—your life, not just the quality of your life."

"But Doc, come on, what kind of life will I have with this bag? I mean, how can I live with this?"

"Matt, all the muscles that control your stool habits were basically shredded. If we put you back together, you might not have any control. As crazy as it sounds, the colostomy is better for your lifestyle. But like I said, let's not worry too much about it right now. Let's get you better. And also, remember, you're young, and the technology used to reverse colostomies keeps getting better. So if it seems permanent now, who knows? In three or four or five years, we may be able to reverse this."

I squeezed my eyes shut as he talked. And kept them shut.

Why had I ever opened them in the first place?

# 9

## THE MIRROR DOESN'T LIE

Like everyone else, I made my New Year's resolutions, and my list always started with something I called No Juice January. It was my annual promise to curtail my time (and intake) at the bars after putting in maximum effort during the holiday season. Heading into 2006, No Juice January was slated to coincide with the kickoff to my Boston Marathon training. Shane, Tommy, Larry, and I had scaled back our training ever since finishing the New York City Marathon, but by the second week of January, we wanted to hit the roads hard, giving us plenty of time to ramp up for our 26.2-mile race in Boston on April 17.

Obviously, with the news that Dr. Eachempati had given me, I wouldn't be doing much running this January, and my plans for doing Boston were effectively scratched, too. And it wasn't just the colostomy bag that had me on the sidelines. During one of our earlier conversations Dr. Lorich had warned me that it might take months before my various fractures healed, and that until they did, he wasn't ready to offer a guess on when I would be walking on my own, let alone running.

My Ironman body was in a total shambles.

Where once I could transition from swimming 2.4 miles to biking 112 miles and then to running 26.2 miles, all I was doing now was lying in a supine position, able to lift my head a few inches and to reach with my left hand the external fixator, which was protruding from my belly while holding my pelvis in place. I had a hole in my midsection the size of a football and titanium rods extending the length of my left leg. Metal screws in my hip, knee, and ankle kept the rods in place. My right pelvis, right shoulder, and left foot were all healing after being shattered. I was more Broken Man than Ironman.

That being said, the doctors wanted to make sure my condition did not worsen. On January 9, hours after I had another surgery on my rectum and 18 days after being hit by the bus, Dr. Lorich and Dr. Eachempati gave the orders for me to begin physical and occupational therapy—starting the next day. "You can push him some and push his heart rate," Dr. Lorich told the physical therapists who would be working with me. "We've seen it already. He can handle quite a bit. This guy is an athlete."

I wondered if that was what he meant to say. I wondered if he intended to tell them, "This guy *was* an athlete."

═══════════

She arrived in my room early that Tuesday morning, around 9:30. She wore a white hospital smock and had a stethoscope around her neck. She came up to the side of my bed, cheerful and smiling, everything I wasn't at that moment. "Matt, my name is Inna Tsykun, and I'll be working with you as your physical therapist," she said. "How are you this morning?"

"Fine," I said, and left it at that.

Fact was, I was annoyed and hurting. I had not slept well after the previous day's surgery. During the night my nurse boosted my morphine level to help ease the pain. Still, I was dealing with more than physical discomfort. When my family had gone home for the night, I unburdened myself to the nurse on duty. The shock of my situation was finally sinking in. I told her I was feeling helpless and sad. It was the first time I had admitted those sentiments to anyone.

It just seemed that with each conservation I had with a doctor, the longer my road to recovery became. Maybe I should have figured out on my own that it wouldn't be easy. My friend Vicky, who visited me almost every day after finishing her shift in the OR, at one point told me that the average stay for most people in intensive care was two days. I was finishing my third week.

And now this perky physical therapist, looking as fit and trim as the runners I used to race with in the park, was here to rehab me, to get me moving again, whatever that might mean. Discouraged and depressed—that was how I actually felt.

For the better part of a month the nurses had been changing my dressings and cleaning me, turning me and making sure I didn't develop any bedsores. That had been the extent of my movement. At the same time I continued to lose weight. On the day Inna started working with me, I was down to 150 pounds from my racing weight of 175 (and I would lose another 25 over the next six weeks). My metabolism was sucking my muscles dry in order to try to heal my injuries. I was deconditioned, my muscle tone withering away.

"Matt, the doctors have told us that you have to start getting up, working toward getting out of bed," Inna said. "The sooner you can get out of bed, the faster your recovery will be."

I snapped back, "And you're getting me up?"

I felt bad that I was short with her; that certainly wasn't my style, especially with women. But a bad night's sleep will do that to you.

"Not today," Inna said. "Today I just want to see if we can get you to sit up higher in bed."

Even weighing what I did, Inna was not about to try to lift me herself. She called for two other therapists, Hope and Tammy. Before they had even positioned themselves near my shoulders, preparing to help prop me up, I started firing questions at them and resisting their efforts. "Do we have to do this? Is this going to hurt? Can't we just try this tomorrow?" The women stayed at it, and after about 15 minutes or so, during which time they had to maneuver around all the wires sprouting from my different body parts and the slings that held my left leg and right shoulder, I was upright in an L position at the head of the bed. They then made sure my heart rate hadn't gyrated too much during the exercise. My resting heart rate hovered around 100 beats per minute, but the doctors had given the therapists the green light to let it jump to 140 during the session.

For the first time since I had hopped onto the bike 19 days ago, I was sitting up. I could look out of my window and see more than the dark waters of the East River. If I looked south, I might catch the tram that shuttles people across the river and over to Roosevelt Island. If I stretched some and looked north, I might see the southern edge of Ward's Island, which is connected by landfill to Randall's Island, home of the FDNY training academy.

I remained in that position for 30 minutes or so, long enough for Mom to see me when she first visited that day. She smiled when she did. Later that morning the occupational therapist, Julie McNichols, came by for her first appointment with me, and she had me eat some applesauce. It was actually part of a swallowing test to see if the trach could be removed from my neck and to determine if the muscles around my throat and larynx would allow me to eat solid food. The trach had been extremely uncomfortable.

I was constantly fighting to cough up phlegm and would start gagging every 15 minutes or so. The applesauce was dyed green, and if the green sauce seeped out of the hole in my neck where the trach was inserted, then I wasn't swallowing properly. On this first try the test came back negative. "Don't worry, Matt, we'll keep on trying," Julie said. "You'll be eating solid foods before you know it."

A couple of days later I was finally transferred out of the ICU and to the hospital's eighth-floor burn unit. It made sense to move me there because my family continued to use the FDNY waiting area on the floor as their own Holiday Inn. Also, with my sensitive skin wounds I could expect to get exceptional treatment there. Besides the holes in my midsection and leg from which the fixators protruded, I had skin grafts taken from my thighs. The grafts were used to partially close the wounds near my abdomen and a hole above my left knee and one on my right side where my pelvis tore through the skin. For all these open wounds to heal properly and quickly, a medical vacuum, or vac, was placed on them. Theoretically, with the vacs sucking all the drainage from the wounds and pulling new tissue to the top, the wounds would heal faster. As it turned out I had the vac on my abdomen for nearly five months. And every couple of days, the nurses had to delicately clean the area around the wounds, carefully cutting strips of tape that kept the vacs in place.

On my first night on the eighth floor, Dad decided to stay with me. He had sent Mom home earlier, and we talked a bit. He was 66 years old and as busy as ever. He still owned the liquor store in Bay Ridge, but through the first three weeks of my recovery, he left my uncle Tom to manage the shop. He also had his political work. In 2006, New York would be electing a new governor for the first time in 12 years. George Pataki, who was elected in 1994 by the margin of Dad's Conservative Party vote, had announced he was not running for reelection. Dad would be instrumental in helping to choose a candidate to take on the Democrat nominee, Eliot Spitzer, New York's attorney general. But before Dad could even think about politics, as always, his kids came first—in this case me, his 39-year-old son.

When we were growing up, Dad made it a point—regardless of how busy the ice cream parlor or liquor store might be or how much political work he might have—to reserve Sundays for the family. We went to church together or to a basketball game together, and we always had dinner together. All this time with a bunch of hyperactive, high-strung kids probably drove him a bit looney, but he knew that came with the territory of being the father of a large family.

He also knew how fragile that role could be.

One night when I was about 12, Dad had a meeting with members of the local Conservative Party at the ice cream parlor that ran late into the night. Around midnight he and Uncle Tom offered to walk one of the attendees back to her car. She had parked near a bar that was popular with some low-level members of the mob. When they got to the woman's car, they found it had been smashed, apparently by another car. Dad told the woman that whoever had hit the car probably hadn't gone too far; there was just too much damage. So he and Uncle Tom started scouting the area for the car that had caused the trouble. They found it in the parking lot of the bar and called the police. But before the cops arrived, a couple of the bar customers came out and spotted Dad and Uncle Tom near their car. As the group approached them, Dad told his brother, another marine, "Let's take down the mouth of the group and the others will scatter." He was right; they were cowards, but the thugs didn't bolt. Instead, they pulled out guns, and one of them shot Dad in the stomach. He was rushed to the hospital, where doctors removed the bullet from just above his kidney. Fortunately, the bullet did not do much harm, and within a few days he was home recuperating.

Still, how much more did the man have to take? A gunshot to

his belly. One son nearly killed on a Long Island road. And now me.

Well, in my hospital room that night, I was about to give him one more crummy memory.

Just about 1 a.m., after finally falling asleep, I started to hallucinate. The wild tonic of medications still coursing through my body had me screaming and blathering, with everything directed toward Dad. I kept yelling at him to stand at the foot of the bed. "Catch the bubbles!" I shouted. "Move the ball!" Then I yelled, "Move over here and keep your hands up. Dad, get in the game!" I was like a basketball coach giving orders from the bench to some nervous rookie. Dad didn't know what to do except hop at my commands. He was afraid I might fall out of bed or pull the IVs from my arms. The odd dance went on for nearly 90 minutes; I giving orders, Dad scurrying around the room obeying them. Finally, around 2:30 a.m., a nurse came in.

"Mr. Long, you've got to stop," she told him. "Please, go home and get some rest. We'll watch him; he'll be okay."

Dad was exhausted and crying, his arms sore from all the flailing I had put them through. He finally agreed to have one of the firefighters drive him home.

---

Obviously I had no intention of staging such a terrorizing late-night drama for Dad. But the reality was, I seemed unable to control my mood or my behavior, no matter the time of day. One afternoon, I remember, Dad came in to tell me that Mayor Bloomberg was in the waiting area hoping to see me. Over the first couple of weeks of my hospitalization, the mayor had stopped by on three or four occasions, but I was unconscious each time. Now that I was awake, he looked forward to speaking with me. But when Dad told me the mayor was just outside my room, I wanted no part of him.

Don't get me wrong. I had nothing personal or political against Bloomberg—though, like a lot of other firefighters, I was still annoyed that it had taken nearly four years after 9/11 for us to receive a new contract from him and the city. Fortunately, when the deal was approved a few months before my accident, it included a retroactive back-pay clause. So when I saw the mayor at the starter's podium of the New York City Marathon, I reminded him of that. "Hey, Mayor Bloomberg," I yelled out, "where's my retro check?" and gave him a big smile. He returned the smile, with a thumbs-up.

No, what bugged me about the mayor's visit was that it smacked of a public relations move—or that's what I assumed. You know, *Let's go see the fallen firefighter risen from the dead*, and I didn't want to be the latest photo op.

"Dad, don't let him in. I don't need to see the man."

Dad was equally insistent. "Listen, Matt, you're going to see him. He's been checking on you every day since you got hurt. This is no stunt." He paused for a moment. For the first time since I had come to, someone wasn't coddling me. "Matt, I'll be frank. Politically, it would help me if you let him see you." And with that, I agreed.

Mayor Bloomberg came in and stayed for 10 minutes or so. He was cordial and talkative, and we laughed about my retro-check comment from marathon day. "Don't worry, Matthew. Your money's coming," he said with a wink. He also said the city would not forget me, and neither would he. He meant it. A few nights later he came back to check on me again, and he made it a routine to stop by at least once a week for the next month or so.

Like the mayor, a number of my friends, relatives, and acquaintances from around the city continued to come by the hospital hoping to see me. And like the mayor, before they could visit my room they had to check with someone—Dad, Mom, one of my brothers, T-Red—to see if everything was okay. Often it depended on how much pain I was in at that moment, or my mood, or how well I knew the person. The Cronies usually got the go-ahead no matter how I felt. And so did Frank Carino and Noel Flynn, my prime training partners. Frank, who looks like the actor Stanley Tucci, with his shiny shaved top and olive skin, would bust through the door with a big "Hello, bro. You looking good. How you feeling?" and before I could answer, he would be riffing on some shopping spree his wife, Renee, had just come back from or the mess his dog had made in the front yard of his house. Goofy, lighthearted chatter: That was what mostly came out of Frank's fast-moving mouth. Noel, on the other hand, arrived a few decibels lower, and often he would just sit, maybe talk a little bit about running, and watch some TV. One time, appropriately, the movie *Forrest Gump* was on the TV when he got there, and we laughed as Forrest ran across the United States. "Run, Forrest, run!"

It was also good to see my running partners from the Rock— Shane, Tommy, and Larry—when they came by, though the experience Shane had during his first trip summed up why I often felt unnerved by visitors. Shane bounded into my room like a linebacker breaking through an offensive line. But then he quietly said, "Excuse me," made a sharp U-turn, and left. Seconds later he was back but a lot less jaunty. Months would pass before he told me what had happened. "Matt, I didn't recognize you at first. You looked like you had aged 30 years since I last saw you. You looked like a cancer patient on chemo."

Shane didn't need to tell me that. I suspected it all along as I lay in my bed; I was no longer the fit, chiseled Matt Long who had finished an Ironman, who had rushed around the city on the back of a hook-and-ladder putting out fires, and who confidently talked up the ladies in bars around Manhattan. Instead, more and more I saw myself as a feeble man, a shadow of my former self.

The image became a reality one morning when I finally had the chance to look in a mirror. For weeks, either a nurse or one of my brothers would shave me or brush my teeth, so I never had the need for a mirror. But this morning, when I was working with Loreen Acevedo, another occupational therapist, I tried shaving for the first time since the accident. She put a mirror to my face, and I lost any self-confidence I had left.

"Holy shit," I muttered when I saw my reflection.

My face looked ghostly—gaunt, emaciated, hollowed. My cheeks were bony, the skin hanging loosely. My eyes, sunken deep within their sockets, were a milky gray instead of their usual hazel. I thought of Grandpa Mike. He looked better than me, and he was 87 years old.

That face—*my face?*—only deepened the despondency I was feeling. *What had happened?* One December morning I had taken off on my high-speed bike, energized by a body hardened by hours of exercise and intense competition. Now, judging from this image in the mirror, apparently I had morphed into a man who looked inches from his grave. How could people come into my room and say I looked great? *How?* They had to see what I just saw. Sure, they wanted to be nice and encouraging. I could understand that. But honestly, now that I knew what I looked like, I'd rather have heard nothing at all than something that wasn't true.

And so, more and more, I asked that my friends be kept away. I let my world get smaller and smaller.

━━━━━

As much as I sometimes wanted to, I couldn't keep my physical therapists away. Every morning for six weeks Inna or one of her partners was at my door, pumped to get me going. They reminded me of Anthony Carillo, my triathlon coach, who could make a one-mile swim workout sound like dinner at the Ritz. I used to dread swim practice. While others in my triathlon club would glide through the water with the ease of Michael Phelps, I chopped my way up the lane of the pool with clumsy, inefficient strokes. Anthony was always there to give reassurance. "Matt, remember, most triathletes struggle with the swim," he would tell me. "Get through your swim, then make up the time on the bike and run."

Inna, who was in her early thirties and had been a therapist for more than a decade, had a similarly soothing way about her. She kept telling me that we would do a little at a time. Sit up one day. Dangle my feet off the bed the next. Try, maybe, to put some weight on my good leg the next. "If you're ready," she would say. "If you're not, then we'll try it tomorrow." Some days I would beg off. The pain I was experiencing was too much. Or I was coming off a bad night's sleep and was out of sorts.

And sometimes I was completely honest with her.

Once, a couple of weeks into our therapy sessions, she asked me to try standing on my own. Up to this point, I had always received help getting out of the bed and into a chair. Now she wanted me to stand by myself.

"Inna, thanks, but, uh, I'm scared to do that."

Just saying *I'm scared* hurt. I was a fireman. We were supposed to be macho guys, ready to take on any emergency. And challenges had never frightened me before. When Noel tried to convince me to attempt a triathlon, he went to his fallback line—"Are you scared?"—and that immediately did the trick. No one questioned my toughness. But now, when Inna asked me to stand up, something I had mastered in the living room of my parents' apartment in Cypress Hills when I was a year old, I panicked. I was afraid, afraid just to try.

Inna persisted, gently. "Matt, you may be scared, but I still think you can do it." She said it too nicely for me to keep protesting.

First, though, I made sure she had someone nearby to spot me. She called over a brawny male nurse to supply cover. Then, with just enough pressure, she put her hands underneath my right forearm for support; with the broken shoulder, my right arm was still weak. I took my left hand and started to push up from the wheelchair's railing. I raised my rear end, inch by inch by inch. Then my knees uncoiled, slowly, slowly, slowly. I could feel the metal rods in my left leg straightening out. They built the Empire State Building faster than I unfurled from that chair. But as seconds passed, I got taller and the soles of my feet felt, for the first time in months, whatever body weight I had left.

And then I started to topple over.

Inna quickly grabbed my rear end, my naked rear end, and kept me off the floor. "Hey, Inna, you're grabbing my bare ass!" I blurted out.

"I know I'm grabbing your ass," she shouted back at me, "but if I don't grab your ass, you're going to fall down."

"Good point. Keep grabbing."

Moments later, she plopped me back into the chair. We looked at each other. She probably thought she had lost any chance of ever getting me out of that chair again. Instead, I gave her a twisted look, and said, "Inna, you just grabbed my bare ass, you know that?"

"Yes, Matt, you've mentioned that already," she said, embarrassed.

"Well, let me say, thank you . . . for grabbing . . . my bare ass."

"Well, you're quite welcome. Let's hope I don't have to do it again anytime soon." And then we both broke out laughing.

Such a moment of spontaneous laughter—the kind I used to have all the time in the firehouse with the guys, dropping water buckets from the roof at some unsuspecting firefighter, or in the bar, when I'd get a slow night hopping with a round on the house—seemed to come so infrequently now. In fact, most of the time I wasn't even looking for a laugh: I was so frustrated with my progress toward getting back on my feet that a good laugh just didn't fit my mood. How could I ever run again, or bike or swim, if I couldn't even stand up? Inna and the other therapists kept telling me not to be so hard on myself, that in a month's time I had gone from lying flat in a bed to sitting for hours in a chair. But I couldn't relate to these accomplishments; they seemed so small, so inconsequential. Months earlier I had run a marathon—26.2 miles—around New York City in three hours and 13 minutes. Now it took my nurses almost that long to wash my body and clean my wounds just so I would be ready when Inna knocked on my door for our daily session. And I understood the logic behind the therapists' "a little at a time" approach. Would-be marathoners apply it to their own training: You start by running a mile, and then, over weeks, you build to five miles, 10 miles, 13 miles, 18 miles, 22 miles. You increase your endurance, strengthen your legs and your heart and your mind, until that improbable total—26.2 miles—seems doable, not daunting. There's a progression to the process, toward a finish line for all the effort.

But this work I was doing now? Where was the finish line? I just couldn't see it. What I had been and what I wanted to be again—an endurance athlete—didn't seem attainable. One look in the mirror told me that.

My time with Inna ended on February 22, when I was transferred from the burn unit to the hospital's in-house rehabilitation center. Officially, the move meant I was discharged from the hospital— after two months and more than a dozen surgeries. But while I could have gone to any rehab center in the New York City area to continue my therapy, Dr. Lorich and Dr. Eachempati worried that I would need regular medical attention from them, so it was smart to stay close. I still had the vac connected to the open abdominal wound, the colostomy bag attached to my left side, and a suprapubic catheter to urinate. My urologist, Dr. Darius Paduch, had hoped I would soon be urinating on my own; if not, he warned, then I likely would be self-catheterizing myself for the rest of my life.

The doctors were right to be cautious. Within two weeks of moving to the rehab ward, I was back in the hospital and under the knife. Dr. Eachempati had to perform emergency surgery on a bowel obstruction caused by tissue scarring. He simply called the incident bad luck.

One morning when I was back in the rehab unit shortly after that surgery, one of my new therapists, Tena Ross, wheeled me into the ward's long hallway. She had news for me. "Matt, you're taking your first steps today."

I immediately fought her. "No, not a good idea. No, I'm not ready for that. Nope."

And in my mind, I wasn't. Just days earlier, I had been in the OR. I still felt woozy. I also was worried about the dressing coming off my abdominal wounds, which would cause the vac to lose pressure and start beeping, and that would mean going back to my bed and having the nurse remake the dressing. And I worried that the colostomy bag might leak, and I didn't need to be responsible for that mess. And I worried that if I fell, and the catheter came loose, then . . .

"No, let's not go there today, Tena," I insisted.

Tena was less of a pushover than Inna. "Matt, don't give me a hard time," she said. "Let's just try." And with that Tena and one of her aides locked my chair's wheels and placed a walker a few inches in front of me. "On three," she said, "try to lift yourself out of the chair. Use your legs, not your arms, okay? All right, one, two . . ."

I had no choice, it seemed, so on three I lifted myself up out of the chair using, well, my arms, and came to the standing position. I grabbed on to the walker. I didn't wobble this time. I stood for a couple of minutes, shaking, but not feeling like I might topple. I bought some time before trying that first step.

"Ready?" I asked the aide. "Have the chair close by in case I need it."

"Yes, Matt," the aide replied.

"Come on, Matt," Tena jumped in. "You can do this. You're ready."

I started thinking, something I never had to do when I ran. Back then, I didn't have to tell my brain to alert my legs to move faster; they just did it naturally. But now it felt like I had to will my legs to move. Imperceptibly, I slid the right leg forward, then the left. Tena said, "Good job," but she wanted me to transfer the weight from one leg to the other.

"Keep hold of the walker," she said, "but I want one foot off the ground."

I tried again. I loosened my grip on the walker just a bit and took a step with my right foot, and then one with my left.

And then I quickly sat down. I was done.

Taking those two steps felt like I had bench-pressed 400 pounds. But I sat down not just because I was exhausted. I had been wearing a hospital gown with boxer shorts and a loose pair of tear-away sweats. And now they were soaked in my urine. The stress from the exercise had caused me to pee uncontrollably.

Tena and her aide took me back to my room. The nurse cleaned me up and put an adult diaper on me. Later that day I cried for an hour.

Now, aside from everything else, I had to worry that with every step I took, I would embarrass myself.

Some athlete I was.

# 10

# SEPTEMBER 11, 2001

One March afternoon just before Saint Patrick's Day, Ronan Tynan came to the hospital to visit.

"Matty, it's great to see you, lad," he said as he bounded into the room. "You're looking terrific."

"Ronan, that's nice of you to say, but I'd feel even better if I were sitting with you at Smith & Wolly's having a cold one rather than lying here in this hospital room."

"You'll get there, lad. You'll get there."

Since our first night of talking and drinking together at Smith & Wolly's, Ronan and I had become good friends. To hear his booming Irish brogue and to see his easy smile brought back fun memories. He filled me in on all the doings at the restaurant. "The crew there is always asking for you, Matty. They haven't forgotten you," he said. "You know, they have a little note in all the menus telling people to remember you in their prayers. It looks like they're working."

We talked about Saint Paddy's Day, which was always one of my favorite days in the city. The Irish firefighters would walk the parade route down Fifth Avenue, and then a crowd of them would wind up at Third & Long for the better part of the night. "Ronan, no beer for me this year," I told him, "and no step dancing, either."

"No worries, Matty. Next year, lad, next year."

We traded stories for a half hour or so, until he said he had to run. But before he did, I asked him to meet one other patient on the floor. His name was Tarrell Lee, a 27-year-old New York City traffic enforcement agent who had lost his right leg when he was hit by an SUV a few months before my accident. At this point, Tarrell had been in and out of the hospital for nearly seven months, but he was still having difficulty adjusting to life with a prosthetic leg. One day, Dr. Lorich and Dr. Eachempati, who also had treated Tarrell, asked me to try to cheer up their patient—a tall order considering my own fragile state. But over the course of a few weeks, the two of us—a white firefighter from Brooklyn, a black traffic officer from Queens—had become friends.

"Ronan, maybe you can help, too," I said as he wheeled me down the floor to Tarrell's room. "Maybe talk to him about living with a prosthesis."

"I don't know, Matt. I'll see what I can do." Twenty years earlier Ronan had lost both his legs after being in a car accident. But within four weeks of getting fitted with prosthetics, he was walking and back on his way to becoming a world-class tenor.

When we arrived in his room, Tarrell's eyes immediately started to beam. He recognized Ronan from Yankee Stadium, where the tenor often sang "God Bless America" during the seventh-inning stretch. The two ended up chatting for quite a while about their respective struggles and recoveries. Finally, Ronan told Tarrell, "It's not going to be easy. You're going to need to work hard. But you can do it, Tarrell, if you put the effort in. I know you can."

Tarrell smiled. It was maybe the happiest I had seen him since we met. And by the end of March, he was discharged from the rehab unit and walking much better. Talk about the luck of the Irish.

It may have been a small gesture, but helping Tarrell gave me some hope that I was returning to my old self, the guy who enjoyed making others feel good. When I was with Tarrell, I could think about someone else, at least for a while, and not dwell on my own problems.

I craved distractions in whatever form they came. When I wasn't being poked by the nurses or exercised by the therapists, I was hungry for something to occupy my time. The TV became a steady companion. I watched Oprah and Martha Stewart and the Food Network regularly—I always picked up some good recipes from Bobby Flay and Giada De Laurentiis; I figured that one day I'd prepare some of their dishes for the guys in the firehouse. I saw every rerun of *Seinfeld* and *Law & Order*, some multiple times. I watched dozens of movies, new ones and classics. One night when Jimmy and Pam were visiting, we got sucked into *On the Waterfront*. When Marlon Brando started kissing Eva Marie Saint in that famous bedroom scene, Jimmy—Serious Jim—blurted out, "Pam, that's the way we used to do it."

I shot him a pained look. "Bro, too much information."

I also watched plenty of news, sometimes more than was helpful for my tormented psyche. One day I turned on NY-1, the local New York news station, just as a report came on about a protest march across the Brooklyn Bridge. The march was led by Roger Toussaint, the transport workers union boss. He was on his way to a Manhattan prison to begin a 10-day sentence for his role in organizing the transit strike. Ten measly days. That was his punishment for an illegal strike that shut down the city, cost New York City millions of dollars in business, and broke my body. But he didn't go to jail quietly. That afternoon he shepherded 1,200 supporters across the bridge, tying up downtown traffic in the process. Later that day Governor Pataki blasted Toussaint while referencing me. "I would prefer that the people of New York think and pray for the firefighter," the governor said, "instead of someone who actually provoked this illegal action." I fumed, too, watching the grandstanding. I took it as a public kick in the face. This guy broke the law and received a hero's send-off to prison. I tried to bike to work and nearly got killed.

The TV went off.

Like the *Seinfeld* episodes, my days became one rerun after another. They typically started at 6 a.m. with the nurses waking me to bathe me and clean my dressings. When they were done, I would sit in my chair by the window for an hour, sometimes two, waiting to be taken to 30 minutes of physical therapy, followed by 30 minutes of occupational therapy. Then came lunch, followed by two hours in my chair. Occupational therapy, again, at 2 p.m. Physical therapy, again, at 3 p.m. Maybe a little rest. Dinner at 5:30. Some visitors for a couple of hours. Then TV. My meds. More TV. More meds. Lights out. Staring at the ceiling. Thinking. Staring out the window. Thinking some more. Finally, by 2 a.m., falling asleep. Sleeping until 6 a.m. And then the nurses were back, and the routine repeated.

Each day, every day. It was so redundant, I couldn't see the advances I was making—or didn't want to. One day Tena actually had me walk the length of the rehab ward with a walker. I shuffled along the hardwood floor, a floor that looked like the basketball courts I used to play on in high school. As I slowly moved down the hall, she was giving me all the encouragement a patient in my shape could ever want. And when I finally made the distance, she leaped up. "Matt, that's fantastic!" she shouted. "Amazing job."

I couldn't match her enthusiasm. I shrugged it off. "Tena, remember, I used to run a mile in six minutes. I'm not getting excited by walking 60 feet."

"Matt, come on," she snapped back. "Look how far you've come."

But I didn't want to look back. And I couldn't look forward. I had always lived in the present. I used to wake up every morning expecting to make that day more fun than the day before. I jumped from thing to thing, as quickly as possible, filling each 24 hours with as much as I could. Then I got run over by a bus, and I couldn't do anything or see anything. I couldn't see that last week I had walked 30 feet down a hallway, and this week I walked 60 feet, and next week I might walk 120 feet. I didn't see that things were doubling. I just saw one thing.

*Me in a damn wheelchair with a damn colostomy bag hooked to my side.*

And that constant image wore on me, tainting the achievements that I should have been celebrating. Instead of making me feel happy, the milestones only made me angrier. I tried not to show my frustration to my college roommate Mark Desautelle and his family when they visited, or to Noel and Vicky and Frank, or to the doctors and nurses, or to my brothers and sisters. But when Mom and Dad were with me, and I couldn't contain myself any longer, they got the full force of my fury. One night was typical of many. As I lay in bed, Mom and Dad were just talking about their days. Idle chitchat, and I heard them but I wasn't listening. I had other things on my mind; it had been a difficult day in rehab. Suddenly I just started to scream at them. "I can't do this anymore! I'm done! This sucks!" I grabbed my pillow and tried throwing it, but couldn't. My body was so weak, and I was connected to so many machines, I could hardly move. So I let the pillow drop to the floor, and I just started crying. Mom and Dad then started crying, and I couldn't take that. So I asked them to leave.

When they were gone, I just kept crying and wondering what had happened to me. And what was going to happen. What was the plan?

I needed to know. *What was the plan?*

A couple of days later Father Jim Devlin, a family friend, came to visit and we had a lengthy conversation. I may have slacked off in recent years when it came to going to church, but I still believed in God and prayed to Him every day. At one point Father Devlin asked me how I felt about God.

"Father, I'm not angry at Him," I said, "but to be honest with you, I'm pretty damn confused. I always thought God didn't give us things we couldn't handle. But now I'm not so sure."

"Matt, there's a plan, you'll see," Father Devlin assured me. "You just need to hang in there."

I told him, "Father, I'm having trouble doing that."

Before I did my first Ironman, Anthony, my coach, had told me to visualize the day ahead of me—visualize the finish line—and then the looming effort wouldn't seem so overwhelming. So I did, and I finished the Ironman stronger than I ever had expected. But when I was alone in my hospital room, sitting in my chair and looking out the window at the city below, or when I lay awake in bed in the middle of the night unable to sleep, I could not visualize a plan. All I could see was the question: *God, why did you let me live when I should have died that day?* And it irked me that I had no answer. I could never bring myself to say, "Well, at least I lived." No, that wasn't sufficient. No matter what face I put on for my family and friends, for the firemen, for the mayor, or for anyone else who came to see me, when they left and I was alone, this is how I felt: *I wish I had died on that December morning.*

And that only made me feel worse—because I once so loved to live.

And because I knew the misery of death. On one awful, unconscionable day, I saw how death, in the hundreds, had ruined families and friends. And almost ruined me.

＝＝＝＝＝＝

Around 9:45 on the morning of September 11, 2001, Ladder 43 finally received the call to report to lower Manhattan.

For much of the past hour, the Twin Towers of New York's World Trade Center had been burning, with hundreds of people trapped inside, after two hijacked jetliners had rammed into each tower's upper floors. Fire companies closest to the Trade Center responded first to the scene. As the magnitude of the emergency grew, crews from outlying areas were called to report.

We had just finished handling a small job in Grand Central Station—we had to free a subway rider stuck in a revolving door—when we got word to head downtown. As we made our way through a midtown traffic mess, I heard some guy yell from his car, "They just hit the Pentagon!" I relayed the news to Lieutenant Glen Rohan and to our driver, Johnny Colon.

"What?" the lieutenant yelled back.

"The guy in the car next to us says they just hit the Pentagon."

The men in the truck looked at each other. Suddenly, we realized we were not headed to another accident scene. Now we knew what was at stake: That morning the United States was under attack.

We approached the Trade Center via the West Side Highway, with the Hudson River to our right. I sat in the rear of the truck, staring at large plumes of black smoke billowing from the towers and up into an otherwise crystal-clear late-summer blue sky. From about two miles away, I could see debris spewing from above the 80th floor, along with flames from the fire. We listened to the truck's radio as calls from people inside the towers came in to the FDNY's central dispatcher. Each voice sounded more desperate than the last.

"I'm trapped on the 83rd floor!"

"I can't breathe; it's getting hot up here!"

"We're burning. Please, help! Please, help!"

As we moved closer to the site, some of the guys started taking pictures of the approaching scene—we often carried disposable cameras in our coats to record fires—until they realized what they were photographing: The debris falling from the towers wasn't debris. "Holy shit!" one of the guys yelled out. "Those are people jumping!" The cameras were put away, and the truck got quiet.

Usually on the way to a fire there's an excitement on the truck; I often compare it to the mood before a marathon. A revelry that signals that we're prepared and ready for the job ahead of us. But there was no chirping now. This was different. We were anxious and scared. We were about to go into hell. Someone had a bottle of Gatorade in the back of the rig. He dumped out the remaining contents, and we started pissing into it.

We drove to within five blocks of the Trade Center and parked the rig along the West Side Highway. The noise around us was incredible, with people screaming and running for safety. In the confusion of the moment we didn't even know that the South Tower, the second one hit that day, had already collapsed. And over our heads the North Tower kept burning.

Amid the chaos Lieutenant Rohan ordered us to huddle up. "Guys, I have no idea what we're going in to. No clue. All I know is that it's going to be a hot day, and we're going to be here a long time. You need to be flexible; you need to be fast. So strip down to just your shorts and then put your bunker gear back on over them."

I had long pants on under my fire outfit, so I pulled them off and tossed them into the truck. When the other five men were ready, Lieutenant Rohan began again. "Guys, remember: We are only as fast as our slowest guy. There are seven of us here; we do not part from each other. Understand?"

"Yes, sir!" we said as one.

"Then let's get going," the lieutenant said.

His entire talk took all of three minutes. As it turned out, three lifesaving minutes.

We headed down West Street, walking toward the North Tower, where we planned to aid in the evacuation. But within seconds of leaving the rig we heard a massive rumble and looked up: The 110-story tower had started to implode.

We did the only thing we could do. We ran for cover, with debris raining down around us, but quickly realized that we couldn't outrace the collapsing wreckage. Lieutenant Rohan ordered us to pile on top of one another, facedown, hands behind our heads, next to a building on West Street—just as a tornado of dust and glass and shrapnel blew by. For the longest 10 minutes of my life, a blackness of dirt and ash smothered us. I kept breathing it in and gagging. For several seconds I couldn't take in any clean air.

All I could think was *The world is ending.*

And why not? By now I had been a firefighter for eight years and had been in dozens of fires. All the smoke from all the fires combined couldn't match the plume swallowing us at that moment. And I had been tutored by some of the most seasoned senior men in the FDNY, guys with dozens of saves to their credit and hundreds of years under their helmets. But none—*none*—had ever told me about something like this.

Now I knew what hell looked like.

We stayed piled atop one another, every so often glancing to see what might be coming or listening for the next rumble. Finally the whirling dust slowed to a point where we could see some light. When we could see maybe 15 feet in front of us, Lieutenant Rohan gave us the order to get up.

"Holy shit," I said to Johnny Colon, his face and body covered in chalky dust. "What are we doing still alive?"

"Matty, this is insane," Johnny said. "What the hell's going on?"

"I don't know, bro. It's scary."

Lieutenant Rohan led us toward an area that minutes earlier had housed two iconic skyscrapers; now it was mostly a massive pile of rubble. Ground Zero, as it became known. We didn't know exactly what we were doing or were supposed to do—save lives, presumably—but where do you start when you are dealing with an entirely new, unmapped piece of real estate?

We tied a lifesaving rope to a pole, and each of us grabbed ahold and walked forward. The air remained thick with dust, and it was still difficult to breathe; I used my fire hood to cover my mouth and nose. It was not until much later that morning that we met someone passing out painter's masks. We walked over the piles of crushed building until we came across a ladder that led to what looked like a balcony, maybe 30 feet above us. Firefighter Frank Macchia and I held the ladder as the first five men climbed up. Before Frank and I could ascend, Lieutenant Rohan called down to say he had found an injured firefighter. He told Frank and me to retrieve a Stokes basket that he could see lying on the ground where we had just come from. They would use the stretcher to carry the firefighter out of the rubble.

"Matty," he said, "it's about 40 yards back in that direction."

It may have only been 40 yards away, but it was up and over stories of the crushed Twin Towers. It took probably 20 minutes for Frank and me to get to the basket, and when we returned with it, we couldn't find our company. Anywhere.

"Uh, Matt, where do you think they are?" Frank asked.

"I'm not sure, Frank. Let's just assume they're okay."

For the next few hours Frank and I moved around the site, working with fire chiefs from different houses and doing whatever we were told—which, unfortunately, produced little in return. Along with hundreds of other firefighters, we crawled on the ground and dug through piles of dirt; we walked up and down stairs that led to nowhere; we came across crushed fire trucks and looked underneath them for anyone who might be injured. We found no one. We walked in, around, up, and down 16 acres of rubble, and we found nothing. I only came across destruction, and other firefighters and police officers as dazed as I was. Word had started to spread about the enormous death toll this tragedy might produce—a toll that was sure to include colleagues of the firefighters and police officers I was working beside.

Around 2 p.m. a firefighter who knew my brother Jimmy well spotted me. "Matt, oh, thank God."

"What do you mean?" I asked.

"Well, I had heard that one of the Long boys was missing, so it's great to see you."

I gave him a quizzical look. "Well, if you heard one of the Long boys was missing, and I'm here, that can mean only one thing."

Ever since I had arrived at the scene, I had tried not to think about Jimmy. Coincidentally, he had worked in my house the night before, filling in for someone who was on vacation. His shift ended just as the first reports came in about the Trade Center, and he went back to his firehouse in midtown. All morning I assumed he was working somewhere near or around me and that he wasn't buried in the ground I was searching.

I put thoughts about the worst out of my mind. I would do the job I was there to do and not agonize over something I couldn't control. I didn't think about Mom and Dad and how they had to be suffering, knowing that two of their sons were in a place central to this terrorist attack. I wouldn't think about Eileen and Maureen and my other brothers and how they were probably wondering if Jimmy and I were okay or dead.

No, I had a job to do. So I tried not to think.

————————

Frank Macchia and I finally reconnected with our company around 3 p.m., just as Lieutenant Rohan and the guys were about to provide one of the few bright spots in an otherwise terrible day.

Hours earlier, as the North Tower was being evacuated, a team of six firefighters from Ladder 6 led an exhausted Josephine Harris down stairwell B of the building, where the 59-year-old woman worked as a bookkeeper. At the fourth floor they stopped. Josephine told them she couldn't go any farther; she had already walked 60 flights. Just then the tower began to collapse, 110 stories toppling in a matter of seconds. Miraculously, stairwell B remained intact between the second and fourth floors, right where Josephine and the firefighters had stopped. They were alive, along with four other rescue workers, but trapped 60 feet or so above the main pile of rubble.

While searching the site, Lieutenant Rohan and the guys heard screams coming from the pocket where the group was trapped. Our company managed to get a ladder down to the men of Ladder 6, who climbed up to safety. Josephine needed to be carried up the ladder and out of the hole. To then get her down the mountain of rubble, the men of Ladder 43, along with several other firefighters, formed a human chain. Frank and I spotted our guys in that line and joined them. Josephine passed through our arms to safety.

The thrill that came from having helped this woman did not last long. By 6 p.m. the scale of the day's devastation hit home when our company regrouped back at our truck along the West Side Highway. As we downed some water and toweled off, we heard a report that Freddy Ill, a former member of our truck, had perished in the rubble. Johnny Colon had worked with Freddy for years, and the two men had remained good buddies after Freddy had been promoted to captain in a downtown house. In the time I had worked with Johnny, a Vietnam veteran with 20-plus years on the job, I never saw him fazed by anything. But when he heard about Freddy, Johnny turned whiter than the ash already covering his face, and he started bawling. Then he dropped his Halligan on the roadway. The sound of the steel tool hitting cement made a ringing noise that marked the hollowness of the day. For the rest of my life I'll never forget that sound.

I'll also never forget the sight I saw minutes later. There, a few yards north along the highway, sitting on the rear end of his rig, was Jimmy. I broke from my unit to race over to him.

"Bro, you're alive," I shouted when Jimmy finally saw me coming.

"Me?" he said. "A few minutes ago someone told me that you were gone." We chuckled for just a second or two, and then I hugged him harder than I ever had before.

―――――――

Around midnight, after 14 hours at the site, our crew headed back to East Harlem. At that hour the city was quiet, almost a ghost

town. There was no traffic, and just a few people walked the streets.
Most bars had closed early; Third & Long and Turtle Bay had shut
down around 7 p.m.

As we headed uptown we made brief stops at a couple of other
firehouses along the way, including Ladder 5, where a close friend
of mine, Tommy Hannafin, was stationed. I had known Tommy for
years; he had played on Jimmy's basketball team in college. When
we got to his station house, we heard that Tommy was among the
missing. In the days to come, *missing* would take on a whole new
meaning.

Back at our house we all showered, almost in silence. After I got
dressed I went over to Lieutenant Rohan and put my arm around his
shoulders.

"Thanks, boss," I told him.

"What for, Matty?"

"That talk you gave us before we left the truck? Those three
minutes kept us out of the building—and kept us alive."

Lieutenant Rohan nodded. At that moment he didn't have much
more to say.

"It's going to be a tough road, boss," I said, "but we're all going
to be all right, together."

I was about to head home, but I needed to call someone first. It
was close to 1 a.m. when Mom picked up the phone. She was crying,
even though Jimmy had called earlier and told her I was okay. When
I heard her sobs, I responded the only way I could: I broke down. It
was at that moment, I think, when I realized that firefighters can
cry, too.

"Mom, you don't know what it was like," I bawled into the
phone. "The worst thing you could ever want to see. People jumping from windows, destruction everywhere. Horrible, Mom,
horrible."

When I got to my apartment, I lay down in bed. I didn't watch the news. I just tried to fall asleep, and to forget.

It would be impossible to escape September 11 for a long time. The enormity of the tragedy became clearer over the subsequent days, when we found out how many men and women died in the attack. The FDNY lost 343 firefighters; in some parts of the country, that's the population of a small town. A good number came from Bay Ridge and Breezy Point, neighborhoods where I had grown up and still spent time. I didn't know most of the firefighters who died, but a number of them were guys I would see now and then and enjoy a beer with at an FDNY fundraiser or a party.

No one from Engine 53 or Ladder 43 died that day, but we weren't spared from tragedy. Rob Curatolo, a member of Jimmy's house, had worked with us the night before, just as Jimmy had. But Rob left our house a little before Jimmy did and ended up being on a truck that made it to the site earlier than Jimmy's. He died when the first tower collapsed, along with Jimmy's lieutenant, Ray Murphy.

Besides the firefighters, I had a number of friends who worked in the Trade Center that never made it out alive. There was Mike Armstrong, who was employed at an investment company. To make some extra cash, he bartended at Turtle Bay on weekends. Mike was one of the hardest workers I knew, and one of the nicest guys as well. In all our years together, I never heard him say a bad word about anyone—a rarity in the cutthroat world of finance. I made sure no one would forget Mike and his kind touch. When Jimmy and I opened our newest bar later that year, we named it M.J. Armstrong's after our good friend.

And there was Rob Scandole, whom I played basketball with on the same summer team, the LD Daddy's, in Breezy Point for 12 years. He was as much a part of my summers as the Fourth of July and cut-off T-shirts. Rob couldn't hit an open jump shot from beyond six feet, but he was the kind of player you always wanted on your team: a hustler and a jokester. Every game with Rob, who had two daughters, ended with a cooler of beer and a round of laughs. Days before September 11, I had had a beer with him at the Bowl, our hangout on summer nights on the Breezy Point beach. We were celebrating my birthday and the end of summer. I never expected that would be the last time we'd toast each other. I won't forget Rob, either. The 9/11 tattoo on my hip has "R.S." stenciled in a cross.

Tommy Hannafin's initials are on that cross as well.

Tommy's funeral was in October, and of the dozens of services for firefighters I attended, his may have been the most emotional. Tommy came from a big family, just like me; he had five brothers, including Kevin, a firefighter who days after the attack had pulled his brother's remains from the wreckage of the North Tower. Tommy had a beautiful wife, Rene, and two young kids, Kayla, five, and Thomas, three. As I watched the members of the Hannafin family hugging each other in the church pews, in need of support, I thought about my own family. When the Longs gathered together for a holiday dinner or party, we tended to tease each other, not toss "I love yous" around. But outside Tommy's funeral I gave Jimmy a hug, and for the first time I told him that I loved him.

When I first joined Ladder 43, a senior man gave me some advice: Never miss a firefighter's funeral. September 11 threw that rule out the window because we were having three or four funerals a day around the city and around the region. At some point not long after Tommy Hannafin's service, burying friends and coworkers got to be too painful. And that's when I stopped going to funerals.

I worked down at Ground Zero as part of the cleanup crew for a month or so, but that also became too much to bear. I decided to return to full-time duty at the house, and I never went back to Ground Zero again. Never. It's too raw. Like a lot of guys in the department, I tried to put the day behind me. I went to counseling a few times, but that didn't help much. I also started drinking like I never had before. In fact, it got so bad that one day, while I was still on the site, I saw a banner unfurled from a building across the way with the words "Friends of Bill W." One of the firefighters I was working with suddenly put down his shovel and started walking off the site and in the direction of the sign.

"Hey, what's up?" I shouted. "Where do you think you're going?"

He just glanced at me and said, "Hey, Big Shot, you'll be joining me someday if you keep going the way you're going."

I later learned "Friends of Bill W." was a reference to Alcoholics Anonymous. It would take me a few weeks, but eventually I started to wean myself from the late-night benders.

But how do you deal with so much sadness and tragedy and death? Everyone in the department had to learn to cope in his or her own way. Some couldn't. Besides the rash of senior men who retired after September 11 because they had seen too much, others turned to religion. Walk into a New York City church on the anniversary of that day and the pews are dotted with firefighters. And still others have promoted the idea of honoring those who died with a holiday. I'm not a big fan of that idea; the FDNY already has its own memorial day each October recognizing firefighters who have died in the line of duty. But I understand the sentiment behind the initiative: Whatever works to remember the dead, then do it.

The point is, just don't forget them.

━━━━━

On September 11, 2005, three months before my accident, I took a day off from the firehouse to do a half-Ironman triathlon in Rhode

Island. Some of the guys in the firehouse gave me a bit of a hard time for racing on such a somber day. But I went to the event with a plan: to compete with Freddy Ill, Tommy Hannafin, Rob Curatolo, and 340 other firefighters on my mind. And the plan worked: I had my breakthrough run. After biking 56 miles, I ran the half-marathon in one hour and 30 minutes, six minutes faster than my previous best at the 13.1-mile distance.

As an athlete, I never felt so strong. As a firefighter, I never felt so proud.

The firefighters who died on September 11, 2001, had lived their lives with a purpose. Though sometimes it's difficult to understand, they died pursuing that purpose—helping people who were trapped in an indescribably awful situation. In a way, knowing that is a comfort.

Now, as I struggled to get out of bed every morning, to walk 60 more feet than I had the day before, and to not piss on myself in the process, I searched for a similar purpose.

And worried that I would never find it in this life.

Our family business was a popular hangout in Cypress Hills, Brooklyn (1979).
*Credit: Michael Long*

On the day of my First Communion
at Blessed Sacrament Church in
Brooklyn (1974). *Credit: Mike and Eileen Long*

A rare court appearance for
Iona College (1988). *Credit: Matt Long*

With my family on the beach at Breezy Point in Queens, New York (2003).
*Credit: Mike and Eileen Long*

With the top four FDNY finishers at the 2005
New York City Marathon: (from left) Shane McKeon,
Larry Parker, Denis Sweeney, and me. *Credit: Matt Long*

On the job with members of Ladder 43 following a fire
in East Harlem: (from left) Jim McEntee, Johnny Colon,
Mike Donovan, George Hear, and me. *Credit: Matt Long*

Stunned by the destruction of the World Trade Center on September 11, 2001.
*Credit: Matthew McDermott*

On stage with Billy Crystal at Madison Square Garden in October 2001.
*Credit: Getty Images via Cory Schwartz*

How the New York *Daily News* reported my accident (December 23, 2005).

*Credit: © New York Daily News, L.P., used with permission*

At New York–Presbyterian Hospital in April 2006.

*Credit: Bryan Smith via New York Daily News*

Two of the doctors who saved my life, Dr. Dean Lorich (left) and Dr. Soumitra Eachempati.

*Credit: Dean Lorich and Soumitra Eachempati*

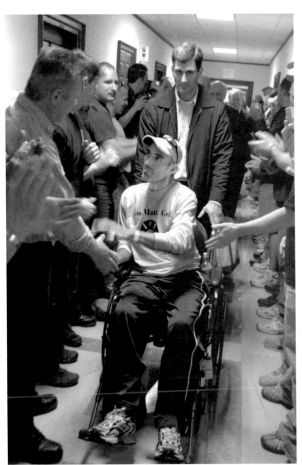

My brother Jimmy wheels
me through the hospital
on May 24, 2006—the day
I finally went home.
*Credit: Matthew Roberts*

Learning to walk again with my physical
therapist, Julie Khan (July 2006).
*Credit: Matthew McDermott*

Running my first postaccident mile in Tempe, Arizona, with trainer Mark D'Aloisio on March 14, 2008. *Credit: Mark D'Aloisio*

My parents, Mike and Eileen Long, waiting for me to run by during the 2008 New York City Marathon. *Credit: David Yellen*

Making my way through Brooklyn during the marathon with
Noel Flynn (left) and Frank Carino. *Credit: Victor Sailer*

Jimmy greeting me at the finish line
of the marathon.
*Credit: The FDNY Photo Unit*

With my brother Eddie
after the 2008 New York
City Marathon.
*Credit: Matt Long*

Running the marathon leg of the
2009 Ironman in Lake Placid,
New York, with Kyle Herrig.
*Credit: Matt Long*

An Ironman again, July 26, 2009.
*Credit: Terri Long*

# 11

# Basic Training

**"Experience Guides Cheruiyot to Record Run and Second Win in Boston"** —*The Boston Globe*

*Boston, April 18, 2006—Robert Cheruiyot had been up and down this bumpy road before, often enough to know that the graveyard is full of runners who have led this footrace at Woodland. "A marathon is a long distance," he said. "Twenty-six miles is a big distance."*

*So Cheruiyot let Kenyan countryman Benjamin Maiyo dash into the Newton hills alone yesterday afternoon, then calmly caught him, broke him on Heartbreak Hill, and went on to win his second Boston Marathon in a course record two hours, seven minutes, 14 seconds on a cool and cloudy day that was ideal for an assault on the clock.*

*"When I was at 40 kilometers [24.86 miles], I think maybe I can run 2:06," said the 27-year-old Cheruiyot, who shaved one second off Cosmas Ndeti's 1994 mark while leaving Maiyo 1:07 behind. "But [training partner/world record-holder] Paul Tergat told me: 'Don't run too fast, you only need to win.'"*

I loved that line: *Don't run too fast, you only need to win.* Two hours, seven minutes, 14 seconds seemed darn fast to me when I heard that that was the winning time of the 2006 Boston Marathon. Even on two good legs (and roller skates) I couldn't have given Cheruiyot much of a battle. He was a world-class marathoner from the running-rich Rift

Valley of Kenya; I was a classic recreational runner from the streets of Brooklyn. But come to think of it, John J. McDermott, the very first Boston Marathon champion, would have been left in Cheruiyot's dust, too. Back in 1897, McDermott claimed the title with a time of 2:55— 48 minutes slower than Cheruiyot's—and he won when the length of the marathon was only 24.5 miles, not today's standard of 26.2.

In 109 years, times certainly had changed.

But a much faster champion wasn't the only difference between this year's Boston Marathon and the original. That first year, just 15 men took part; this year, the race attracted a record 22,000 entrants. The field had become so big, in fact, that the organizers needed to schedule two wave starts—one wave of faster runners starting 30 minutes before the next one—in order to reduce the bottleneck of athletes departing from the tiny town of Hopkinton, Massachusetts, where the starting gun has been fired since 1924. For 99 percent of those runners, the goal was not to win Boston; they were just happy to *run* Boston. To enjoy the local color and crazy traditions of the most recognized foot race in the world. Hopkinton. Heartbreak Hill. The winners' wreaths made of olive branches. The women of Wellesley College prodding runners on around mile 13 with their Screaming Tunnel of Noise and "Please, Kiss Me" posters.

Yes, I had lots of reasons to want to run Boston, with the kiss-me posters way up on the list. Obviously, it didn't happen. Instead, I got reports about the day from the newspapers and from my buddies at the Rock. Shane McKeon, Larry Parker, and Tommy Grimshaw had trained through the tricky winter months, and through the memory of waiting for me on the morning of my accident, to run their first Boston. They started together but then spread out over the course of the race, with Larry finishing in 2:58, Shane in 3:13, and Tommy in 3:44. Afterward they went out for some cold Sam Adams and toasted me. "This was for Matty, the brother who should have been here today," Shane told the other two. "Next year he'll be running with us."

While those guys tackled Boston, I was in New York, where my various therapists kept trying to push me up my own set of hills. Each day I returned to the rehab gym, a room the width of the hospital at the far end of my floor. In a lot of ways the facility looked like your typical New York City fitness club, with tables for stretching, parallel bars, Swiss balls, and light weights. Windows ran the length of the room, providing views of the East River. But instead of featuring supertoned gym junkies working out with their iPods or *People* magazines, the room usually was filled with men and women struggling to get back on their feet, just like me.

Loreen Acevedo, who was in her mid-twenties and had long, dark hair that made her look a bit like Jennifer Lopez, had been an occupational therapist at the hospital for two years. Her job was to retrain me to handle the tasks of a typical day, from tying my shoelaces to turning faucets on and off in the bathroom. Simple, mundane tasks that could drive a person in my condition nutty. The two of us were alike in many ways. Loreen grew up not far from the city and had a street-smart edge to her, which often made for a fiery dynamic between us. She would hear me whine about some exercise I didn't want to do, and bluntly say, "Matt, just try it," and I would say, "No," and she would say, "Try it anyway."

One of her favorite exercises was called the Valpar. I had to stand about an arm's length from a wall and reach out and grab tiny shapes that hung on pegs. I then had to put the shapes back on the wall but on a slightly higher row. A two-year-old standing on his mother's knee could play this game. The exercise was intended to work on my shoulder's range of motion. Since the surgery to repair my humerus, I was able to raise my arm only a few inches above my shoulder, an impairment that didn't bode well if I wanted to climb fire ladders again or swim the length of a pool. Loreen had more immediate concerns: She wanted to make sure that once I got back to living on my own—an eventuality that was starting to loom larger—I could reach life's essentials: a lock on a door, a bottle of shampoo in the shower, a light switch on a wall.

The first time I finished a row of 10 shapes, I glanced at Loreen with a know-it-all look. "Done," I said sharply. "You happy?"

"Great," she said, "now move them to the row above that one."

"Huh? You said to do the second row."

"I know. Now I'm saying try the third row."

"But it's getting late. Let's do it tomorrow."

"No, let's start now. You have five minutes. Keep working."

So I started on the next row, but after reaching for the first shape, I felt a twinge in my shoulder. "Tomorrow, Loreen. I'll do it tomorrow."

"No, Matt, keep trying."

"Loreen, *tomorrow!*"

"Matt, *today!*"

The sparring would go on until one of us gave in; each day seemed to produce a different winner. Every time I "won," I really lost, because it only slowed my recovery. And Loreen knew this, but she had also come to realize that she could push me only so far. From talking to my brothers and the Cronies when I wasn't around, she had drawn a bead on my former life—my former in-perpetual-motion life. The insights only made her job trickier. One night, months after I left the hospital, we saw each other in a restaurant in the city, and she admitted my case had stressed her considerably. "Matt, a lot of times after I worked with you, I went home and cried," she told me. "Your damage was tenfold what my typical patient has. Normally, I'll talk to my patients about what they did before they got hurt and say, 'We'll get you back to that.' But you were this independent guy; you had tons of girlfriends, your hands in a lot of businesses. You had a lot going for yourself." She paused and looked away for a second. "I couldn't talk to you about past stuff because I honestly didn't know if you would ever get back to triathlons and running and all the things you did. I wanted to avoid all the things that made you happy—and there were a lot of things that made you happy."

There certainly were.

Fortunately for Loreen and me, Julie Khan entered the picture. And when she did and hatched a plan with Loreen behind my back, my rehab work—and my days—suddenly became a little more meaningful.

Julie's job was to advance my mobility beyond where Inna and Tena had taken me, even though I remained almost as fragile as when I first got out of bed in January.

As my doctors, my therapists, and I were discovering, my skeletal structure had been changed forever the day the bus ran over me. When salvaging my right pelvis, Dr. Lorich needed to raise it an inch or so higher than my left pelvis, which made my right leg shorter than my left. Another complication involved the gluteal muscle in my right buttock. The glute is one of the body's most powerful muscles and helps provide the push-off needed to propel a leg forward when you walk or run. My glute had been severed, along with many of the nerves connected to it, and Dr. Lorich couldn't tell yet if this major muscle would ever work as it once had. That meant I had virtually no control over my right leg; it wobbled like a chicken bone soaked in vinegar. Each time I tried to take a step, I thought my leg might buckle. And I never knew how my right foot would plant; it might flop to the left, it might flop to the right. I just never knew. It was a scary sensation.

Then there was my midsection, or what remained of it.

In a way, the abdominal muscles work like a cocoon, keeping such key organs as the stomach and intestines in place. But my intestines had swelled so much from the injuries I sustained that they forced my abs to retract to either side of my body. Until the intestines could heal—Dr. Eachempati wasn't ready to hazard a guess when that might be—my abs stayed separated. During this wait-and-see period Dr. Eachempati and Dr. Lloyd Gayle, a plastic surgeon, performed a skin graft that temporarily encased the intestines and gave them a little privacy. No one, including me, needed a window into the inner workings of my gut. Unfortunately, the doctors did not want to reconstruct the area until I became stronger and the scarring around my intestines decreased.

But while the graft covered my organs, it didn't provide my core with much support—at least not the kind of support the abs regularly supply. Instead, my stomach looked like a water-filled balloon: sagging, constantly jiggling and jostling, stretched by the parts floating around inside. My soft belly also compromised my balance. The abs help keep you from spending your life hunched over; a water balloon doesn't.

So I was basically a five-foot-ten-inch jellyfish, placing my hope of moving around, tall and erect as I once had, in the hands of some 28-year-old woman I didn't know.

Julie took over as my full-time physical therapist in mid-March. She was new to the hospital, and I was her first patient. She was a brunette with a sweet, easygoing way about her, and immediately I tested her toughness. At our first session together I peppered Julie with questions as I might a probie at the fire academy. "Why did you become a therapist? Where did you go to school? Where did you work before you came here? Why did you leave the other hospital?" I wasn't being nosy. I wanted to know the person who planned to get my body working again.

Because my body no longer worked the way it once had.

Each morning at 11:30 Julie and I met in the gym. For the first couple of weeks we kept the small talk to a minimum. With Loreen, whom I had known longer, I felt comfortable voicing concerns; I would tell her how I slept the night before or how the nurses were treating me. But with Julie, I just did what she asked me to do, and then we moved on to the next task. A workmanlike relationship, which was fine. Loreen must have noticed, because one day—as I only learned later— she filled Julie in on my story beyond the injuries. Loreen told her that I had been a serious runner who had raced marathons and competed in Ironmans. She also told Julie, "I don't know if he'll ever run again."

That's when Julie offered a peek into her own life: She told Loreen that she was a runner and was planning to run the New York City Marathon the coming fall.

"Does Matt know that?" Loreen asked.

"No, we don't talk much about anything."

"Well, you mind if I tell him? Because maybe—and I'm not sure—but maybe if he knows you're a runner, he might feel more comfortable with you."

"Go right ahead. I need something to move us along."

During our therapy session the next day, Loreen ever so subtly filled me in on some new information about Julie, or New P.T., as I called her. I took the bait. When I saw Julie later that day, I said to her, "So, I hear you're a runner."

"Who told you that?" Julie asked, barely looking at me. She was a good actress as well.

"Loreen, and she says you're planning on doing the marathon. Have you done it before?"

"I've done a few half-marathons, but this will be my first full one. I'm pretty nervous."

"Why do you want to do one?"

"My dad sort of inspired me. He's done a lot of them."

"Yeah, how many?"

"About 25."

*Twenty-five.* I had done only four. "Okay, he's legit. So, have you started training?"

"Well, officially not until June."

"June? Glad to hear you're in no rush. Come on, now's the time to start getting some extra miles in. You can start doing speedwork. And you're doing tempo runs, right? You got to do tempo runs!" For a second I felt like Burgess Meredith in *Rocky:* "Julie, you're gonna eat lightnin' and you're gonna crap thunder!"

From that point forward I felt more comfortable around her, and maybe she around me. I kept on Julie about her training, and she pushed me a little harder with my therapy. We moved from partial squats to full squats; we added push-ups and kneeling exercises. We progressed from stationary lunges to lunges on the balance board or foam mat. She slowly built my strength and my confidence.

Case in point: I never came to rehab without a bottle of Gatorade; it was a habit left over from my Ironman and marathon training days. Usually, I'd leave the bottle on a table, and then ask Julie to retrieve it once we finished an exercise. One day when we were working on the stretching table doing knee bends, I asked Julie to pass me the Gatorade.

"Get it yourself!" she said, and walked out of the room.

*Get it myself. What do you mean, get it myself? It's 10 feet away. Get it myself?*

Julie was nowhere to be seen.

I sat on the edge of the table, staring at the bottle. There were probably 10 other patients in the room at the time, all involved in their own workouts. To get the bottle I needed to stand up and move 10 feet—two body lengths. That's all. It seemed like the length of the Brooklyn Bridge. I put my left foot down on the floor first, followed gradually by the right, and stood up. I steadied myself on the table and stared at the bottle. *Do I really need a drink?* I took a half step with my left leg and didn't fall. I shuffled with the right. Still standing. Half step. Another half step. Another half step. Reach . . . *reach.* I grabbed the Gatorade and turned, slowly, around. I steadied myself for a second, then began the shuffle back. When I got to the stretching table, I leaned my butt against it and gulped the Gatorade.

A few minutes later, Julie returned. She saw the empty bottle.

"How was it?" she asked.

"Delicious," I told her.

And we went back to work.

More breakthroughs would come. For a couple of weeks Julie worked with me on climbing a small set of stairs in the rehab room, four steps at a time maximum. At first we practiced doing one step, then two steps, and so on. Each time I started with my stronger leg—the left—then hitched my right leg next to it. One day, though, with no prompting from Julie, I went step over step straight to the top step.

"Where did that come from?" Julie shouted to me.

I just kind of shrugged. At that moment Barry White's "You're the First, the Last, My Everything" was playing on the rehab center's sound system. Still up on the top step, I clicked in to a little dance move. Julie saw me. "That's the way I used to do it," I called down to her, smiling.

―――――

The goal of all this rehab work, of course, was to get me out of the hospital and living independently at home—without nurses giving me sponge baths, or handrails lining a hallway, or hospital aides wheeling me wherever I needed to go. I had to prepare myself for the contingencies that crop up in everyday life. Like, what do you do with a pair of crutches when you need to walk up a flight of stairs? Loreen showed me how to simply hook one crutch to the banister and slide it up on its side as I rose. And when I wanted to climb into bed, they showed me how to use a leg lifter—a pole that looked almost like a shepherd's crook—to pull my legs up. We practiced walking in and out of crowded elevators, stepping into a shower, getting out of a wheelchair and into a car, and even cleaning my colostomy bag. They kept feeding me all this insider information—meaningless stuff to a healthy person—with the hopes of making my life at home a little more bearable. Their help reminded me of how Vicky used to supply me with simple, practical advice before a marathon or triathlon. At my first Ironman, for instance, I made the mistake of buying reflective tape to put on my bike. When Vicky saw the tape, she rang me up. "Put that away. If you're still biking when it's dark out, then you're going to need more than tape to help you out." Another time, on the morning of one of my first marathons, I ate a bowl of pasta and drank a strawberry smoothie—and by mile five I felt like I was running with an oak tree in my stomach. Afterward Vicky, a nutrition expert, set me straight. "You don't need to be carrying around 2,000 calories in your belly for a three-hour event. You just need to top off what you have stored already. Just eat a bagel with peanut butter and half of a banana. That's plenty." And that's exactly what I ate before running my 3:13 New York City Marathon.

So, I listened to what Loreen and Julie told me, even when it came to my apartment.

In early May, about two weeks before my scheduled release from the hospital, we left the rehab center for a few hours to do what Loreen and Julie called a home evaluation. They wanted to make sure my apartment was safe. (I wanted to make sure it was still there. I hadn't been back since the morning of the accident, nearly five months earlier.) In a lot of ways the apartment was a typical New York City one-bedroom: It was no bigger than 600 square feet; "cozy" in the lingo of city realtors. It was on the fourth floor tucked in the back of the building, and my bedroom window faced the blackening brick façade of the neighboring building. The sun had little chance of sneaking in, which was okay with me. Buried back there, unconscious from a long night at the bar or a 24-hour shift in the firehouse, I never heard the noise of midday traffic. I just slept in my urban cave.

The place looked fine when we walked in. In fact, better than fine. Someone must have come by to give it a good cleaning. I hadn't seen the top of my kitchen counters since moving in seven years earlier. But Loreen and Julie became antsy right away.

"Matt, we're going to move these rugs," Julie said. "I can see you tripping on them all the time."

"And the couch. Where can we put that so you'll have more room to walk?" Loreen wanted to know.

Wow. Suddenly it seemed like I was returning from my honeymoon, not the hospital, with *two* wives to show for it. They scoped out my bathroom and checked out my shower. They told me I needed to install handrails to use the shower safely. They looked through all my cabinets and closets. Then they stared at my bed.

"Matt, that bed's pretty high," Loreen said, her eyebrows arched. "It's going to be hard for you to get in and out of that, even with the leg lifter."

I was getting tired and itchy. "Thanks, ladies. I'll figure it out. Now, you two: Let's get out of here. You're starting to make *me* nervous."

Plus, we had one more stop to make before heading back to the hospital.

Smith & Wollensky, with its distinctive forest green and white exterior, is impossible to miss. Located on the northeast corner of Third Avenue and 49th Street, the restaurant was one block up from my apartment—and in many ways more like home than my apartment. Over the years I had spent so many nights at Smith & Wolly's that I felt like family among the waitstaff and bar crew. There were Major, Ollie, Pat, and the two Ciarans, who all worked behind the bar; Danny, the head waiter; and Tommy Hart, who ran the place. A friend of Dad's, George McGuinness, introduced me to the steakhouse when I was just out of college, and I knew right away it had a charm and character that fit my personality. Sure, Smith & Wolly's could seem like some old boys' club, a place to talk football and the markets over a steak and a cigar. But it was also classy enough to impress a first date. The menus were the size of the Ten Commandments, and the prices on them just as imposing. The wine selection was one of the finest in the city. The walls showcased photos of famous athletes, actors, and politicians. Rudy Giuliani. Ted Kennedy. Keith Hernandez. Liza Minnelli. I had hung around the place so much that Tommy put my name on the wall behind table 35. When I came in with some of the boys, we'd go to that spot and wait for Danny to bring us the usual: the shrimp, lobster, and lump crab appetizer (seafood shit, as we called it), followed by sirloin on the bone with cottage fries and creamed spinach. If I came in solo, I took the corner spot at the bar; it looked out on the front foyer and I could watch everything and everyone. I would have a glass of Pinot Noir and wait to see how the night might go.

Smith & Wolly's became the place where I celebrated life's highlights. Jimmy and I came here to toast the opening of Third & Long. We brought Dad here on his sixtieth birthday. And Noel and I enjoyed a big blowout at the restaurant after I finished my Ironman.

And now on an early spring afternoon, I sat down to lunch at Smith & Wolly's with Loreen and Julie. I reached over to get the basket of bread with my left arm. "Matt," Loreen quickly said, "use your right arm. You got to keep practicing."

"Come on, guys," I shot back, "how about a little time off for good behavior?"

A few minutes later, Danny came by to take our orders and to give me a big hug.

"Matty, it's so good to see you," he said in his Bronx twang. "We missed you, kid."

"Danny," I told him, "the feeling is very mutual."

=====

For sure, I was making progress toward something. But I still couldn't grasp exactly what. And was it what I wanted, or just what the people around me—my family, my doctors, my friends—wanted? Loreen and Julie were preparing me to live on my own, and a lunch at Smith & Wolly's would never be enough to repay them for all their efforts. But as slowly as I climbed a makeshift stairway for Julie, I descended again into depression. I didn't want to be taking baby steps. I wanted to be rushing down a pole in the firehouse, strapping on my bunker pants, and hopping into a rig as it pulled out to a fire. I wanted to be rushing around Turtle Bay, making sure everyone had a drink and grabbing someone to have a fast dance with. Most of all I wanted to run and run and run. It was springtime in New York City. Central Park was awake and I wanted to be there with everyone else, running its collection of loops and transverses.

And to run—to *really* run, like a nine-year-old playing tag in the schoolyard, or like a high school basketball player hustling after a loose ball, or like a Kenyan marathoner winning a race in Boston— meant being able to ever so briefly lift both feet off the ground at the same time with each step. Because technically *that* is running; that ability separates running from walking. Now, nearly five months after my accident, I was nowhere close to doing that. For God's sake, my ability to walk amounted to barely a shuffle.

Each night after my rehab sessions, I returned to my room and couldn't forget that fact. And if I tried to, someone wouldn't let me.

I received hundreds of cards and letters while in the hospital, mostly from friends and relatives but also from strangers. People who happened to hear my story on TV or read about it in the newspapers and kindly thought to write me. Dozens sent cards offering to have masses said in my name in Catholic churches around the city. I got a note from a high school kid from Brooklyn, Frankie Loccisano, who was undergoing cancer treatment at a Manhattan hospital. He wrote that my story had given him hope, that if I could live after getting run over by a bus, maybe he could beat cancer. I appreciated all these thoughts and wishes—until one day when I opened a card from a woman who wrote that she was a friend of a friend. She wanted me to know that she was thinking of me and wished me the best and told me to stay strong. She knew I was a runner and said not to give up hope. She wrote, "I'll save a spot for you on the Achilles team."

When I read that line, it hit me like a 20-ton bus.

She was referring to the Achilles Track Club, an organization that trains people with disabilities to take part in running events. They work with everyone from kids with visual impairments to adults with prosthetic legs. I often would see Achilles athletes training in the park, and I always gave them a shout of encouragement. Talk about inspiring. One year Third & Long hosted the Achilles' after-marathon party, where a number of disabled American war veterans who had run the marathon were honored. Their stories made you immensely sad and incredibly proud.

But as I read the card again—"I'll save a spot for you . . ."—it only upset me. I thought to myself, *I don't want a spot with Achilles. I'm not disabled. I'm injured. I have a broken leg, a broken pelvis, a fractured foot. And, yes, I need a colostomy bag. But none of this is permanent. I'll get better. I'm not disabled. I'm not an Achilles athlete.*

I called my friend who knew the letter-writer. "I don't get it," I said. "Your friend thinks I'm disabled. I'm not disabled!"

"Matt, calm down. You're overthinking all this. She meant well . . ."

"I'm sure she did," I told him, "but I'm not disabled! Okay? I'm not disabled!"

*I'm not disabled.*

Or that's what I wanted to believe.

The picture the medical team continued to paint for me, though, seemed to show something different. A week or so before I left the hospital I met with each doctor. I would continue to see them in the weeks and months ahead, but these meetings gave me an indication of where I stood as I was about to return to the world—and what my future might hold. Dr. Eachempati said my internal wounds, especially my intestines, had not yet healed sufficiently for him to reattach my abdominal muscles or to consider reversing the colostomy. "We'll continue to monitor everything, Matt," he told me. "When the time seems appropriate, we'll make some decisions." Although the catheters had been removed, Dr. Paduch, my urologist, remained concerned that my ability to clear and control my bladder had been compromised. And although most of my broken bones had healed, Dr. Lorich warned me that it would take at least two years before we would know just how far my recovery would take me to walking normally—or running as I once did.

———

On the morning of May 24, Mom, Dad, Jimmy, and Robert came to my room around 11. I was dressed in a white, long-sleeved T-shirt and blue sweatpants and was sitting in my wheelchair. I hadn't slept much the night before, thinking about what this day would bring.

It was checkout day, and while I was excited about finally leaving the hospital, I was also more scared than at any moment in my life— more frightened, in fact, than when I was lying on West Street as the North Tower crumbled. I didn't have a clue as to what the future held or how I would deal with it. I wouldn't have the early morning wakeup call with a dozen or so doctors coming by to check on me. I wouldn't have the attendants bringing me my breakfast. I wouldn't have a button on my bed that I could press at any moment if I needed help with something. I wouldn't have someone to clean the colostomy bag.

I was going home a much different man than the one who had tried biking to work on that December morning. I weighed 40 pounds less, my cheeks looked hollow even behind my unshaven stubble, and my arms and chest appeared not just thin but deflated. Mostly, though, I lacked the confidence—the C—that I once had in excess.

Just as we were leaving my room, Jimmy told me that the FDNY and the hospital wanted to hold a press conference downstairs in the lobby. My story had generated a lot of attention early on and now the newspapers and the TV stations wanted to wrap everything up. I asked Jimmy, "That's it? Nothing else? You don't have anything big planned for me, right?"

"No, don't worry about that, bro. You'll do the press conference," Jimmy said, "and then we're off for home."

"Great."

We got on the elevator, Dad carrying a duffel bag, Mom clutching a bag filled with cards and letters, Robert holding my crutches, and Jimmy, behind me, resting one hand on my shoulder. It was a quiet ride down.

The silence ended with a roar as soon as the elevator door opened. Jimmy rolled me out to the lobby—and into a crowd of hundreds of family members, firefighters, medical staff, and friends from my different worlds. Later, one of the newspapers estimated that more than 500 people were there. As Jimmy wheeled me along, the clapping and cheering got louder. I sat in the chair feeling awkward, not knowing if I should smile or cry. I saw all my other brothers and sisters, including Eileen, who two days earlier had given birth to her first child, Joseph. I had told her not to come to the hospital so soon after having the baby. "Matthew," she said, her eyes red, "I wasn't missing this day for anything." Off to another side I saw Frank and Vicky and some of our teammates from the Asphalt Green Triathlon Club. I saw firefighters I hadn't seen in years, like Lieutenant Carroll—Uncle Kenny, we called him—who leaned in and gave me a big, wet kiss on the cheek. There was Anna, my nurse from the rehab wing, who each morning delicately bandaged the wound near my abdomen. She had even come in on Saturdays, her day off, to do the job. All my doctors—Lorich, Eachempati, Gayle—and Fire Commissioner Nicholas Scoppetta circled around the podium at the front of the lobby.

I had the strange feeling that I was attending my own funeral.

Jimmy kept wheeling me down the hallway toward the podium, where a microphone had been set up. As we rolled, I could see Ray Paprocky, my oldest friend, standing a few feet away. I tapped Jimmy on the hand.

"Bro, there's Ray," I said. "I'm walking for Ray."

Jimmy stopped the chair, and I raised myself up. Robert handed me the crutches, and then I shuffled the next 30 feet into the lobby. The cheering seemed to get louder. I got to the microphone and saw the reporters waiting. I had nothing prepared to say. I just started by thanking the hospital and all the doctors. "With each step I take, I feel lucky. Thanks for being with me on my long journey. Thanks to everyone at the hospital. Thank you," I said. My voice sounded scratchy and hoarse. "Dr. Lorich let me know it's a two-year journey. But with all your help, with all my friends' and family's help and the support I got from all over New York . . . I wouldn't have gotten this far without you."

One reporter asked me about the wheelchair I came down the elevator in. "No worries," I told him. "It's just a rental." And everyone laughed.

Being on stage felt good. When another reporter asked about how much weight I had lost, I joked, "When I decided to become a fireman, someone said you'll become bald and fat. Well, I'm definitely bald," and I lifted up the white Ironman finisher cap I had on my head, "but I ain't fat." And everyone laughed again.

But then the room got quiet when someone asked for my feelings about Roger Toussaint, the transport workers union leader. I could feel myself getting tense as I prepared to answer. "It's against the law for civil servants to strike," I said, my voice now edgier. "If the Fire Department went on strike, and it was his neighbor's house or his house or someone else's house on fire, and we stood idly by watching that burn while you had to wait for firefighters from Jersey or somewhere else to come and put it out, how would you feel, Mr. Toussaint? That's my question for you."

The questions kept coming for a few minutes, until someone asked if I could see myself one day competing in Hawaii in the Ironman Championship, which I had once set as a goal. I said, "Maybe, but that's not for today. I can only say I wish this was the end, and I know it's not."

The press conference broke up, and we headed out of the hospital and into a gorgeous spring day, the kind of day that begs a runner to go a little longer on his run. The FDNY Emerald Society Pipes and Drums were playing. A dozen or so fire trucks were lined up, with guys hanging off them and cheering. They made me seem like a hero, as if I had been injured while saving lives in a burning building. I wasn't a hero; I'd just gotten run over by a bus on the way to work. Jimmy pulled up in his 1963 Ford Galaxy convertible, which he usually kept mothballed in his garage. The top was down, and we drove over to Turtle Bay for lunch. Pretty soon the place was packed with the faces I had just seen at the hospital.

It became a party, but I didn't stay long. After an hour, I said to Jimmy, "I'm tired."

It was time to go home.

# 12

# OH, BROTHER

We called him Fast Eddie for a good reason: The Runt could run.

Eddie Long may have been the baby of the family, as well as the shortest and slightest of the nine of us, but put him on a cross-country course with a pair of spikes on, and he left the rest of us chasing his shadow. In high school Eddie ran the half-mile in two minutes, three seconds. Was that world-class speed? No. But in our corner of Brooklyn, his quickness caught people's attention. Eddie enjoyed enough success at Bishop Ford, my old school, to earn a track scholarship to St. Francis College, a Division I school not far from Bay Ridge.

Even though I was 14 years older than Eddie, I could never catch the kid. I used to bet him dinners at Smith & Wolly's or Peter Luger, another top New York steakhouse, every time we raced. The winner? Let's just say Eddie ate well on my dime.

Which made that 5-K race in November 2005, just a few weeks before my accident, all the sweeter.

It was the annual FDNY Turkey Trot, a firefighter-only race held the Tuesday before Thanksgiving at a park in Queens. This was Eddie's Turkey Trot debut; he had joined the department earlier in the year. He was stationed at Engine 69, the Harlem Hilton as it was called, in upper Manhattan. Unfortunately—at least for Eddie—he was still recovering from minor knee surgery at the time of the race and had done little training. Me? I was in the best shape of my life, still pumped from my New York City Marathon finish a couple of weeks earlier.

*Today*, I told myself at the start, *is the day Fast Eddie goes down.*

Off the line, Eddie looked his old self. For the first two miles he led me by a comfortable margin, maybe 50 yards, but at least I could see him. I started to pick up the pace. When I was about 10 yards from him, and gaining, I said to myself, *Holy crap, I'm going to catch the kid!* I could tell Eddie was now laboring; his usually easy stride had broken down. But this was a race—no time for sympathy cards. I notched another gear, and with just about 500 yards to go, I caught him.

"How you feeling, little brother?" I yelled over to him.

He turned and looked. "Oh, damn!" was all he could say.

"Yeah, your older brother is beating you. This is *unbelievable!*" Then I accelerated, cut in front of him, and left Eddie with one last memory: I gave myself a wedgie. "Eddie!" I called back. "Look at this the rest of the way." I enjoyed my best, and most satisfying, Turkey Trot finish ever.

I was 39 years old and gloating like a 9-year-old in front of my kid brother. But it was all in fun. By now, Eddie understood about good-natured ribbing. He had picked up the firefighting bug from Jimmy and me and followed us into the department. He knew how firefighters taunted one another. He also knew that the more razzing you could take, the tougher you became—and the more the house could depend on you. The same held true for two brothers, even two separated by 14 years.

Now that I was back home in my apartment, I was about to depend on my little brother in ways I never could have imagined.

———

When I left the hospital, I was in no shape to live on my own. I needed full-time, live-in help. The options came down to my six brothers: Michael, Jimmy, and Chris were out. They had wives and kids to take care of. Frank and Robert worked jobs with inflexible schedules. That left Eddie. He was single, and by working double shifts in the firehouse, he could sock away the days off and spend them with me.

For the first time in years I had a roommate. I wish I could say I gave him a grand welcome. Instead, within 20 minutes of being in the apartment, and after Jimmy had left us, we were both crying. The excitement of leaving the hospital and the drama of the press conference had worn off. Reality had set in.

Sitting in the middle of my tiny living room, in my wheelchair, I broke down in tears. Eddie soon followed. "I'm not going to be able to do this," I told him. "This is going to be my life and I can't live like this, confined to a wheelchair needing my younger brother's help. You have your life; you shouldn't be here."

"Listen, Matt, we're a big family. We're going to be here for you, you're going to get through this," Eddie said, kneeling in front of the chair and wiping away his own tears. "We're going to do whatever we have to, to get it done."

We didn't embrace; we didn't go all Oprah. For 10 minutes we just cried.

Yes, we were off to a rousing start, and the afternoon was still young. A few minutes later I told Eddie I had to go to the bathroom to clean out my colostomy bag. "You stay out," I said. "I'll call you if I need you." I lived with the constant fear that anyone close to me might smell the darn thing. Before I left the hospital I had practiced detaching the bag from the opening on my left side, cleaning it, and reattaching it. The bag was beige, about eight inches long and four inches wide. It was a two-piece system: A two-inch-round hole at the top snapped into place over the stoma, a hole in my abdomen where a small part of my intestines stuck out. The bottom of the bag had a small opening that locked shut with a plastic snap, which I could use to clean it out. As I stood in front of the toilet in my narrow bathroom, leaning on my crutches, I got more and more nervous. Once I had the bag off my side, my fingers turned all thumbs. The bag fell on the bathroom floor and the contents flew everywhere: on the tile floor, on the toilet, on the outside of the bathtub. I tried bending down to clean up the mess, but I couldn't with the crutches under my arms. I became enraged and embarrassed. I had no choice but to call for Eddie.

"What's the matter?" Eddie said as he pushed open the bathroom door. All he needed to see was the mess on the floor to know. He immediately helped me out of the bathroom and into my bedroom.

"Matt, listen, fix the bag or get a new one on; just do what you have to do," Eddie said, walking me into the bedroom. Now I was taking orders from my little brother. "And I'll clean up the bathroom."

I sat on my bed, seething, as Eddie looked for a mop.

———————

While not every day involved latrine duty, I kept Eddie hopping. For the first few weeks, each time I got into bed I needed him by my side to lift my legs up off the floor. When I took a shower, Eddie guided me onto the medical chair I had in the tub and then hung around to pass me the soap and shampoo. He did the shopping, the cleaning, the last-minute sprint to the pharmacy for my medicine. He was my personal Lurch. I rang, he fetched. I wore him out. One night, just before midnight, I was in bed trying to fall asleep. I could hear the TV blasting from the living room, where Eddie was stretched out on the couch, his temporary bed. I tried yelling to him—"Eddie, I need you!"—but my voice was too weak and the TV too loud. So I tried knocking on the wall between my bedroom and the living room. That did no good. I grabbed my cell phone and called the house phone. He didn't pick up. Now he had me slightly crazed. I called his cell phone, and the ring finally kicked him out of a dead sleep.

"Hello?"

"Eddie, I've been calling for you for 20 minutes, what the hell?"

"What's the matter?" he asked in a panic. "What's the matter?"

"Nothing. Can you just turn down the TV?"

"Matty, that's it? You scared the hell out of me. Oh, bro, don't do that to me again."

Eventually, Eddie and I settled into our routines. In the morning when he went to work, I went to rehab. I needed to maintain the conditioning I had gained back. Three mornings a week, a firefighter from Ladder 43 picked me up in a van supplied by the Fire Family Transport Unit, a service the department offers to injured firefighters. First we went to Starbucks—I needed my Grande Soy Mocha—then to New York–Presbyterian, where I continued to do outpatient rehab. Usually I followed those sessions with a visit to an acupuncturist, who worked mostly on trying to restore flexibility to my right hip. I also joined a gym, where three times a week a trainer, Ed Rhodes, stretched my legs and arms before helping me step in and out of Nautilus machines for strength training.

As if all that weren't enough, Julie and Loreen stopped by once a week to work with me after they had finished their shifts at the hospital. Loreen continued to concentrate on my shoulder rotation, while Julie took me on progressively longer walks outside. She would time me as I attempted to go around the block, stopping the clock each time I needed to take a breath. I would tell her that the walks were harder than the mile repeats I used to do in Central Park when I was training for the marathon the previous summer.

At the end of the day Eddie and I would have dinner together and talk shop. We were like a married couple, relaying what had happened since we last saw each other. Eddie was still a young firefighter, learning the tricks of the profession and the psychology of his house. He would ask my advice about dealing with certain guys or how to handle a situation better when out on a call. Sitting there listening to Eddie and offering suggestions, I finally felt like the senior man I always wanted to be at Ladder 43.

A few nights a week, Jimmy or Frank or one of my other brothers might stop by and join us for dinner. And for a while Kevin Torrey, Pat Ginty, or some of the other Cronies came by, too. We'd joke a little and tell stories. Sometimes I would even play the pity card. "Hey, Pat, mind grabbing me a beer? You know, I'm kind of stuck in this chair?" Or, "Kevin, can you run to the diner and get me a chocolate shake? I would do it but, well, I can't walk." The eyes would roll, along with a laugh or two.

But after everyone went home, it would just be Eddie and me. The conversation would lag, and by 9 p.m. I'd start making my way to bed. In less than a year's time, I had gone from being a night owl to a senior citizen. My octogenarian grandparents were staying up later than I was. I'd lie there in bed, watch some TV, fall asleep for a while, wake up, watch some TV. And think.

I would think about Eileen and her husband, Joe, and their new baby. And about my cousin John, who had gotten married a couple of months earlier, and his new life. And about Maureen and her husband, Brian, who had their third kid, Timmy, a couple of weeks after I got out of the hospital. And about my buddy, Frank Carino, whose triathlon career was on hold due to the recent arrival of his first child.

And about Jimmy and Pam, who were now expecting their first kid in December.

I was happy for all of them; their lives kept getting richer, fuller, and busier. They kept moving forward. But honestly, I envied them, too. What they had I wanted. But more and more I knew I had little chance of ever having it. I could go to rehab 24 hours a day. I could seek the opinions of more and more doctors. I could go to church every day and pray to every saint in heaven. None of it would matter. The life I always wanted—the wife, the kids, the family like Mom and Dad's—was now a pipe dream.

In fact, it was nearly an impossibility.

———————

I can remember taking health class at Bishop Ford and and having to stare at the funky illustrations of the human anatomy. Our teacher tried to explain how all those squiggly parts—the bladder, the kidneys, the colon, the prostate, the urethra, the scrotum—all worked. That was as good as a sex education class gets at a small Catholic high school.

But whatever I may have learned in that class, Dr. Darius

Paduch, my urologist, schooled me again during the months he treated me in and out of New York–Presbyterian.

They were lessons I could have done without.

Essentially, when my bike's seatpost rammed through my perineum, my urethra sustained devastating collateral damage. In medical terms, it had been transected; in layman's terms, it was torn apart. In addition, arteries leading to and from my penis were slashed, and Dr. Paduch found bone fragments from my pelvis lodged in the organ. I was unable to urinate, and that's why I needed to use catheters for several months. Through various surgeries and procedures, Dr. Paduch managed to repair my system to the point where I could pee, but with a hitch: Because of irreparable nerve damage, I now don't know when my bladder is full. Whether I need to or not, I urinate at regularly timed intervals to avoid making a mess of myself.

Unnatural? Certainly. But this method sure beats using a catheter for the rest of my life. And for that I am immensely grateful to Dr. Paduch.

Unfortunately, trying to restore another function proved more difficult.

During surgery and follow-up exams, Dr. Paduch determined that the injuries I had suffered had left me with severe erectile dysfunction. It was devastating news to get. Before a bus ran over me, I had been a young, single guy in the city with a very healthy social life. Now, as Dr. Paduch honestly yet compassionately told me, my condition could have drastic implications. I faced a future where I could have trouble developing any kind of lasting personal and physical relationship with a woman. He also encouraged me not to get too down, though, because thanks to drug treatments, continual medical advances, and, of course, the most understanding woman, one day I could still have what I always dreamed of.

But at that point in my rehab, such a day, and such a woman, was well beyond my imagination.

━━━━━━━━━━

Living in Manhattan for so many years, I had dated lots of women. Some I knew quickly weren't right for me; with others I kept the relationship going a little longer, hoping that maybe, eventually, she might turn out to be the one. I went on blind dates that my sisters arranged. I met women in bars when I was out with the guys. Some people might have thought I was a Casanova—heck, maybe I was.

But in my heart I always wanted the next girl to be the only girl.

Now the chase seemed over. How could I ask a woman to join me in this life sentence? I couldn't ask Shelly. She had been a steady, caring girlfriend through the five months I was in the hospital. We listened to the CDs that friends had brought to the hospital—especially Jack Johnson, the laid-back singer with the upbeat tempo whom I had gotten Shelly hooked on when we first started dating—and she kept me posted on the doings outside the hospital. She came to know my family well and helped to cheer them up with her lively personality. Still, even before the accident had happened, I wondered about our relationship and whether or not it had legs. We had different interests, different ambitions. I was an FDNY lifer; she was successful in real estate. I was closing in on 40; she was barely 30. Maybe the accident kept us together longer than we were meant to be. Maybe a Florence Nightingale syndrome was at work. Maybe I was afraid to end something when everything else around me was ending.

Ultimately, though, I realized we couldn't continue, for her sake or for mine.

One night when she was at my apartment, I told her that we needed to talk. "Listen, Shell, you're 30 years old," I said. "You don't need to be involved in this situation. I'm holding you back. You need to move on."

"What are you talking about, Matt?" she said, starting to tear up. "You want to break up now? After all these months? After I've tried to be there for you?"

"Look, Shelly, I don't want to make it harder than it is, but I don't know what kind of recovery I'm going to make. Go out, live your life. I'll always feel like I'm holding you back."

The conversation went on for some time, and not well, until Shelly finally left, angry and hurt.

I felt terrible, but also relieved. No longer did I have to worry about how my life was affecting hers. She was free to pursue and find someone with a real future. Someone she would want to live with the rest of her life. I already knew what it was like to find such a person. Someone committed to being there for me *for better or for worse.* And someone I was committed to as well.

Committed, that is, until I let that someone go.

---

She came into Third & Long one night in the summer of 1993. She had long, light brown hair and a cheerful, athletic face. I was at one end of the bar with my brother Chris. He saw me staring at this girl as she breezed through the front door and to the end of the bar.

"Bro, what are you thinking?"

"Chris, see that girl over there?"

I pointed with my forehead. Chris nodded.

"Matt," Chris said, "the one standing next to her, um, boyfriend?"

"Yeah, her."

"What about her?"

"Chris, that's the girl I'm going to marry."

And the chase was on.

After that first night, she came in more and more with her girlfriends and less and less with the guy. I was curious, and I began to chat with her and her friends. She had grown up on Long Island, graduated from Fordham University, and, best of all, had just broken up with her boyfriend. I saw the door opening and went through it. We talked whenever she came in, and I played songs on the jukebox like "Second Hand News" and "Mr. Wendal," which I knew she and her friends enjoyed. When they came over to the bar, I had their favorite drinks ready. I made all the right moves, and she was receptive to them.

Like most things I did in life, I moved fast. This time, maybe too fast.

After we started dating we were rarely apart. We went skiing together, went to all the big concerts in the city together, and even ran together. She was fit and trim. She had as much energy as I had, and when she walked into a restaurant or bar, her beautiful face lit up the place. I would watch guys' heads turn when she came into a room and smile to myself. *Sorry, fellows, she's with me.* And I wasn't about to lose her to anyone.

We were engaged after just nine months. We bought an SUV and a dog—a yellow lab named Taylor. We went house hunting and started to plan the wedding. We had the wedding hall picked out, a band booked, and the gifts registered. Our families met and everyone got along. It was perfect.

Too perfect.

Speed is essential when racing to a fire, but once you're there, you need to slow down, pace yourself, assess the situation, not make rash decisions that may do more harm than good. And running a marathon? Speed only comes into play when kicking those last 500 meters. Otherwise it's a race of stamina, of endurance.

The two of us never seemed to slow down, to figure out who we were and what we wanted. I saw a finish line—a wedding, a wife, a family—but maybe not the speed bumps that come before and in between all that. So when little things, and then big things, started to crop up in our relationship, neither of us was prepared to step back and assess. Now when other guys eyed her, I got angry. Now when she started talking to old boyfriends, I worried, even when she told me not to. But I did. And soon, instead of rushing to the altar, we were fighting, constantly, and roaring to a breakup. I asked for the engagement ring back, and she gave it.

The romance ended almost as fast as it started. We talked a few times afterward, but there was no chance of getting back together. She soon met another guy and got engaged again. And then they married and had kids.

I dated Maggie, Shelly, and dozens of other women, but never got engaged again.

And now I may never.

———————

Throughout that first summer after my accident, my family and friends tried to keep me involved in their lives—and out of my apartment. Ladder 43 had a regular Thursday afternoon softball game that I often got a ride to and would watch from the dugout. And one night I met some of my training partners from Asphalt Green for pizza. It was great seeing them, even though each one looked fit enough to bench-press me. While I was in the hospital a number of them had volunteered to bring dinner to my family and me on Sundays, which let the firefighters enjoy a night off from cooking. The pizza dinner was my first chance to thank them in person. Then, for my 40th birthday, Jimmy put together a party for me at a Mets game at Shea Stadium, and a hundred or so friends from the bar business joined us in the bleachers. The Mets lost, but otherwise it was a nice day.

I also made it out to Brooklyn one morning to watch the Kenneth Dolan Memorial Run in Prospect Park. Fifteen years earlier—long before I had gotten into running seriously—some friends and I helped to start the race in honor of Kenny, a college buddy, who was killed in a car accident when he was only 23. The race had raised more than $50,000 over the years, with the money going to a scholarship fund in Kenny's name. But mostly it kept alive the memory of a friend who had died all too early. Until this year, I had never missed running the 5-K race. This time I showed up in my wheelchair, still looking gaunt. But everyone who saw me seemed to say the same thing: "Matty, you're looking good." Even members of the band Hell or High Water, which often played at Third & Long and was performing at the race's after-party, spotlighted me. "Matty, you'll be running here next year," one of the band members told the crowd in between songs. I nodded and smiled. "Definitely," I said. After an hour I said to Robert, "Drive me home."

More and more, "Drive me home" became my default line. For all the years I had lived in the city, my apartment had mostly been a stopover point between work and play. Where I once appreciated its darkness and quiet for the easy sleep it induced, now the place fit my daily mood. Each time I went out socially, I seemed to regret it. I couldn't be the person friends remembered me as—the guy rushing around getting drinks and telling stories—and I was worried about the person I had become. I hid the colostomy bag under baggy, extra-large T-shirts, hoping no one could see it, and fearing that someone would smell it. I was out one night with friends for dinner, when someone shouted, "Wow, who farted?" Everyone at the table laughed like a bunch of junior high students. I just squirmed; a few minutes later I checked out for the night.

I just stayed in my apartment and let my circles of friends shrink. When the phone rang, I would look at the caller ID and try to decide if I would answer it. Was it a Crony just checking in? *All right, I'll take that one. Maybe.* Was it someone wanting me to meet him for a burger and a beer? *I can't do burgers and beers right now. My stomach's a mess.* The phone rang a lot. I constantly had a decision to make. Answer it or don't answer it. *Nope, not that one,* I'd say to myself. Then two minutes later, *Okay, I'll pick this one up.* For weeks and then months, this game of roulette played on, filling my head with dilemma after dilemma. And no easy resolutions. When I used to feel stress at the firehouse or at the bar, I had the simple solution: Throw on a singlet, put on the shorts, lace up the running shoes, and do a hard six-miler in the park. Every run solved a problem or reduced its significance. I liked to say a run cleaned the chalkboard of life.

But now, when I needed running more than ever, I couldn't have it. I couldn't even bring myself to go to Central Park and watch others run. My chalkboard only became more cluttered, my psyche darker. Was there really no future, no hope?

# 13

## RIDING THE CYCLONE

One day while I was in my living room sorting through more of the cards and letters I had received when I was in the hospital, a magazine clipping fell from a card onto the floor. I tried picking it up but couldn't reach it from my wheelchair. Later, when Eddie got home from work, he saw the clipping.

"What's this?" he asked, bending down to get it.

"I have no idea. It came from one of these letters."

When he handed me the clipping, I noticed it was from a cycling magazine called *VeloNews*. I glanced at the headline, "Near-Fatal Accident Can't Break an Athlete's Spirit," and I started to read the story.

*In September 2000, Fabio Selvig, then 33 years old, had just returned to a job in high-end sales at nationally renowned bicycle retailer Belmont Wheelworks of Belmont, Massachusetts. At the time, Fabio was an active, successful multisport competitor. It was 10 days after Fabio started at Wheelworks that tragedy hit. While riding his bike in historic Lexington, Massachusetts, Fabio was knocked down by an oil truck that proceeded to "make a right turn right over me." Conscious for about 10 seconds, Fabio later learned that police and medical teams on the scene were certain that he wasn't going to survive. The next day, surgeons at Boston University performed four to five surgeries on Fabio. For the next four days, Fabio says, "I was completely out," and his doctors didn't know if he would live.*

*Nevertheless, roughly one week later, his prognosis changed, primarily, Fabio recollects, because "I was in great shape when the accident occurred, and my doctors were top-notch. I think it was the best-case scenario for all involved—I was fit and strong, and they were excellent doctors. The impression I got was that people who suffer the type of damage that I did don't usually recover as quickly as I." Despite Fabio's upgraded status, orthopedic surgeons said that there would be a slim chance that he would one day walk without a cane. Competitive sports? Forget it . . .*

As I continued to read the article, I couldn't believe how eerily similar this guy's story was to mine. He was about the same age as me, he had been run over while on his bike, and he had only a slight chance at first to survive. As I read further, it turned out he needed rehab to relearn many of the simple life skills, like how to shower and how to open a door, that I had to relearn. And, unfortunately, the early indications were that he would never regain his athletic lifestyle.

I was both saddened and fascinated. I kept reading.

*Fabio remained in a wheelchair for three months after the accident. On December 19, he was released from the hospital and given the green light to go home on crutches. At first, he lived with his parents, but eventually moved back into his own place. Being on his own, he was routinely tempted to try new things. Moving without crutches was one of those. Slowly, he began to regain his strength. Formal rehab sessions continued to be a part of his everyday life. At last, on January 9, 2001, he was given the go-ahead to "try standing up on your own." With that major accomplishment under his belt, Fabio went home that very same day and got on his trainer. No matter what, he said, he was going to push for 10 minutes. Fabio recalls that "it hurt like hell, and I had absolutely no power. But over the past three months, I'd experienced a lot more pain than that." Fabio gritted through his 10 minutes, got off his bike, and cried. The tears were those of happiness as Fabio realized that all he needed to do was work hard, and hope that nothing would limit him from riding again someday. And that first day back on his feet was a great way to start out.*

This story was too good to be true. I needed to find this guy. I went to my computer and Googled *Wheelworks*, Fabio's company. I found a phone number and contacted the company. Someone there gave me Fabio's e-mail. I wrote him a note that detailed my story, from getting crushed by the bus to the status of my rehab. I hit send, and then waited.

Fabio returned my e-mail a day or so later, and over the ensuing weeks and months we stayed in touch regularly. In one of his earliest notes to me, Fabio relayed much of what he had been through and what he had since accomplished. It turned out that within a year of his accident, he had managed to return to racing. He said that with hard work, his body was able to do things almost as well as it had in the past—and that mine would, too. He also said not to lose hope. "Matt, all the best things in my life happened after my accident. I met my wife and had a child," he wrote. "It can happen to you, man. Just believe."

Without a doubt, I wanted to.

━━━━━━━━

I always considered myself a bit of a risk taker, an adventure seeker. I tried snowboarding, horseback riding, downhill skiing; heck,

Ironman triathlons are one daylong adventure. You name it—open a bar in big, bad Manhattan, become a firefighter at age 27—I tried it.

Except, that is, for roller coasters.

My fear of roller coasters began when I was young, maybe six or seven. Dad had taken us to Coney Island, the old-fashioned Brooklyn amusement park, and I saw the Cyclone, the legendary roller coaster: 2,640 feet of twisting wood, with people screaming from its roaring seats as if they were being chased by Godzilla. Dad and I went on it— "It will be fun, Matt, you'll see"—and for the duration of the two-minute ride we looped and spun and turned, but I saw nothing. My eyes had been shut tighter than a bank's vault at closing time.

After that experience, I waited until I was in college and Mark Desautelle, my roommate, talked me into taking him to Coney Island. He had heard about the Cyclone and wanted to ride it. I didn't want to admit my childhood fear to him, so I got on. What a mistake. The same sickening, scared feelings came back. I vowed that would be the last roller-coaster ride of my life.

But now it seemed my life was one never-ending roller coaster. I enjoyed moments when I felt up, on a high that could get me through a day and give me a reason to look toward tomorrow. Corresponding with Fabio, for instance, and reading one of his reassuring e-mails. Or getting a phone call from one of Maureen's kids, Matthew or Kate. They seemed to call their uncle to fill me in on the games they were playing and the fun they were having just at the right time. Or driving back after a rehab session with one of the drivers from Ladder 43—usually Matt McSweeney or Dan O'Keefe—and eating a turkey sandwich and drinking a Jamba Juice. Those trips reminded me of the times Noel and I used to end up at the Silver Star Diner on Second Avenue after a hard run or a long training ride. Noel and I would plow through pancakes, eggs, and sausage and rehash every moment of our workout.

For those 20 minutes with Matt or Dan, wolfing down a sandwich and smelling a little sweaty, life seemed right.

But I had become almost conditioned to know that with every rise, like on the Cyclone, came a drop—and when it did, I was afraid to open my eyes. So that's one reason I was not looking forward to my visit with Dr. Toyooki Sonoda one morning that summer. While no man my age wants to see his colorectal doctor, I knew I was in for more than a routine checkup.

My sphincter, one of the pelvic-floor muscles that allows for the control and discharge of stool, had been sheared in the accident. Dr. Eachempati stitched it together, but there was no guarantee that the nerves and blood vessels would regenerate to allow the muscle to work again. Prior to this appointment I had seen Dr. Sonoda's partner, Dr. Jeffrey Milsom, who had told me a sphincter repair could possibly be attempted. Such a procedure might pave the way for a colostomy reversal, my ultimate desire. On this day Dr. Sonoda was going to do a preoperative exam of my anus.

I asked Mom and Dad to take me to the exam with Dr. Sonoda; I needed the support. We arrived at his Upper East Side office around 11 a.m. Mom and Dad stayed in the waiting area while the doctor performed a 15-minute exam. It was as grueling as it was invasive, but as I kept telling myself, it had to be done.

When the procedure was over and I was waiting for the results, I called Dad into the office.

"How did it go, Matt?" he simply asked.

"Let's just hope it was worth it," I said.

It didn't take Dr. Sonoda long to return with his findings—and he didn't let me dangle waiting to hear them. He said the exam showed that the muscles used to move my bowels remained in a weakened condition and that my anus was minimally functional. He didn't offer an opinion as to whether or not to go forward with a sphincter repair—that would be up to Dr. Milsom. What he could tell me was to stay positive.

When he was done talking, I stared at him, not sure what to say. *Stay positive? Minimally functional?* To me that meant *primarily nonfunctional.* My head lowered to the ground as I tried not to cry in front of him. The room had become achingly quiet. Finally, I looked at Dad and told him I wanted to leave.

I walked out of the doctor's office wondering how much longer I had to wait until this part of my roller-coaster ride finally would turn upward.

---

After we left the doctor's office, Mom, Dad, and I drove to Turtle Bay. "Let's get you something to eat," Dad said, "and talk things over." Not surprisingly, I wasn't very hungry or talkative.

I was drained, sad, and depressed. In my mind, I took Dr. Sonoda's news to mean that the colostomy bag would be a permanent part of my life, as critical to my daily functioning as my heart or kidney or any other organ in my body. I needed the bag for survival, as much that day as on the day when Dr. Eachempati had done the colostomy. *Matt, performing the colostomy was necessary, absolutely necessary, if we were going to save your life. At that moment, that's what we were worried about—your life, not the quality of your life.* And on the chance that it would be permanent, I had started to look for ways to manage with it. Using the Internet I scouted support groups for people in my situation. I found a few in Manhattan, but couldn't bring myself to contact them—at least not yet. It seemed an admission of acceptance, and I wasn't ready for that.

Emotionally, I also knew what this bag meant: It would continue to drain me in ways it was never intended to. How could I ever get back to running—or biking or swimming for that matter—if I was tethered to this bag? Why bother going out to a restaurant to see old friends and meet new ones with this bag playing on my mind? Why bother with life when there really was *no* quality to it? The doctors had told me they had other patients who were enjoying happy, active, social lives with colostomy bags. But I didn't want to listen to these stories.

Already the bag had kept me from enjoying things that had been such a part of my life. Like Breezy Point. Ever since I was nine I had been going out to the family's summer bungalow on the dunes of the Rockaways. No, it wasn't a Southampton-style retreat—it had three bedrooms for 11 people to share, a washer and dryer on the back deck, and space for just a single couch—but it was the perfect beach pad for the Longs of Bay Ridge. From Memorial Day to Labor Day we went there to escape the city streets and just have fun. That first weekend of summer the Atlantic Ocean's temperature might only be in the low 60s, and if you put just a toe in it, you would be scared away by the cold until August. But I attacked the surf as if I were a linebacker blitzing a third-string quarterback. First I would spend a couple of minutes lying on the beach, heating up, then I'd rush across the sand, jump into the water, and keep charging until I broke my first wave of the season. Sure, I would turn purple, but I was in the water . . . on the first day of summer . . . and I would be back for more. Breezy Point—the bungalow, the beach, playing hoops with the LD Daddy's, and drinking beers at the Bowl. That had been my summer life for years.

My family kept urging me to come out to Breezy Point that summer. Eileen and Maureen said I could relax there and spend more time with the nephews and nieces. It sounded like a good idea, but the couple of times I ventured out, I found that negotiating the dunes on a pair of crutches was a battle. And then once I made it into the house, I felt squeamish; in 30 years the place had never seemed small. Now it seemed miniature. Sitting there with people around, I worried about the *bag*. I know I was with mostly family, but it still got on my nerves.

So I started to stay away from Breezy.

And I couldn't go into Smith & Wolly's without thinking about it. There I would be, in one of the city's most popular restaurants, surrounded by executives in their Brooks Brothers suits, while I wore a floppy T-shirt and sweatpants, trying to conceal the bag. Everyone around me was laughing and slapping backs and talking up deals they had just made that day. My deal? Only Ollie, who was behind the bar, knew about it. If he came back to my spot at the bar and saw that I had disappeared, Ollie knew it wasn't because I had walked out on the check. I was good for the money, but my upset stomach needed me home.

The damn bag controlled my mind. Often, when I was at home and Eddie was out and I couldn't watch anymore TV, or roam the Internet any longer, or read another letter, I sat there and thought about friends. Friends who were no longer around. Kenny Dolan. Rob Scandole. Mike Armstrong. Tommy Hannafin. And I thought about my cousin Richard, who died when he was only 19 from epilepsy. I was sad that all these people were gone, but in a way I envied them. Their pain was over. They no longer had to suffer anything like I had to.

I remember once telling Noel, "I don't care if I ever walk again, but I got to get rid of this bag." Now, after this morning's session with Dr. Sonoda, it looked like it would control me forever. And Mom and Dad wanted to talk about it. Over lunch. At Turtle Bay.

I was quiet for some time, just ordering a turkey sandwich when the waitress came by. Mom and Dad tried some lighthearted conversation. Dad asked about the bar business, and Mom wanted to know how Eddie was doing. When they realized I wasn't engaging, they tried cheering me up.

"Pal," Dad said, "stay positive. Look how far you've come. Don't let this slow you down. We'll see Dr. Milsom in a few weeks and see what he has to say."

Then Mom weighed in. "Yes, Matthew. You've had so many obstacles to overcome, and you've tried your best to handle them. We're so proud of you. This is just one more. You can do it."

Their words ricocheted in my head. *Stay positive. Obstacles. Overcome. Your best. Obstacles. Overcome. Stay positive.* And then every bit of anger, frustration, and stress poured out of me.

"Mom, I'm tired of all the obstacles! You know, you two are so happy that I'm alive. But I'm miserable because I'm alive. If I had died, at least it would have been short-term pain for you. But I got to live with this every day of my life."

The outburst, so sudden and sharp, shocked them both.

Mom held her breath for a moment, tears welling in her eyes. Physically, she didn't get hurt on December 22, 2005, but ever since she had suffered. She watched me almost die that day and night. She barely slept for weeks, and when she did they were fitful hours. The whole time I was in the hospital she also had to worry about her two daughters, Eileen and Maureen, both pregnant. The months had been rough on her, too.

Mom looked over at Dad, glassy-eyed. For 43 years they had been together and been through a lot. Celebrations, for sure. Baptisms, graduations, weddings, the births of grandchildren, Christmas. She saw him become important in politics; still, she always waited up for him to come home from his party meetings, usually with a sandwich ready for him on the kitchen table. They dealt with enough anxious moments, too. Raising nine kids. Operating an ice cream parlor that never seemed to close. They lived through September 11 when Jimmy and I went unheard from for hours. They waited to see if Frank would live after his car accident. Mom waited by Dad's side the night he was shot. Yes, she had ridden a roller coaster, too.

Then she looked at me, her sobbing middle-aged son. She knew I had been unhappy for months, since shortly after I awoke in the hospital. She knew how devastating the injuries were. That's why, when Roger Toussaint was given only a 10-day jail sentence for his role in the transport union strike, Mom wrote letters to the newspapers blasting the decision. She fought for justice, my justice. She also understood how important running and biking and swimming were to me. The previous fall I had called her on the day one of the TV networks aired the Ironman World Championship from Hawaii. I told her that I would be competing in that event someday. She watched—horrified—as men and women my age tortured themselves to complete 140.6 miles in less than 17 hours. She told me I was nuts. But she never told me not to pursue it. Mom knew it was what I wanted. And now she knew I probably would never have a chance to go after that goal, and I was hurting. Hurting, perhaps, more than at any point when I was in the hospital. It was in the hospital that Mom kept saying that she was there for me and to tell her what she should do. Too often I would just shrug, give her the cold shoulder. I didn't act like a man happy to be alive.

For months all that ate at her. Still, she kept silent. Until this moment.

"Listen," she said, in a voice I hadn't heard in a long time, "if you want to miss family parties and sit around in your apartment feeling sorry for yourself, go ahead. But let me ask you, do you want to be a miserable bastard all your life?"

She surprised me with her outburst. But I didn't hold back. "Maybe I do," I shouted at her.

"Well then, be miserable, but let me tell you, Matthew. You have a lot to offer people other than misery. If you want to be a piece of crap the rest of your life, great. But don't do it around us; we're not going to stand for it. You're going to be doing it alone." She paused a moment. I didn't look up. "Remember, Matthew, we struggled and we fought and we hurt just like you did during that whole period."

"Not like me, Mom! Not like me."

"No, Matthew, maybe not like you, but damn it, we hurt! And we still do!"

Her words rolled through my head, but I didn't know what to say. Finally I told her, and Dad, I didn't want to hear any more. "Get me out of here! Drive me home!"

I got my crutches and made my way out of the bar to Second Avenue, and into Dad's car. They dropped me at the doorstep of my apartment. I got out of the car, closed the door, and went inside. Alone.

———————

Yes, as I told Mom and Dad, I wished I had died on December 22.

But in no way did that mean I now wanted to die.

I know it sounds cockamamie. What I mean is that even on my worst days, when depression overwhelmed me and when the pain from all my injuries made me want to stay in bed, and when I was attached to things I didn't want to be attached to, I never thought about taking my life. That's just not my style. Rushing into a burning building? Yes, that was my style. Pulverizing my body over 140 miles of swimming, biking, and running? Yes, my style.

Suicide? Not me.

But as the blowup with Mom revealed, I kept struggling to figure out what I was supposed to do if I was going to be *alive*. What was the purpose of everything I had gone through and was going through? I had no job to get up for in the morning. I remained on disability from the FDNY, and with my injuries it was becoming less likely that I could ever return to Ladder 43 and to the job I once had. As far as the bars went, I let Jimmy and the other partners handle the business. I didn't have the stomach to spend nights at Third & Long and the other spots. I was usually in bed when those places got going.

What I had mostly was time—and my apartment, where I killed the hours waiting for something to happen. I waited for someone to come and drive me to rehab. Or for Eddie to come home so we could have dinner. Or for someone to call whom I felt comfortable talking with. At times the apartment seemed more cramped than I could ever remember it being. Maybe that was because I was spending so much time there, and I was constantly maneuvering around tables and chairs with my crutches. But the tight quarters also let me notice things that previously had just seemed to blend into the scene. I sat there, some days, and just looked at the pictures on the wall.

And they told a lot—especially the one of me standing alone on the rubble of Ground Zero.

The photographer, Matthew McDermott, shot it shortly before the guys from Ladder 43 helped save the firefighters of Ladder 6 and the bookkeeper, Josephine, from the trapped stairwell. In the photo you see me from the back, my hands on my hips, glancing up at rubble. It appeared on the cover of *Men's Journal* magazine and in a few other publications. Some days I would stare at the image and think how sad I seemed glaring at the destruction around me. Other times I'd look at it and wonder what I was thinking at the moment the picture was taken: *What should I do next? Where can I help? How did all this happen?*

For me and other firefighters, that day will always have lots of different meanings. We lost plenty of friends on 9/11, but we also helped countless strangers. In an odd way, the FDNY seemed to raise New York City's spirit with the sacrifices it made. A few weeks after the attacks, people from all over the world showed their appreciation at a concert at Madison Square Garden that raised money for the families of firefighters, police officers, and emergency workers victimized by the events of the day. Two dozen entertainers performed that night, including Billy Joel, Paul McCartney, Elton John, Jay-Z, The Who, and Bon Jovi. A number of firefighters came onstage to be recognized. I was one of them, representing Ladder 43. What an opportunity. Billy Crystal, the evening's host, introduced me to the 18,000 people in the Garden. We joked for a while about each other's hairline—well, the lack of one. Then Billy told the crowd how I was part of Ladder 43's effort to save the firefighters and Josephine. "Lady Luck drove Matt's truck that day," Billy said to cheers. Then he gave me the microphone to fill in the rest. "What 43 did," I told the crowd, "is what any firehouse would have done. I am proud to be a member of that company." Then I got to introduce the next act—the Goo Goo Dolls—and to give Billy a hug.

It was some night, and it helped bring smiles back to many faces. More nights like that would do the same. A few weeks later a couple of flight attendants from American Airlines and United Airlines, who used to stop by Third & Long when they were in town, asked Jimmy and me to take part in a fundraiser called Americans Are United, for families of airline employees killed on 9/11. The event's draw? An auction during which Jimmy and I would go to the highest female bidder.

We showed up in formal attire, then had a sash with our bachelor number placed across our chest. Jimmy was four, I was five. To sweeten the pot, Jimmy offered his winning bidder a tour of his firehouse and a ride on the rig. Big spender. I went a bit more upscale: I put up a dinner at Smith & Wolly's. With about 300 women eyeing him, Jimmy strolled the runway, strutting his stuff. We were told to do something extra to get the ladies' attention. So Jimmy did a little dance, punctuating it with a perfect split. Then he jumped off the stage, picked a woman from the crowd, brought her onstage, and flipped her over his head. A killer move and finale. The ladies went wild. Jimmy sold for $3,300.

He came backstage and I tore into him. "Damn, Jimmy, how am I going to beat that?"

I had no shot. I simply walked out on the runway with a sheepish look and said, "I'm his brother." I went for $2,700, mostly on sympathy.

The event at the Garden and the auction reminded me of how people, even after the worst tragedy possible, will be searching for something. Mostly for other people. We came together after 9/11, especially in the FDNY. For a time, that day crippled the department—343 veteran firefighters can't be replaced with a simple call to the academy. It would take years to rebuild the crew. In the short term, though, we just tried to look out for one another. To make sure no one around us was having too many bad days in a row. And eventually, a year or so later, things got to the point where the events of September 11 were no longer top of mind. We felt we could move on.

And then, several months after my accident, we heard something about one of the Cronies, and we knew we never really could move on. My buddy John Kelly had cancer. It was related to the pollutants at Ground Zero.

John and I had become close soon after he joined our firehouse. We played basketball together on the house's team; at six foot four he was one of our top rebounders and scorers. His upbeat personality matched his size; he was always one of the favorite bartenders at Turtle Bay when he filled in on weekends.

When John found out about the cancer, he went on part-time disability and started treatment. As part of his limited-duty activity, he drove me to see my different doctors, including one day to a psychiatrist. Yes, after dealing with depression for months, I finally sought help; as it turned out, my one visit to the psychiatrist was my only one. I didn't like the advice he gave me after an hour. He said, "Matt, instead of you trying to make everyone else feel good, maybe you need to let people make you feel good." I gave him an odd look. I wanted to say, *No, Doc, you don't get it. I want that life back.* Then he tried to make an analogy between my injuries and one he had suffered. He said he loved to play tennis but couldn't anymore because of his elbow. I heard that and said to myself, *This guy's a quack. I was run over by a bus, and he's comparing it to tennis elbow.*

After the appointment I got back in John's car and told him what had happened. He could tell how frustrated I was. But then John started telling me more about what he was going through with his cancer and how it was affecting his life and his family. And for a few minutes, I stopped thinking about myself. The conversation got so heavy that at one point we were both on the verge of tears.

Just as John was about to drop me off, I asked him, "Man, why do you think God did this to us?" Neither of us had an answer.

Later that night I went to my computer. There was an e-mail from John. It was a note about our conversation from that afternoon. He told me to hang in there, that we were both strong guys and that we could handle what had been thrown at us. He finished by saying, "Matt, you asked me why God did this to us. Well, I'm not sure, but I think he believes we can handle it. And maybe inspire people as we do it. We both had everything, and now we've lost something. But we can still help people."

At that moment I didn't know how to respond to John.

I soon would.

# 14

## ONE YEAR LATER

"Yo, Lance! Lance! Got a second?"

There he was. The greatest cyclist of all time: Lance Armstrong. The man could take on the Pyrenees as if they were speed bumps in the parking lot of a suburban shopping mall. He won the Tour de France, the world's most famous and challenging cycling race, seven consecutive times. Amazing. And he did it all after surviving a killer form of cancer. Armstrong was only 25 when doctors discovered he had testicular cancer, which had spread to his lungs, abdomen, and brain. After having surgery to remove the cancer, he underwent radical chemotherapy. It worked, and two years after his last treatment he was racing again—and winning his first Tour.

An incredible story. But I had one, too. And I wanted to share it with him, if he would only give me a few minutes.

"Lance! Yo, Lance!"

Granted, I chose an odd moment to try and get the guy's attention. It was minutes before the start of the 2006 New York City Marathon, which would mark Armstrong's first attempt at running

26.2 miles. Word had it that he had skimped on his training for a
race of this magnitude and distance; he would be relying on raw
ability—and a team of world-class pacers running beside him—to
negotiate the 26.2 miles. At this moment he was standing just to the
side of the starting line on the Verrazano-Narrows Bridge, stretching, with earbuds in his ears, and encircled by handlers from his
main corporate sponsor, Nike. He looked like a man who wanted to
be left alone.

I was with my boss from the Fire Academy, Lieutenant Mike
Cacciola, and a group of other firefighters. They had driven me out
to the marathon start in Staten Island so I could help send off the
150 FDNY runners on that chilly November morning. I had mixed
emotions as I waited for the race to start. Sure, it was great to be
with the team, whose goal once again was to beat the tar out of the
NYPD marathon squad. Still, I was bummed. A year earlier I had
run the greatest race of my life, finishing fourth on the FDNY
team and qualifying for Boston. While I was now back on the deck
of the bridge, the picture was much different: This time I was
standing on crutches, my shapeless stomach drooping over my
waistline, and I was still 20 pounds below what I had weighed at the
time of the accident. I had grown a bushy goatee to try to fill out my
drawn face.

And I wanted to be running with my buddies, not watching
them.

The guys must have anticipated how I might feel. As they took
off their warm-up jackets and sweatshirts, I got a huge lift: The
back of their racing shirts read "Go Long!" I would be running
with them after all.

Lieutenant Cacciola spotted Armstrong first. "Matty," he said,
"you got to talk to Lance." So we started shouting out to him. But

Armstrong didn't hear us, or didn't want to. "All right, I'll be right back," Lieutenant Cacciola said.

I gave Shane and the guys a little last-minute encouragement—and razzing. "Boys, who's stepping up to fill my shoes?" I wanted to know, trying not to smile. "I had big shoes. Who's up for the job?" Just then, and just minutes from the starting cannon, the lieutenant returned with someone.

"How you doing, man?" Armstrong asked, reaching out to shake my hand, his earbuds still jammed in his ears.

"Hey, Lance, it's awesome to meet you," I said, a bit in shock. "Thanks for coming over. Listen, I know you don't have much time, but get this. The doctors gave you a 50 percent chance to live, right? Well, they gave me a *5 percent* chance!" That seemed to catch his attention; the earbuds came out.

"Damn, man, what happened?"

With the countdown to the race on, I gave Armstrong the CliffsNotes version of my story. *Bus. Run over. Sixty-plus units of blood. Crushed bones. Running career on hold, perhaps for good.* Finally, Armstrong looked at me and said, "Man, that's rough. Listen, I got to go, but hang in there, okay? Lots of luck."

I called out as he rushed off, "You, too, Lance. Have a good run."

Seconds later the race was on, and Armstrong and 38,000 other marathoners took off on their five-borough run. I climbed into the FDNY van for the ride back into Manhattan and to Central Park, where later we watched the guys come in at the finish line. It was my first time in the park since my accident. We once again beat the cops, and later at a hotel in midtown the guys congratulated themselves for retaining the Mayor's Cup, given to the winner of the FDNY-NYPD challenge.

I stayed just a few minutes at the party; it had been one of my longer days outside of the apartment. As soon as I got home, I turned on the news and watched the race highlights. Lance Armstrong was the lead story. He finished the marathon in 2:59:36, a remarkable time considering his limited training. He later said, "For the level of conditioning that I have now, that was without a doubt the hardest physical thing I have ever done. I think I bit off more than I could chew; I thought the marathon would be easier."

I clicked the TV off and went to my computer to check the race results for some of my friends. Shane had a rough day, finishing nearly 9 minutes slower than the year before, but Tommy went 10 minutes faster—go figure—in his 21st New York City Marathon. The man will be running the race when he's in a rocking chair. And then there was Julie Khan, my physical therapist. I had seen her at the start, shaking from the breeze off the Narrows as well as from nerves. But she succeeded in what she had set out to do months earlier: She ran her first marathon, in four hours, 25 minutes.

And that was it: another Marathon Day in New York over. Its passing always seemed to signal the coming end of the year. The days begin to get shorter, the city streets feel chillier, and the trees in Central Park start to thin out, along with the number of runners using the park. The calendar says the holidays are getting closer, and all that comes with them.

Including an anniversary.

---

Just before Christmas that year, I sent my folks the following letter:

*Mom and Dad,*
*I don't know where to begin. I think it's best to let you know how lucky I am to have the family I have. I am sorry I put you*

*through that incredibly tragic experience last Christmas and the first half of 2006. It's very important to realize that without all of you pulling for me, I would not have gotten this far along in my recovery. No one is luckier than the nine Longs; you gave us the gift of life and taught us the value of family. A gift that is acknowledged best when it is re-gifted to your grandchildren. So far you have been lucky enough to see that come back to you.*

*I am very confused about how I feel about my accident. I ask "Why?" knowing that is a question never to be answered. I ask to have a full recovery and that will only be answered in time. I find myself negotiating with God day in and day out: "Take away the running and the biking and I'll limp around the rest of my life. But please, God, I beg of you, please put me back together again." Now as a mother and father, you wish and believe I will fully recover, but we can't make that happen, can we? I am also fully aware that I am loved by you regardless of my physical appearance, and I thank you for that as well.*

*In the next couple of months I will find out just how much recovery God is going to send my way. I hope and pray it's a full recovery, but when the moment comes and the doctors say this is it, this is how it will be for the rest of your life, I'll find out just how tough I really am. I can't imagine being this way the rest of my life. I know it's not the right attitude, but I have to be honest with you: I just don't believe I can be the person I want to be if things don't change. I even feel bad writing this, because I don't want to have a negative thought about the outcome of future surgeries. But I have to be prepared.*

*If we must search for the good that comes from evil or this horrible tragedy, then you'll be happy to know that I've been to church more in the last six months than in the last six years. Also, I wasn't a witness to the strength and courage that our family displayed last December in the hospital, but it amazed hundreds of people. That was the best late Christmas present I ever received. Thanks!*

*I am very proud to be your son and couldn't imagine life with*

*any other parents. Thanks for teaching us the difference between*
*right and wrong and allowing us to learn from our own mis-*
*takes. I know this Christmas will be an emotional one, but let's*
*keep the tears to a minimum. I love you both! Matthew*

I wrote that letter one evening with the memories and feelings
of the past year raw in my head. They were hardly the thoughts I
had expected 2006 to produce when I originally plotted out the
year. No, this was to be the year when I challenged myself like never
before, visualizing the results of long-anticipated goals and then
pushing my body to achieve them. Run Boston. Qualify for the
Ironman World Championship. Compete in Kona.

Well, I certainly faced physical tests, but instead of challenging
me they only annoyed me. Learning to lift my butt from a wheelchair. Walking a couple of steps with a set of crutches. Exercising
my blunted shoulder by reaching up for a saltshaker. Flexing the
toes on my left foot to see if they would ever straighten again. Small
tasks, small results.

As often as I complained to my family about my issues or
pouted about my situation, fortunately I didn't give in totally to the
depression and the anger. I'm not exactly sure why. The only reasonable explanation was that a long time ago I had been taught that
you don't quit, at anything or on anyone. Dad and Mom had made
that clear when I wanted to give up on my high school basketball
team. "You don't quit on them, Matthew." And so did Lieutenant
Dan Thompson when he told me, in slightly different terms, that
you don't walk out of a fire simply because your air tube breaks.
"Bro, shit happens. You got to get back in there. Let's go." And so
did Noel Flynn when he kept after me to sign up for a triathlon,
even though I kept coming back with reasons not to. "Are you
scared, Matt?" which I took as *Are you a quitter, Matt?* because once
you run from new challenges, you're quitting on life.

I couldn't quit. I had to get back in there. I couldn't be scared.
Most of all I had to keep searching for a reason to live.

One night I finally found it.

———

It was nearing 10 p.m., and I was lying on the couch getting ready
to watch TV. Two of my brothers, Frank and Chris, had just gone
home after stopping by for a late dinner. Eddie was in the kitchen
cleaning the dishes. A commercial came on for the New York State
lottery. "Tonight's Mega Million jackpot," the announcer said, "is
$118 million."

*Hmm,* I thought, *we still have a few minutes to get a ticket before the
drawing.* I called in to Eddie. "Hey, can you make it to the deli across
the street and get a ticket in time?"

"I'll try," he said.

But before Eddie could put on his coat, I said, "Wait, wait. Forget it. Just another thing I wanted to do, win the lottery."

"Doesn't everyone?" Eddie chirped.

"Yeah, you're right. Everyone wants to win."

For the next few minutes my mind stayed stuck on the word
*want,* and I began thinking—again—of all the things I had wanted in
life. It was the same old laundry list, and I was tired of reciting it. My
eyes began to swell. Then, just like that first afternoon when I was
back in the apartment, I started crying in front of my little brother.
"I can't live like this," I wailed, jerking Eddie from out of the kitchen.
"I had so much, and now all my life involves is sitting in this apartment. What kind of a life is that?" I paused for a second. "Hell, I even
wanted to win the lottery, but we know that isn't going to happen."

Eddie chuckled. "Got that straight, Matt, and if it ever did,
then half is mine for putting up with you."

The line was enough to break the tension I had worked into the evening. And then, just as randomly, I started to riff in the other direction. I ticked off everything I already had. Great friends who were as close as family—Noel, Frank, Vicky, Ray, Mark, the Cronies, T-Red. Eight incredible brothers and sisters who had put up with me while trying to coax and coddle me through so much over the past year. Two strong parents who had endured their own pain.

After all that, I just stopped talking for a second. I rubbed my eyes and felt the tears. I shook my head. "You know, Eddie, just forget all the 'I want' crap. It isn't enough to just want things and expect to get them. Everything I have I worked for—the bars, the career at the firehouse, the running. None of it came easy. If it had, then everyone would be out doing Ironmans."

I started to think about seeing Lance Armstrong at the marathon, and the e-mails from Fabio Selvig, and Mom's lunchtime harangue from a few weeks earlier. "Eddie, I'm telling you, Mom was right. I'm tired of being miserable. That isn't me. My body's a mess, but I don't have to be." I stopped again. For the first time in a long time, I could feel myself liking who I was. "I don't know how the hell I'm going to do it, Eddie, but I will push myself harder. I will start getting out more. Let me tell you, Eddie, I will start to live again."

I was rolling, so much so that Eddie became jumpy. "Bro, it's late. Calm down."

"No, Eddie, and let me tell you one more thing, all right. I don't know how, but I will run again. You hear me. I will. Just wait."

That did it for the night. Eddie walked over and turned off the TV. "You're tired, Matt. Let's get to bed."

He helped me into my bedroom. At that point we had been living together almost six months, and I still needed him to get me ready for bed. A few days later, though, I would tell Eddie it was time for him to move out—and live his own life.

That night as I lay in bed staring at the ceiling, I started visualizing again, just as my coach, Anthony Carillo, had taught me. I visualized running the six-mile loop of Central Park, not alone but with my buddies—Frank, Noel, Vicky, Shane, and whomever else wanted to join us. And then we would all go out for beers. A lot of beers.

In my head, everything looked great. Now I just needed to figure out how to get my body to play along.

———

Nearly a year after my accident, I was still physically a mess and nowhere close to walking even one mile, let alone running six. My abdominal muscles remained retracted, and a skin graft continued to hold my stomach organs in place. I had given up the wheelchair, but I needed crutches to get around; only on the rare occasion would I try a cane. I woke every day in crippling pain; my first steps felt like I was walking on shattered glass.

And, of course, I still had the bag.

But now I had a dream—as well as some hope. A few weeks after seeing Dr. Sonoda and getting his assessment about my colorectal issues, I met again with Dr. Milsom, one of the country's leading experts on complex colorectal diseases. Over his career Dr. Milsom has done close to 3,000 colon and rectal operations around the world. Obviously, he knew his ass from his elbow.

During my exam Dr. Milsom explained that when the bike's seatpost impaled my rectum, it ripped and detached nerve and muscle from the rectum's right side. But his exam also revealed what he thought was enough healthy muscle tissue on the left side to use in reconstructing the rectum. He said it would be a painful surgery, and once everything was healed, I would need to spend weeks—maybe months—strengthening the pelvic-floor muscles to determine if they could regain their functionality. And even after all that, he said, "there is no guarantee that a colostomy takedown can take place."

"Doc, whatever you say," I told him, "I'll do."

So that fall I had the surgery, and Dr. Milsom was right: My rear end took a beating. I remained in the hospital for days recovering, a period when the slightest movement below the waist seemed to set off an avalanche of pain. And in the weeks that followed, I could do little physical therapy for my legs. But with each follow-up visit, Dr. Milsom said he liked how the area was healing. Finally, just after New Year's, he told me that I was ready for phase two of the procedure.

"Okay, Matt, I know you were a runner and an Ironman. So you know about exercise and endurance training. Are you ready for a whole new type of training?"

I looked at him. "What do you mean?"

"Matt, your pelvic-floor muscles now need to be strengthened. They haven't been working for over a year. Like any muscle that's gone dormant, you need to retrain them."

He then called for one of his nurses, who came in with a long syringe and a bowl filled with what looked like oatmeal. He explained that the rectum is the critical last portion of the large intestine that is essential to storing the body's waste, and when it's full, like the bladder, it signals for you to go to the bathroom. But for the past year, my waste had been diverted out of my system via the colostomy. "Matt, you need to retrain your rectum to store and eliminate your waste. We also need to expand its walls and make them more elastic."

Again, I understood all that. I just didn't understand why the nurse had the syringe and the oatmeal. Dr. Milsom soon explained. "Matt, this is actually Cream of Wheat. For the next few months, you need to inject it into your rectum and then try to hold it as long as you can. The longer you can hold it, the stronger those muscles will become."

"Doc, you're not serious, are you?"

"Matt, I know it sounds unusual but I am. Unless you do this, we can never reverse your colostomy. You need to train those muscles to hold stuff." And then, with the help of his nurse, he demonstrated how to do it.

I won't share all the details. Safe to say, though, I never felt so desperate in my life. *This is what I have to do to make my life better? Shove Cream of Wheat up my butt?*

During the cab ride back to my apartment I said to myself, *Hell, I'm not doing it. Nothing is worth doing that.* And besides, how was I going to do this hideous job on my own? I didn't have a wife whom I could lean on for help. I wasn't going to ask Jimmy or anyone else in my family. This chore was well beyond their line of duty.

But there was no alternative. As Dr. Milsom reminded me as I left his office, "There's nothing elective about this, Matt. It's critical to the rehab process. If you don't train that muscle, we can't reverse the colostomy."

For three weeks I woke up every morning facing that dilemma—and for three weeks the Cream of Wheat stayed in my kitchen cabinet.

Finally, I broke down. I called a friend who was a nurse. I told him of my situation and what I needed to do. He was familiar with colorectal surgeries, and he agreed to help me with the injections. And we agreed to keep everything between us. I can only hope that one day I can repay him for his support, understanding, and discretion.

Starting in early February, he came to my apartment twice a week. I kept a log of how much cereal I was able to hold and for how long. It was as if I were tracking my miles during the buildup to the marathon. At first I could keep about four ounces of the solution in me for all of 10 seconds; by the end of a month, I held twice that amount for close to one minute. The goal was for me to keep increasing the volume and the length of time that I could hold it.

I went to see Dr. Milsom for monthly checkups, and he liked my progress. But for all the encouragement, it couldn't diminish the sadness I felt every time my friend left my apartment. "This sucks," I would say as soon as I heard the apartment door shut. After a session, I didn't want to go out or see anyone. I was getting demoralized but trying not to sink back into depression.

Fortunately, I hadn't forgotten one important lesson I learned while training for the Ironman.

———

Never in my life had I worked so hard as in the weeks leading up to that race in Lake Placid in the summer of 2005. I had to—I was playing catch-up. Most of the 2,500 competitors in the July Ironman sign up a year in advance and use a good portion of that time training for the event. But I didn't enter the race until qualifying for it by doing a half-Ironman—a 1.2-mile swim, 56-mile bike, and 13.1-mile run—in May with a time of five hours and seven minutes. When I called my coach with the news, Anthony said, "Awesome! Now take two days off, Matt, and enjoy. But then we've got to get back to work. We only have nine weeks to train you to go twice as long."

In those two months I crammed in as many miles per week as I could with Frank and Vicky, who were doing Lake Placid, too. Every Saturday we biked 80 to 90 miles; on Sundays we ran 12 to 18 miles. In June the three of us traveled to upstate New York to spend a week at a triathlon training camp that Larry Parker, the Fireman Ironman from the Rock, puts on each year. Over those five days we swam, biked, and ran a total of 300 miles, then topped it off with a weekend half-Ironman. And when I wasn't training with Frank, I was calling him three or four times a day for pointers on everything from fueling up while on the bike to saving strength for the final marathon leg. My repeated calls started to make Frank's wife, Renee, suspicious. One night she asked him, "Frank, do I have to worry about you two guys?"

Still, for all my work, Anthony wasn't satisfied.

"Matt, it's great that you're training so much with Frank and Vicky," he said to me one day, about four weeks out from Lake Placid. "Physically you're going to be ready to start an Ironman. But what are you doing to prepare yourself mentally to finish one?"

"Anthony," I said, "I'm not sure what you're talking about."

"Those guys aren't going to be by your side on race day. What happens when you start to struggle?" He paused a second. "Listen, you need to go out by yourself and bike 90 miles."

"By *myself*? What's the point of that?"

"Because then it's just you. It's you dealing with the mental demons that show up during a race like the Ironman. It's you battling you. It's you finishing 90 miles by yourself regardless of what might go wrong out there: a tire pops, or you get dehydrated, or whatever. Whatever issues you have, you deal with them and you overcome them."

I said okay, and right away I started to plan for my solo ride the following Saturday: a 90-mile round-trip from the East Side of Manhattan to Bear Mountain State Park.

That morning I awoke to a forecast calling for temperatures in the low 90s. Immediately, the ride was irking me. Then, before I could get out of the city, I hit trouble. The George Washington Bridge was closed to traffic into New Jersey. *Damn it!* I said to myself when I saw the signs at the bridge. *I'll do this tomorrow.* But then I stopped myself. Anthony had said I would need to fight through frustrations like this if I wanted to hear my name announced as an Ironman come July. So I got off the bike, tossed it on my shoulder, and walked the bike along the pedestrian path. When I was on the other side of the bridge and riding, I started to play mind games to stay distracted. I looked down at the bike computer and said, *Okay, Matt, at 10 miles it's on—you're ramping up to half-Ironman pace for the next 12 miles. Got it?* I would repeat the same command two more times on the ride. But trouble came again just after the 45-mile mark, after I had turned back for home. I was getting hungry, so I reached into my bento box for an energy bar. *Damn you, Matt*, I said once I had a hand on it, *you should have cut it open before you got on the bike.* I fumbled with the bar trying to unwrap it and, sure enough, I dropped it. *Okay, these things happen,* I told myself. *Hang in there.* I knew I had packed enough liquid calories to get me through the ride; I would just have to stretch them out.

After five hours I made it back to my apartment, ravaged but done.

What did I discover during my solo—besides learning to unwrap my energy bar ahead of time? That you ask yourself a lot of questions when you're alone on a bike for that long. One question more than others: *Why the heck am I doing this?* When I was done, I think I had found the answer: for the satisfaction that comes with pushing your body to the breaking point and conquering the unknown.

That night I called Anthony. "All right, coach, now I understand."

A month later I completed my first Ironman. I was so mentally prepared that when it came to the event's final leg—the marathon—and my legs felt crushed after biking Lake Placid's wicked course for more than five hours, I still had enough in me to run a 3:44:38.

I had never run 26.2 miles faster. And I had learned something that years later I would put to use under circumstances I never could have anticipated.

On October 4, 2007, after nine anxious months of training my bowels to work again, I entered New York–Presbyterian Hospital for one more operation. If everything went according to plan, Dr. Eachempati would perform a colostomy takedown and Dr. Gayle would finally fold my abdominal muscles back into place and close my stomach.

Two months earlier the two had done a preliminary surgery during which they inserted silicone implants on the right side of my stomach. In the weeks that followed, I received weekly injections of silicone. The intent was to expand the skin surface around my midsection enough so as to cover my abdominals once the muscles were back in place. In subsequent weeks my oversize stomach started ballooning like that of a pregnant woman. I needed to buy triple-X-size T-shirts to cover it. One day at the gym I saw a man on the treadmill staring at my stomach. "We think it's a boy," I told him. "He's due in December." The guy stopped staring, while I smirked a little.

I knew none of this unease would matter if I woke up without a colostomy bag. Shortly before I was put under, Dr. Eachempati told me that he expected the surgery to take two to three hours.

"Take as long as you need, Doc," I said. "Just do a good job."

I should have kept my mouth shut.

The surgery lasted 13 hours, and when I finally awoke, 20 hours after being put under, I was back in the ICU. I couldn't move my arms; they were restrained by straps to the railing of the bed. Tubes clogged my mouth. I was disoriented. Mom and Dad were there at my bedside, but I couldn't talk to them because of the tubes. I lay there feeling imprisoned—and like I had gone back in time.

For a moment I thought a bus had hit me again.

Later, when Dr. Eachempati came in, I mouthed to him, "What happened?"

He explained to me that the surgery had taken so much longer than planned because several of my other doctors, including Dr. Milsom and Dr. Lorich, came in to examine their previous work while I was open. Dr. Eachempati also found a massive amount of scar tissue in my midsection, which had accumulated over the 22 months since my accident. As a result of the surgery, my stomach and digestive tract were temporarily shut down. "Matt, you'll be on a liquid diet for the next two weeks," he told me.

But that's not what I wanted to know. Dr. Eachempati could see that just from the way I was looking at him.

"Matt," the doctor said, "overall the surgery was a success."

*And?*

"Yes, Matt," Dr. Eachempati said, finally showing a smile, "yes, it looks like the reversal worked."

I shut my eyes and for the next few minutes just rested.

# 15

## THE FIRST MILE

If I could have gotten out of that bed the moment Dr. Eachempati told me the news, I would have rushed outside, hailed the first cab I saw, and headed straight to Central Park. And then run its six-mile loop—right then and there—in my hospital gown, flapping open in the back, so the whole city could admire my beautifully reconstructed rear end. Then I'd do another loop. And maybe a third.

Then I would have called Eddie and told him to drop everything and go out and buy that lottery ticket. "Eddie," I'd say, "I'm feeling lucky. Very lucky." I was that pumped—well, as pumped as a guy can be lying on his back with tubes coming out of his mouth and 100 staples covering an 18-inch swath of his chest.

Fact was, I wasn't going very far very soon. I spent the next two weeks in the hospital recovering and restricted to the liquid diet. I ended up losing almost 30 pounds; I was back to weighing approximately 135 pounds, close to what I had weighed when I first started rehabbing more than 20 months ago. I also needed to learn to take care of myself again. For the first time in two years, my midsection was completely sealed. Those 100 staples kept in place a combination of cadaver skin and silicone that Dr. Gayle had used to close my abdominal area. When I could finally sit up, it felt like a zipper was holding my stomach shut.

"Don't worry about the staples, Matt," Dr. Gayle said. "We'll remove them when it's time. But just so you know, you're going to have one heck of a scar."

Stuck in bed, I also wondered if I would lose even the limited conditioning and mobility I had gained prior to the surgery. Dr. Eachempati told me not to worry. "Matt, the work you've already done has given you a base. You've lost some of that, but it won't be like starting from scratch."

And, of course, I thought about the reversal and what it meant to my daily functions. Dr. Milsom explained that the nerves to my rectum, which would normally alert me to go to the bathroom, were extremely damaged. Without those signals, I would have to experiment with various methods to keep from having to use diapers for the rest of my life. Ultimately, medications—and a good deal of patience—helped me to come up with a workable solution: To this day, my morning routine includes spending an extra 30 minutes in the bathroom waiting for something to happen.

So, was everything perfect when I left the hospital on October 22? No. But I wasn't looking for perfection. I was looking for hope. And that—as well as 100 staples—was what the doctors had given me.

One of the first things I did when I got home was box all my triple-X T-shirts that I had been wearing to conceal my midsection and donate them to charity. Then I started looking for a new apartment. For some time I knew I needed to get away from my dungeon in midtown, which was doing nothing to help my mood. I found a good-size one-bedroom on the Upper East Side, not far from the hospital, with a balcony that looked out onto the East River and the sun rising over the city. In the morning when I woke up, I no longer needed to turn on the TV news to learn about the weather. I just looked out my window and took it from there.

I also began to push myself a little more at the gym once the doctors gave me the okay to start rehabbing again. With the two-year anniversary of my accident not far off, I made it a goal to put away the crutches for good on that day. Going forward I wanted to rely only on a cane.

It was a short-term goal to propel me toward my ultimate one: to run again.

━━━━━

When I was seriously training for and racing endurance events, running had made me fitter, spiked my competitive juices, and supplied me with a closet full of race T-shirts. But it also added a new dimension to my world at a time when, more and more, I needed one.

For much of my life I couldn't do anything without Jimmy, and I didn't want to. Remember, we were the Long Twins. We went to school together, played hoops together, opened bars together, joined the fire department together. But then he met Pam and got married. Jimmy and I were still best friends, but just different kinds. I was single; he wasn't. And for a long time I had the Cronies to pal around with, and we had plenty of great nights out together. Maybe too many. But then those guys started getting promoted to new jobs at different firehouses or moving to the suburbs once their kids came along. I stayed at Ladder 43, hoping the new firefighters might think of me as a senior man, and stayed single. We were still the Cronies, we just didn't see each other as much as we once had. And

I still had Third & Long and the other bars, and I talked to T-Red and the other partners almost every day. But suddenly, when I stopped in at the bar for a pop, I noticed the crowd seemed younger than it once was. And then I realized it was just me getting older.

A hole was opening in my life. Running came along and filled it. Sure, I was also swimming and cycling, but those two sports were more companions than sidekicks. You can't do a triathlon unless you do all three. But swim workouts never thrilled me; if I wanted to get wet the first thing in the morning, I'd rather take a shower. With the cycling, I loved the buzz from speeding down a hill and passing someone who had dusted me in the triathlon's swim leg. But so much of cycling depended, naturally, on the bike. You had to have it with you when you needed it. Or wanted it. Biking was cool, just not always convenient.

Running, on the other hand, was simple and satisfying. Shoes, shorts, maybe a shirt, and you're on your way to a good sweat. I could go for a run on my own, and the only thing I had to worry about breaking down was me. Or I could run with a friend, pushing each other while catching up with each other. When I was training for the marathon, Mark Desautelle would often come down on a Wednesday night from Connecticut. We'd meet in the park and rip off mile repeats at six-minute pace. Between miles he'd fill me in on how his daughters were doing, and I'd tell him how my love life was. We ran, we talked, we kept a 20-year friendship from our college days on course. Then on Saturdays, Noel and I might go out for a 10-miler; it would take us 70 minutes or so, but by the time we were done, he had the latest news from the firehouse and I had a couple of stock tips from his business world. And a few more hours deposited in the friendship bank.

Running became that little extra glue in a friendship. And sometimes it cemented it. When I first got to the Rock in March 2005 to begin my detail training the probies, I had only known Tommy

Grimshaw a bit from seeing him at various FDNY events. Then I started working with him and getting a sense of his energy and enthusiasm for life and firefighting—and running—and realized he was another senior man worth emulating. That became even more apparent during a run we took together on a smothering hot August day, a few weeks after I did the Ironman. It must have been 93 degrees at noontime when Tommy and I decided to go out. "Matty, maybe we'll do 10 miles, maybe a little longer," Tommy said as we changed into our running gear. "Let's see how we're feeling and how the heat is."

We left the Rock and headed across the pedestrian walkway that connects Randall's Island to Manhattan. I figured we'd run along the FDR Drive to the Williamsburg Bridge, about six miles, and then turn around and come back. Twelve miles on a day like this would be plenty. After half a mile, in fact, the sweat was rushing off my temples. Tommy didn't seem to notice. He had been locked in on telling firefighting stories since the moment we left the Rock. By now Tommy had 25 years on the job, the first 20 at the Harlem Hilton, the firehouse where Eddie was stationed.

"Matt, back then we might put out three or four fires a night," he said, hardly huffing as he talked and ran.

"You must have been stressing out your lungs every night, Tommy."

"It could be brutal, Matt. But you know, I worry about the young guys today. With the buildings so well designed and fireproof now, it's strange to say it, but I'm not sure they're getting enough work—you know, enough practice with the Red Devil."

We kept talking and we kept running. We made it to the Williamsburg Bridge, with Tommy chattering away. I wanted to cut him off—*Tommy, you ready to turn back? We're at six and it's hot out here*—but I didn't have the guts to make that call. We kept going. We looped around the lower edges of Manhattan, looking out toward Brooklyn. At this point Tommy started advising me on my running. "Matty, your form has gotten a lot better, but keep the arms straight, not across your body."

"Okay, Tommy, I'll remember that," I said, but I wasn't sure I would. With the heat, my head was starting to ache.

When we moved closer to Ground Zero, where the Twin Towers used to stand, we talked a bit—just a bit—about September 11 and the buddies the two of us had lost that day. We curved up the West Side and ran along the Hudson River. Finally, I said, "Tommy, I have a twenty. Let me treat you to some water."

"Sounds good."

We guzzled the water, then Tommy looked at me. "You know, Matt, at this point"—we had gone about nine miles—"it might be easier if we stay on the West Side. It may be a little cooler."

"Works for me," I said as we pushed on.

It wasn't any cooler. A hot breeze was blowing off the Hudson, giving us more resistance than relief. We ran along the river, past the ship terminals and the Intrepid, the aircraft carrier that had been converted into a museum. We dodged tourists and bikers heading in the other direction. A dank smog seemed to cover New Jersey on the other side of the river. The talk had lapsed into trying to figure out the best way to get back to the East Side.

"We should cut over at 59th Street and into the park," I suggested.

"Matty, I'm not so sure. Could be stifling around those sky-scrapers. Let's keep going along the river."

So we did. We shuffled along. Miles 14, 15, 16. We stopped for another bottle of water. "Tommy, you treating this time?"

"Love to, Matt, but I don't have any money."

"No money! Tommy, how do you go for a run on a day like today with no money?"

"'Cause I knew you would have some."

Just north of 100th Street we finally decided to turn east, making our way over to Central Park. Suddenly, some shade. But then I looked down at my legs. A whitish paste was caked to my shins and calves.

"Tommy! Is this normal?"

"Matt, wow, that's your salt, I think. Let's get you something more to drink, bro."

One more stop, and one more chance to treat Tommy. We walked a bit, drinking Cokes, until I told Tommy I was ready to get this run over with. We had at least two and a half miles to go. The conversation had dwindled to just the now-and-then "I'm hurting" or "Damn, we there yet?"

We got to the walkway that led to the Rock. "Matt, do we finish strong?" Tommy asked.

"Of course."

We ran our butts back to the Rock. We had been gone for more than three hours and covered close to 23 miles. We took long showers. "I don't know, Matt," Tommy said later as we were dressing. "Seemed like a pretty good run to me." And then he laughed.

Tommy and I would talk about that run a lot over the next few days. "Matty, tell Shane about our little run . . ." "Tommy, has Larry heard about the 23-miler?" That's all either of us needed to say to get the chattering started again.

Running got me fitter and faster, and friends like Tommy Grimshaw. It gave me the chance to be a part of people's lives and they a part of mine. I wanted running back because it made my life better, more interesting.

Now that I no longer had any holes in my body, it was time to fill that other hole again. And to see if I could make my life whole again.

One night in mid-December, a week or so before the accident's two-year anniversary, I was talking to Noel on the phone. I told him that I was worried that my rehab may have plateaued. I was making little progress with my walking, and although I was close to meeting my goal of using a cane, I could walk only a couple of blocks before tiring, thanks to a pronounced limp. In order to go even a couple of feet, I essentially needed to first anchor my left leg—the one with the titanium rods in it—and then swing my right leg forward. The glute muscle in my right leg, which should have helped me to push forward, just wasn't responding.

I also told him I was thinking about leaving New York for a while. I was worried about spending another winter in the city, trying to maneuver around the crowded and sometimes icy streets—and looking out for buses. I still had no recollection of the accident, but each time I walked down a street and saw a bus getting closer to the curb, I thought about everything that had happened to me.

"And one more thing, Noel. I'm tired of people constantly asking me how I'm doing."

It could be my family or friends or even strangers—once they found out I was "the fireman run over by the bus"—but all too frequently the first thing anyone said to me was, "How are you doing?" followed soon after by "Well, you look great." Everyone meant well. I appreciated their concern. But each time I heard either the question or the compliment, I was reminded that, well, I *was* that fireman run over by the bus. And I just wanted to be Matty Long.

"Matt, Matt, you're right," Noel said, once I shut up. "Get out of town for the winter. Go somewhere warm, to Florida or California. Find a place where you can work out and train a lot. And relax. Man, you've been through a lot."

"But Noel, I've never lived anywhere but New York."

"Matt, you're not going forever. Go for three or four months. If it helps, treat it as work, not as a vacation. You're working to get back in shape for the rest of your life."

He had a point. A little sun. Some intense training. A little more sun. When we hung up, I went to the computer and started searching for rehab facilities. I zeroed in on ones in south Florida, Southern California, and Arizona. When I found a dozen or so, I e-mailed each one. I gave them the facts about my accident and my current condition—"recovering from a broken shoulder, leg, pelvis, foot, and assorted internal injuries." In case they needed any more proof, I added a link to a New York *Daily News* story with a picture of me in a wheelchair. I ended each e-mail with one last note: "I want to run again. Can you help?"

The first five I heard back from basically answered the same way: "We'd be glad to work with you, but you need to be realistic. Running seems unlikely based on your injuries." I scratched them off my list. Be realistic? They were making excuses before they had even met me. I needed help, not excuses.

Just when it seemed that I had heard back from every facility that I was going to, I got one last response. It came from Mark D'Aloisio, a physical therapist who worked at a rehab facility in Tempe, Arizona, called the Functional Performance Center. He wrote that he had read my story and talked about it with one of his partners, Kyle Herrig. At the time, Kyle was training for an Ironman, so he was especially interested in me. He said they worked with both patients rehabbing from injuries and athletes looking to get stronger and fitter. I seemed to qualify for each category. He finished by writing, "If you want to run, all the better. I would never tell anyone they couldn't do what they wanted to do."

That's all I needed to know. Mark and I talked later that week, and he confirmed what he had written. If I wanted to run, he and Kyle would do their best to make it happen. I told him my idea: to spend three months at the center and rehab as much as my body could take—and that my insurance would cover. A couple of days later Mark sent me a proposed schedule: I would do physical therapy with him on Monday, Wednesday, and Friday, 1 to 2:30 p.m. I would do sports training with Kyle on Tuesday and Thursday, same time.

It sounded aggressive and ambitious. Just what I needed. Just what I wanted.

I arrived in Phoenix on February 8, a day before starting my new rehab program. My flight from New York had departed in dreary skies and a temperature of 39 degrees; when I arrived out west, it was close to 70 degrees and gorgeous. I was feeling better already. From some suggestions Mark had offered, I found an apartment about 10 minutes from the rehab facility. It came with just enough amenities to further remind me that I was no longer in Manhattan: a balcony that looked out onto a quiet lake and off to a distant view of the desert, and an outdoor swimming pool that was heated even in the mild winter months. That same day I joined a gym a few blocks from my apartment. I planned to use the mornings before my sessions with Mark and Kyle to lift weights on my own. Except for my shoulder, I had done little strength work on my upper body, and I was looking pretty soft; I wanted the ladies to notice that I had been away once I got back to New York.

The following day, a little before 1 p.m., I made my way to where I would be spending most of the next 10 weeks. The Functional Performance Center was located in a low-key office park by the edge of a canal that fed water into Phoenix. As I walked into the reception area, I noticed photos on the walls of some of the athletes who had used the facility, including several former major league baseball players and a couple of Olympic swimmers. I hobbled around on my cane; it was easy for Mark and Kyle to spot me.

"Hey, Matt, welcome to Arizona. It looks like you made it out here okay," Mark said.

"Okay? I've already called some of my Cronies back home and told them to book their flights."

The two of them chuckled. Both Mark and Kyle looked like they could be anchors on ESPN. Athletic, clean-cut, cheerful, easy smiles. Mark was originally from Ontario, Canada, and had moved to Arizona to work at the center in 2005. Kyle came from Iowa, and, as he told me later, the desert winters had made it hard for him to think about heading home anytime soon.

Before we started our first session, Mark gave me a quick tour of the workout room. It was the size of a college lecture hall, with only a dozen or so pieces of equipment along one wall—sparse compared to the gym I had been using back home. There was a treadmill, a rowing machine, and something Mark referred to as the Cage. "Matt, you're going to be spending a lot of time in there," he said.

The Cage looked like a playground's monkey bar set that had been reconstructed to form one half of a spaceship. It was tall enough for one person to stand in and wide enough to easily grab the bars on either side for balance. Mark explained that they used the Cage for a variety of stretching and strength-training exercises.

"Matt, from the little I've seen so far, it looks like you're hiking up that right hip when you walk," he told me.

"Well, I am," I said. "That's the side where the pelvis shattered. When they patched me up, my right leg ended up being an inch shorter than the left."

"What we're going to start working on is getting that leg stronger so it provides you more balance," Mark said. "When we talked, you said your right glute is still pretty weak. If we can strengthen that muscle so it's firing more, you'll get more lift. But you need all the major muscles working together to achieve the kind of balance you want." He outlined some of them: the hip flexors, the hamstrings, and the quadriceps. "Got it?"

"Sure."

"All right, then step into the Cage."

The first exercise zeroed in on my hip flexor. Mark told me to grip the bars while putting my left foot on the slightly elevated plank in front of me; my right foot stayed behind me, flat on the ground. I was then to rock my left hip forward and backward. He checked my range of motion: It was about three or four inches in either direction.

"Not bad, Matt. Pretty close to normal for a person of your size," Mark said. "Now let's turn it around and try the right hip."

So I flipped everything. I put my right foot on the elevated plank and the left foot behind me. When I rocked this time, though, my range was maybe a quarter of an inch.

"No worries, Matt," Mark said when he noticed me grimacing. "Now we have a baseline to build from."

Over the next 45 minutes, we went through similar stretching routines for my quads, hamstrings, and glutes. Then Mark showed me some lunge exercises. With these, I would look to bend my knees deeper and deeper with each step forward. Like the exercises in the Cage, my right side significantly underperformed my left side with each lunge. When I finished one and looked annoyed, Mark stayed upbeat.

"Matt, this is day one. Remember, we're building toward something."

Through the rest of that first week, I continued with the same set of exercises. In fact, the routines didn't change dramatically the whole time I was there. They seemed so simple. A lot of bending, a lot of pushing, a lot of stepping. I could probably have found similar stretches and strength-training exercises in the dozens of fitness

magazines that crowd the newsstands of New York City subway stations. For $4.95, I could have clipped them out, taped them to my
bedroom wall, and practiced them whenever I wanted to. Did I really
need to travel across the country for the same kind of routines?

Every day I got to the center, I realized that yes, I did. For those
90 uninterrupted minutes, I was getting something no magazine
could deliver: Mark and Kyle's attention, expertise, and encouragement. They played coach, cheerleader, and dime-store psychologist.
After a couple of weeks, they also played host, taking me out with
their wives for dinner. More and more, we got comfortable with
each other. I told them stories about being a firefighter in Manhattan and where the better bars (besides Third & Long) were in the
city. I also gave Kyle some tips on the Ironman; he was training for
his first one that coming spring. "Kyle, my buddy Frank told me
this when I did my first: Enjoy it. Just enjoy the experience. For
your second Ironman, you can try and kill it, but with your first,
have fun. Take some of the pressure off."

Not long after that conversation, Kyle would say something
very similar to me. It was during a session in March, five weeks into
my training. My repetitions in the Cage had tripled by then, and I
was even using the cane less to maneuver around the gym floor.
Still, I was worried that the key walking and running muscles
weren't responding as much as I had hoped they would by now.

"Kyle, I go home exhausted, so I know I'm working hard. But I
just don't seem to feel my glute getting stronger. I got to tell you, it's
kind of frustrating."

"Matt, you have to remember," Kyle immediately said, "muscles
can atrophy without use after just a couple of weeks. Before getting
out here, you hadn't really used some of your muscles in two years.
Getting them to work is a process, a slow, tedious process. That
goes with any kind of therapy. Progress can be imperceptible, but

Mark and I are seeing it." He talked in measured bites; he never seemed to get too emotional.

"Kyle, I know. But the Cage work—I'm in there every day, stretching and bending. What's it doing for me? How's that going to get me to run?"

"Matt, when you look at that exercise, it's kind of an exaggerated version of what your body is doing during a run. Sure, you might not squat as deep as we're having you do, but you're basically going through the motions of what your body does when running. If you're running, then your right foot goes forward, your left arm swings forward. The same thing with the knee and the glute. Each has a job, but they also work in tandem—and they have to be trained to work together. In your case, you're retraining the muscles to work together and to fire at the right time. To pick up that pattern again. Okay?"

"I get it, Kyle, believe me. It's just . . ."

"Just what, Matt?"

"I just want to run."

"Believe it or not, buddy, you're almost there."

———

On March 12, Mark filed a report to my doctors in New York updating them on my progress. He noted that my balance had improved and my risk of falling had decreased. At the bottom of the report, where it asked for "the patient's stated goal" for being at the rehab center, he wrote: "He wants to run. The goal is very attainable."

He wasn't bluffing.

The next day, following my session, I was packing up when Mark came over to me. "Matt, can you get here a little earlier tomorrow?"

"I guess so. What's up?"

"You're ready."

"For what?"

"We're running."

"Huh? What are you talking about? I'm not ready."

"You're ready. We're going a mile or three falls. I have my money on the mile. So get a good night's sleep."

━━━━━

That night I went home and made a little pasta and poured a glass of wine. I went out to my balcony and ate while watching a lightning storm off in the desert. And I thought about the next day.

*You're ready.*

Was I really? I was going for a run tomorrow, something I had waited so long to do. I should have felt excited, relieved. I had undergone dozens of surgeries to get to this point, and plenty of stress. A run should be fun, especially if Mark said I was ready. But I felt nothing but terror. I was scared. Noel would hate to hear that. But I was. There had been so many setbacks over the past couple of years, followed by so many doubts. I rarely saw the progress that other people did. Inna and Julie and Loreen saw it. My doctors always saw it. Mom and Dad and Jimmy always said they saw it. And now Mark and Kyle were saying the same thing. *And now they want me to run. God, what if I can't do it? What if I go one-tenth of a mile and I can't go any farther? What if I fall? What if my right foot flops all over the place? What if I can't plant it? What if I can't run?*

No, that night I didn't sleep well.

━━━━━

Around 12:30 p.m. the next day, Kyle, Mark, and I walked over to the path beside the canal, about 100 yards from the training center.

I was wearing a blue FDNY T-shirt, a white baseball cap, and a pair of Brooks Adrenaline running shoes. Back in New York I had a shoemaker glue a one-inch piece of rubber to build up the bottom of the right shoe so my left and right sides would be balanced.

When we got to the canal, I noticed right away that there was a noticeable grade on one side. It was also rutted with pebbles. The sun was warm at that hour, and the smell of manure from the horse ranch on the other side of the canal hovered. "Hey, guys, real scenic spot you took me to for my first run," I joked.

"Only the best for you, Matt," Kyle launched back.

Mark lined up on my left, Kyle on my right.

"Okay, Matt, half-mile down, half-mile back," Mark said.

"Or three falls," I added.

"Yes, three falls, but let's not worry about that."

I looked at my watch, then pushed the start button of my stopwatch. And then I pushed off.

I started with my left leg, the stronger one, the one that I had come to lean on. I was concentrating so much I could actually feel the ground push into my toes. And it hurt. Ever since my left foot was broken in the accident, the toes on that foot had curled under to become almost hammertoes. The pressure from the ground on the toes caused a biting pain. But I couldn't complain yet. It was just my first step. Then I slid my right foot out; I did it by barely raising my knee. If the foot left the ground, it was only by a millimeter. I repeated the routine. *Left foot push-off, right foot slide. Left foot push-off, right foot slide.*

I just kept inching down the canal path, looking out for every rock and rut. And mindful of every muscle in play, or at least every muscle that was supposed to be in play. It seemed in so many ways unnatural, not like the way I could remember running. Before everything happened, before the bus, I ran to clear my head of the stresses in my life. The girl who dumped me, the bartender I was thinking of firing. Or I eavesdropped on conversations of other runners, enjoying a piece of their lives without their knowing. But I never thought that much about the mechanics of running. About what my hamstring was doing at the very moment I was lifting a leg. And the same thing with the quad. And the glute. They just were part of the package. They just worked without me worrying about them.

But not on this run, along this canal path. I thought about my right hip. *Rotate!* And my hamstring. *Drive! Drive!* And mostly that right glute. *Are you working? Damn it, I don't feel you working! Will you ever work again?* And I worried about falling. I never worried about falling when I was with Frank or Vicky or Noel. But now, with these two guys that I had known for just over a month, I worried about falling and whether they would let me.

Mark and Kyle stayed inches from me on either side. They were all but running in place; they could have walked the route faster than I was running it.

"Nice work, Matt, nice work," Kyle said.

"Up here, Matt," Mark said shortly after, "we'll turn around here."

So we turned around. One half-mile done. *Push, then slide. Push, then slide.* Still no falls. I now was heading in the direction of Phoenix and Camelback Mountain, which towers over the city. For a second I just looked at the mountain. And I stopped thinking of my glute. At that hour, the face of the sandstone mountain appeared as red as I'm sure my face looked. *Push, then slide. Push, then slide.* And for a moment I stopped worrying about my legs. I noticed how my arms were pumping back and forth, just the way Tommy Grimshaw had told me to do it. Maybe I really was running. *Push, then slide. Push, then slide.* No, I really was running.

And then I wasn't . . .

"Matt, buddy," I thought I heard Mark say, "we're done. You did it. You finished a mile."

———————

I got home later that afternoon and grabbed a beer. And my cell phone.

"Noel."

"Hey, Matt, how you doing?"

"Get this, Noel. I just ran a mile."

"You're shittin' me!"

"No joke. I did it in 17:24. Seventeen minutes, 24 seconds, Noel. I used to run a 5-K almost as fast. But I did it, Noel."

"Matt, that's amazing. How did it feel? Did it hurt?"

"Noel, it's the toes on the left foot. Of all things. They ache. And I'm sure something else will hurt tomorrow. But, bro, it feels good. Now listen. Remember I was telling you that someday you and Frank and I were going to do a six-miler in the park together? And then beers?"

"Yeah, we're there for you when you're ready, Matt."

"Well, scrap those plans, Noel. We're not doing six."

"No?"

"No, we're doing the whole thing."

"What are you talking about?"

"Noel, I'm doing the marathon."

"Huh?"

"New York, Noel. This November. New York. Are you in, Noel? Or are you scared?"

# 16

# THE FAST BUILD

Even before traveling to Arizona, I had thoughts of attempting the marathon again. Someday. Say, seven or eight or nine years down the road. I thought by then I might petition the organizers of the Boston Marathon to see if they would let me run based on my previous qualifying time. But I kept those thoughts to myself.

I figured that telling my friends I wanted to run six miles was enough to motivate me *and* them. It didn't sound too far-fetched. In fact, it sounded quite reasonable. They knew me well enough to understand that given a goal and the time to rehab (which I had plenty of as a firefighter on disability), I would limp, hobble, and waddle my way to six miles and a bunch of beers. But a marathon? Had I so much as whispered such a stunt before Arizona, I would have been rushed back to the hospital for a CAT scan.

The fact was, I knew that I could never be the athlete I once was until I could go 26.2 miles again. After getting a taste of running in Arizona, I realized that the sooner I could do the marathon, the sooner I could feel like my old self.

Just after the marathon in 2005, someone took a photograph of me at the finish line in Central Park. I may have been exhausted after sprinting the last half mile or so, but in the picture I'm smiling. I was satisfied that I had just met my Boston qualifying time and proud that I had helped our team of firefighters beat the NYPD. That photo defined who I was before a bus crushed me: someone who set big goals and then did all he could to achieve them. I wanted to play college basketball, and with my final chance to, I succeeded. I wanted to start a bar in Manhattan, and for close to two decades Third & Long had been a mainstay of midtown. I wanted to find a way to honor my friend, Kenny Dolan, who died too young, and the road race I started with some buddies in his name had only gotten bigger, and its proceeds more substantial, with each succeeding year.

Yes, I would only feel whole again when I could set a goal like running the marathon, and then set about to do it. And then I could look at that picture without wondering, *Whatever happened to the guy with the fat smile?*

After that first run with Mark and Kyle, I went out two or three more times on my own around Tempe Town Lake, in the park near my apartment. I usually ran in the early evening, when the air was cooler and the paths around the lake were filled with other runners working out after a day in the office, before they eased into their nights. They reminded me of my former self, when I used to leave the firehouse in the late afternoon after a shift and wind my way through the streets of East Harlem and over to Central Park. On a summer night the shirt would come off and get tucked into my shorts, and I hoped that the ladies might glance my way. I looked fit and I felt confident. But on these runs in Tempe, I had a clumsy gait because of my collection of ailments: a hip that hitched, a right foot that slid (not stepped), and hammertoes that crunched with each footfall. And I never thought to take the shirt off and expose a chest with a zigzagged scar running through the middle of it.

Along Town Lake I would only go a half mile out and a half mile back, but every time a runner approached—it didn't matter if it was a man or a woman—I would mutter to myself, *Come on, Matt, try to straighten up. Try to look like you know what you're doing.*

I'm not sure why I worried so much. Everyone just trotted by me, never saying a word. Until one night when some fellow in his early forties, about the same age as me, came up on my left side at a good clip. He called to me, "Hey, man, keep it up. Good luck." That's all he said as he rushed by. But it was enough to remind me again of the times in Central Park when I would see a runner with a prosthetic leg or a blind runner jogging with a guide, working themselves around the loop, unhurried yet purposefully. They were disabled athletes and members of the Achilles Track Club. I would yell out, "Go, Achilles, go!" and hope it might help a little.

As this guy ripped past me, I thanked him with an "I hear you, bro," and then finally felt okay being noticed. From that point on, I never again cared how I looked or how I ran. No one on the paths of Tempe Town Lake knew me or my story; to these people trying to shake free from the bothers of the day, I was just another runner getting in his miles before dinner.

———

I came back from Tempe with more than a couple of runs in my log. My bottle of Confidence—that magical juice my buddy Matt DelNegro and I used to imagine splashing on before we hit the bars of Manhattan—had been refilled. I felt more comfortable dealing with life, both its small challenges and big ones. For instance, until I got to Tempe I hadn't driven a car in two years, and it showed. I spent the first couple of days driving my rental car slower than my 90-year-old grandfather might, cautious of how well my wobbly right foot would handle the accelerator. But within a week I could picture myself behind the wheel of 43 Truck, chauffeuring the guys through the double-parked streets of East Harlem in 40,000 pounds of red-plated metal. Yes, the driving came back.

And more and more the show-mes reappeared, too. The show-mes were the muscles I used to like to show off to the ladies. Some days I spent an hour in the gym before my sessions with Mark and Kyle, working on my core and upper body. Mostly I would hit the machines: one day, chest and triceps; the next day, back and biceps; the day after, shoulders. I started by lifting as little as 10 pounds. In about six weeks I was up to 40 pounds. At the start I also set a goal of doing 200 pull-ups before I left Arizona, even though I was able to do only five in my first attempt. But two months later I chinned 200 times in just 26 minutes. The show-mes were back.

I also became more willing to go out and socialize. A couple of times I met a friend who worked in the Tempe fire department for burgers and beers, and a few times I ventured out on my own. One night I was at a restaurant not far from my apartment when I met a woman named Jamie. We talked for a while that night. Right away I felt at ease with her, so much so that I told her everything that had happened to me and everything I worried about, especially when I was with a woman. She didn't seem to care. Jamie was a sweet, hardworking single mom of two. We went for drinks and dinner a couple of times after that, and I even asked her to come with me to Las Vegas when my trip out west was winding down. We had a nice time; I think I made her weekend when I was able to snare two tickets to an Elton John show at Caesars Palace at the last minute.

But mostly we talked late into the night while watching the scene pass by us in the hotel bar.

The last night we saw each other, Jamie told me her life was in Arizona with her kids. I told her that I had things to get back to in New York City. We talked about my returning home; she thought I was ready to get back to my life and my routines. I said, "Jamie, maybe I am, but Arizona has been good for me. There are a lot of reasons why I sometimes think about staying."

My family said they noticed the change soon after I returned to the city in mid-April. No, not my improved balance or steadiness of foot or even my fitter look. It was my attitude. "Matthew, it's good seeing you smile," Mom said one night after I stopped by unexpectedly to see her. I started coming by for dinner more often and picking up the phone to call Matthew and Kate and the other nephews and nieces instead of waiting for them to call me. And I was back to teasing my sisters, just like the old times. "You might think about cutting out those cigarettes," I told Eileen one afternoon, trying not to smirk. "Little Joseph shouldn't be around secondhand smoke."

"Oh, Matt, it is *so* good to have you home," she shot back, the sarcasm oozing as much as ever.

I told the Cronies, too, that I was back, and I didn't mean just back in the city. When I saw the guys, I put it to them that they could cut out the white-glove treatment. Bust me about the cane or my goofy walk. Whatever. But the official mourning period was over. Pretty soon we were meeting again at Smith & Wolly's, table 35, for steak and wine and the latest stories from around the FDNY.

I took the same approach with everyone I met. When someone said I looked good, I said, "Thanks, and you do, too"—not leaving the window open long enough for them to ask for a progress report on my health. As much as I could, I tried to keep "the fireman who got run over by the bus" out of the conversation. And even when the accident came up as an aside, I was prepared to handle it. One night I took a girl out for drinks. In her case, a lot of drinks. The next day I called her to see how she was doing. From the sound of her voice I could tell she was still groggy, even though it was well past noon. "Oh, Matt, last night was rough. It felt like I got run over by a bus—*oh-my-God*, I didn't mean that!"

"No problem, no worries," I told her. "I know the feeling." When I hung up, I started to laugh.

Not much could get me down. You might say I had a little bounce in my step. Truth was, I did. When I walked, it looked like I was hopping forward, not striding. I continued to rely mostly on my left leg for propulsion, then letting the right leg simply swing around. I made it down the street as if I were bobbing in three feet of water; I listed, left to right, right to left. Somehow I moved ahead. The effort would leave me aching by the end of each day. At night in bed, I often woke up in agony. But the worst times were the mornings. Imagine waking up to the thought of walking from bed to bathroom over barbed wire. And now that I was more active, the discomfort it caused only seemed to intensify.

Fortunately, my desire to push through the pain did as well. I had something now motivating me to get up each morning.

---

On April 29, I had an appointment to see Jim Wharton. Since returning from Arizona in mid-April, I had been searching for someone who could help me accelerate the progress I had made with Mark and Kyle. Wharton's name kept coming up. One friend put it this way: "Jim's worked with some of the best runners in the world. Go see him—right away."

With all the hype about Jim, I was surprised when I stepped into his small West Side office, a block from Central Park: It was just a studio apartment with a reception area the size of my bedroom closet. I could see a stretching table and some metal contraption rigged with a few weights and a pulley. Where were the StairMasters, the Nautilus equipment, the sushi bar? The receptionist gave me paperwork to fill out. At that point, after two years of seeing doctors and dealing with insurance companies, I had grown bored with detailing every last malfunction in my body. So when I got to the line on the form that asked for a "Brief History of Musculoskeletal Problems," I thought for a moment and then just scribbled "FUCKED!!!"

I few minutes later, a short, skinny fellow with shaggy, graying hair walked in the office. He looked like Mick Jagger, just fitter. He grabbed the chart with my paperwork. Then he chuckled.

"Fucked! I like that. Matt, I'm Jim Wharton. So what can we do for you?"

Over the next few minutes I gave Jim the rest of my story, as well as my goal: to run the marathon in November, six months from that point. When I told other people that wish, they often shot me an odd-looking glance that seemed to ask, "Why so soon, Matt? Can't you wait another year until you're stronger?" I gave them a simple answer: It would soon be three years since my accident. Already I had lost a lot of time. I wanted to be an athlete again, and I didn't want to wait any longer. When I told Jim my goal, he didn't flinch. Having worked with a number of Olympic athletes—including the gold medal sprinter Michael Johnson and the marathon medalist Meb Keflezighi—he said that he understood my mind-set.

"Matt, obviously you've sustained some traumatic injuries," Jim told me, with a bit of a southern twang left over from his days living in Florida. "But you haven't lost your competitive nature. That's what got you through an Ironman and what's kept you going." And like Mark D'Aloisio, Jim said he would never deny anyone the chance to fulfill an athletic dream.

He did explain, though, how his therapy program differed from Mark and Kyle's: Where their rehab concentrated on using different muscle groups at once, Jim based his approach on something he called activated isolated stretching. "We ask individual muscles to respond in the way they are supposed to respond," he explained. "Matt, I want to work on each key muscle individually and see if we can get each one working. That way, you will regain the kind of balance you once had."

Jim recommended that I come in for twice-weekly sessions. Either he or one of his therapists, Tom Nohilly or John Alsop, would stretch me for 50 minutes or so, before ending the session with a light strength-training workout using the pulley contraption I saw when I first walked in his office.

"When do I start running?" I asked Jim as we wrapped up.

"We'll see how you're doing in eight weeks or so," he said.

"*Eight weeks?* What do you mean? I've got a marathon to run."

"Matt, we'll get you to the marathon, but you need to be patient. We need to pinpoint those muscles that need attention. Stretching can be tedious, time-consuming, painful work. Can you be patient?"

At that point, I didn't have much choice.

━━━━━━━━

Think about all the design and work that goes into constructing a skyscraper, from the plans an architect renders to the manpower and equipment and supplies and months (sometimes years) required to turn those plans into reality. And then think of how the human body comes about—a nine-month phase that produces an exquisitely crafted form in which muscles and bones and nerves and tendons are all, God willing, perfectly aligned and working in unison. And its functioning only improves as the years go by.

Until old age or a 40,000-pound bus comes along and ruins the masterpiece.

In my therapy sessions, Jim explained that the aftereffects of my accident had, in a sense, returned me to the infant stage; essentially, I needed to learn how to use my muscles to walk before even thinking of running. To start off, he had me lie on the stretching table to see just how high I could lift my feet. I lay on my right side and raised my left foot; even though I had titanium rods stretching the length of my left leg, my flexibility was close to normal. But when I switched to my left side and tried to lift my right foot, I could barely raise it a couple of inches off the table. He pointed out where the breakdown was occurring—the right glute—something I was all too aware of. "Those muscles are supposed to help lift the leg, working together with the other muscles," he said. "We'll see if we can get that glute firing on its own."

Those first sessions proved to be painful and frustrating. Often I worked with John, Jim's associate, a barrel-chested former college football player with strong hands but an easygoing personality. John concentrated mostly on my lower extremities, twisting, stretching, and manipulating every muscle and joint, from my hips to my big toes. Usually the most I might feel was a slight twinge. But when he took my right knee and locked it into his right shoulder and started to push my leg back toward my hip, all I could do to keep from letting out a scream was clench my teeth.

"Matt, let me know if it hurts," John would say.

"No, not yet," I'd say, lying through my clenched teeth.

For weeks, every session was the same, and yet I wasn't seeing the results I was hoping for. One afternoon Jim asked me to lie on the table and "fire off that right glute and lift your leg up." Essentially, he wanted me to tell my brain to activate the nerves connected to my glute and see if it would respond. Nothing happened. The glute stayed locked. Jim read the tension in my face. "Matt, don't get frustrated. We're just training the brain to recommunicate with those muscles. Remember, they've been traumatized. We'll get there." I wanted to believe him, and in his office I would stay positive. But when I got home, I'd often say to myself, *This isn't happening.*

What kept me going? Something Jim would always remind me of before finishing a session. "Listen, Matt, don't worry about the glute. If we don't get it to respond, we'll get the other muscles— the hamstring, the quad—to compensate. We'll get you to the marathon."

After eight weeks of treatment, my glute remained inert. But Jim noticed that my overall leg strength had improved significantly. When I first tried that odd-looking weight-lifting machine in his office, I could lift only five pounds with my right leg; by the end of June, I hit 45 pounds. As Jim had predicted, other muscles had started to make up for my weakened glute.

"Matt, we're going to use those muscles to get you to the starting line," Jim told me one afternoon, "and, hopefully, to the finish line."

That day he also outlined a 16-week training plan for me. In many ways it was similar to one that many marathoners use to mount their assault on the 26.2-mile distance. The difference? In advance of their formal marathon training, most marathoners have run for weeks, building up a mileage base. They've been running 15 or 30 or 45 miles a week, so when it's time to intensify the load, their bodies can adapt more easily to the added work. The goal for many recreational marathoners is to do one "long run" per week, starting, say, at six miles in week one and moving toward 20 or 22 miles by the end of the 16-week cycle.

In my case I was working off a zero mileage base. And Jim wanted me to run only two, maybe three times a week, with my longest run in week one covering just a single mile. At that rate there was no way I could do a 20-mile long run before marathon day, November 2.

"Matt, don't worry about that. You can work on your cardio in the gym with the recumbent bike and with the swimming," Jim advised. "Let's keep the pounding on your hips and other muscles to a minimum."

And then he reminded me of one important fact in my favor. "Remember, Matt, you're an Ironman. Just the memory of that feat will help you on marathon day. Your mind knows what it takes to be on the course for a long time. Most people out there won't have that to call on."

My official training began on July 1—at, of all places, the Rock on Randall's Island. It was my first day back to work after two and a half years of being on disability leave. Due to the extent of my injuries and the fact that I still needed a cane most of the time, it had become clear that I could never return to Ladder 43 and resume my career there. So I rejoined the physical training staff at the academy to help get the next probie class ready for life in the fire department.

During my lunch break that first day back, I went to a nearby track for my first training run. I asked Tommy Grimshaw to join me. It was humid and muggy, almost as warm as the last long run Tommy and I had gone on—that 23-miler around Manhattan. This time we just looped the quarter-mile track. I hitched and hopped; just as in Tempe, my left leg did most of the work to move me forward. Tommy jogged slowly, as if in place. And the whole time we talked. We talked so much that after four loops, which equaled a mile, we kept going. We ran two more circuits. "Don't tell Jim Wharton we did a mile and a half," I said to Tommy with a chuckle. When I hit the stop button on my watch, we had clocked 24 minutes, my longest training run in three years.

As we walked back to the Rock, Tommy seemed more excited than I was. "Matt, what you just did is amazing. To think how far you've come."

"Thanks, Tommy, but slow down. I got a long way to go."

"You do, Matt, but we're all here to help you. Just like before. Matt, I can already taste the Guinness we'll be drinking after the marathon. And it tastes good."

---

I appreciated that Tommy was willing to run with me at my pedestrian pace, but after that first run I decided that until I got my legs under me, I would spare others the chore of plodding along. I also looked forward to being on my own and enjoying Central Park at my speed. I might do a loop around the reservoir and search for the faces I used to see years ago. Amazingly, Alberto Arroyo was still among them. He was a white-haired man, probably in his early nineties, whom everyone referred to as the Mayor of Central Park. Legend had it that Alberto was the first person to use the park as a place to run, when he was training as a boxer back in the 1930s.

Now he made the reservoir his daily destination, circling the loop with a walker; he had no trouble going at my pace.

When I did my workout, I would often laugh to myself if I saw a fellow runner go by listening to music. *Whatever gets you through your run*, I'd think. But for me, I enjoyed the park's ongoing soundtrack, from the thumps of softballs being whacked on the Great Lawn to the cries of little kids rushing around the jungle gyms of Heckscher Playground. And I wanted to listen in on all of it. Maybe after all the months I had lost sitting in my apartment, depressed and wondering if I would ever be able to just run the park, I had become even more mindful of all the park had to offer.

Besides the running, I pushed myself even harder at the gym to build up my upper body. I knew I would need my arms as much as my legs to drive me through 26.2 miles in November. I also tried to swim at least twice a week. A sport that I once avoided had become a go-to outlet to increase my aerobic capacity without enduring a lot of pounding.

But perhaps the biggest breakthrough came in late July, when I decided to try to ride a bike for the first time since the accident. I had been using the stationary bike in the gym, and, thankfully, its seat didn't bother my reconstructed rear end. My mind, on the other hand, needed some coaxing. While I had no memory of actually being hit by the bus, after all the years of talking about that day with family and friends and of reading about it in the newspapers, I couldn't help but have a few worries when I finally decided to take the Cervélo P3 out for a ride.

I started pedaling from the corner of First Avenue and East 76th Street, and went crosstown toward the park. I rode slowly, cautiously, more so than I could ever remember having done. I didn't want to get sideswiped or have the door of a parked car suddenly open in front of me. Most of all I didn't want to get near a bus. Each time I approached an intersection—at Second Avenue, then at Third, at Lexington, at Park, at Madison, and finally at Fifth Avenue—I waited until no bus was in sight, then I continued to pedal. Once in the park I made two six-mile loops; they took 60 minutes to complete. I used to do the same set in less than 40. But I wasn't in a rush; I was biking again for the first time in a long time.

Biking was back, joining a list of items—the running, afternoons in Central Park, a pleasant disposition—that had been taken away when that bus ran over me on that December morning. Still, I couldn't avoid being reminded that I would never completely be the person I once was, and some reminders were more painful than others. One afternoon I went upstate with Allison Caccoma, a friend from the Asphalt Green Triathlon Club, to watch Noel compete in a triathlon. We took my SUV and put a pair of bikes on the roof thinking we might have a chance to squeeze in a ride ourselves. But as we were driving down a hill not far from the racecourse, I got pulled over by a New York State park police officer. I suspected that I may have passed someone illegally while trying to get my bearings.

"All right," I told Allison, "I'm going to get yelled at. But whatever I did, it couldn't have been too big of a deal."

The officer walked over to my car window. He said, "License, registration, and . . . what the heck? Who is handicapped in this car?" He had noticed a handicap-parking sticker on my windshield.

The question came out of the blue, and suddenly I was shaking. I said, "I'm disabled."

"You? What's your disability?"

At that moment I was wearing a cutoff T-shirt, and from all the lifting I had been doing I looked fit, at least in the upper body. I said, "I don't know how to answer that question, officer."

"It's pretty simple. What's your disability?"

And I said, "No, it's not that simple. Let me get out of the car and I'll show you."

"Stay where you are. Listen. You have two fancy racing bikes on your car. You have a fire department sticker, a license plate that says 'IWILLRUN,' and a handicap-parking sticker. You got to be kidding me—disabled?"

He left for a moment, only to come back with a ticket. At this point Allison was almost in tears; I already was. I took the ticket but then said to the officer, "Do you mind if I say something for a minute?"

"Go ahead."

"The license plate says 'IWILLRUN' because that is something I say to myself every day when I wake up in the morning. It keeps me moving every day and keeps me from wasting my life because of the accident I was in. The fire department sticker is for a job that I did for 12 years, and that I can't do anymore because of my disability. And the handicap-parking sticker is mine, and it was earned because of my disability." I paused for a second and collected myself. "Officer, I'm going to fight this ticket. I cannot believe you treated me this way."

When I finished, he didn't say a word. He just turned in silence and walked away. A couple of months later I got the ticket dismissed.

———

Gradually, as if I were filling a bucket with sand with one of my nephews or nieces on the beach at Breezy Point, the number of miles on my long runs began to rise. By the last week of August my long run was up to seven miles, and two weeks later I did a nine-miler. I was progressing just as Jim Wharton had laid it out. On September 14 I scheduled a 12-miler, a run that I expected to take close to three hours to complete. Knowing that, I called Frank and Noel to join me.

At the start of my marathon preparation, my two longtime training buddies had agreed to run the race alongside me. I wanted them there on Marathon Sunday for the company as well as for the protection; I feared that with my shaky gait, one of the other 38,000 runners might easily bump into me and send me flying to the blacktop. In a way, Frank and Noel would serve as bodyguards. But they needed to appreciate what they had signed on for: a slow slog through the city. They would be running at a ponderous pace compared to their normal one. This 12-mile workout would give them a taste of what lay ahead.

That morning, as we did loops in the park, it felt like the training runs the three of us had done so often in the past. The presidential election between John McCain and Barack Obama had become the major news story, so we spent one five-mile circuit tossing out the pros and cons of each candidate. As the son of the New York State Conservative Party chairman, I definitely had my thoughts on both men. Later we moved on to the Mets and Yankees and the start of the football season. And then the two single guys wanted to know how married life and fatherhood were treating Frank.

"Matty, be glad Renee likes you so much that she lets me spend this much time with you," Frank said, chuckling. "But guys, one thing you need to remember. You two are always moaning about wanting to get married and having kids. Well, it's great and all, but unless you find a sweetheart like Renee, your days doing long runs in the park will be long gone. So enjoy this, okay?"

Amid all the jabbering we managed to finish the 12 miles. Afterward we took a cab to Frank's firehouse on East 67th, where the guys in his house filled a garbage can with ice water and dunked me in. The next morning, though, I felt a tweak in my left foot. I went to see my foot doctor, who gave me a warning: He thought I had the makings of tendinitis in my left foot.

I trimmed back the running over the next two weeks, hoping the soreness in my foot would subside. All I had to do, though, was look at the calendar and realize that the date of the marathon continued to creep closer while my longest run remained stuck at 12 miles. So on Friday, September 25, around 2:30 p.m., I decided to go to the park and run—run until it was too dark to go any longer—and see how many miles I could collect. I started from my apartment and entered Central Park at 79th Street, then headed north, up to the top of the park, toward Harlem Hill, the most ruthless incline in the city. I trudged up its curvy slope, getting passed by other would-be marathoners, probably on one of their last long-distance workouts. It took me 10 minutes just to climb the third of a mile. But when I crested the hill, I knew the next five miles—until I was again back at the foot of Harlem Hill—would be fun and almost painless by comparison.

I ended up running 14 miles that day, my longest outing since I had run the marathon in 2005. It took me three hours and 35 minutes. I laughed to myself. The last time I ran 26.2 miles, I did them faster—*much faster*—than these 14 miles.

━━━━━━━━━━

As satisfying as that training run felt, it delivered damaging aftershocks. I woke up the next morning in excruciating pain—nothing like the usual achiness I had become accustomed to after a night's sleep. As soon as I put one foot on the floor, I felt a sharp twinge in my right hip.

*This isn't good,* I thought to myself.

That afternoon I made an appointment with Dr. Bryan Kelly, a hip specialist who previously had worked on my shoulder. He suspected pretty quickly what my problem was: a tear of the labrum. The labrum is cartilage that forms a ring around the edge of the joint and provides stability and flexibility. "We could operate on it, Matt, but I don't think you want that right now," Dr. Kelly said.

"No, Doc, that wouldn't be too helpful. Anything else?"

"The best you can do in the short term is take pain medication and give it a lot of rest."

After I saw Dr. Kelly, I called Jim Wharton, who gave it to me straight. At this point, four weeks from the marathon, he said I needed to shut down my running. "Matt, you want to finish this race, correct?"

"Sure, of course."

"Well, you've done all the mileage your body will allow for now. Let it rest, cross-train, and be confident that you'll have enough in the tank on race day."

The nice thing about Jim was that he had a mild, reassuring, Zenlike way about him. He also had a history of working with some of the most gifted runners in the world and getting them ready for world-class competition. So if he said I could do the marathon with my ailing hip and the tendinitis in my foot and with a dead glute, then I had to trust him.

But it wasn't easy.

More than ever I worried about whether I could pull this race off. I began doubting myself. Everything I had accomplished in a relatively short amount of time seemed tenuous as the pain mounted while my mileage plateaued. *How am I going to run 26.2 miles in a month,* I asked myself one early October day, *when I can barely run a mile today?* And even if I got to the starting line, I wondered if I would be able to finish the race without constantly worrying that my gimpy body would get even more battered, either by the sheer distance I needed to cover or by the jostling of fellow runners.

Increasingly, I started to think about the letter I received when I was in the hospital, the one in which the writer suggested that I could someday run with the Achilles Track Club. At the time I couldn't accept that I was permanently impaired. But now, nearly three years after my accident, it was becoming clear that my glute would never work again. And that my right leg would always be shorter than my left, and that I would never fully be able to control what my right foot wanted to do. And that my digestive system would never give me peace of mind during a run, or at any time for that matter.

The evidence was substantial: I was a disabled athlete, and to run the marathon I would need help. So I called Dick Traum, the founder of Achilles. He started the program in the early 1980s after becoming the first person to ever run the New York City Marathon on a prosthetic leg. Today more than 500 Achilles athletes run marathons each year. I asked Dick if I could be a part of his team for the upcoming New York race. He must have noticed some hesitancy in my voice, as if I was conceding that I was no longer the person I once was. Dick told me, "We would be glad to have you run with us. And just remember, Matt, you may be disabled, but you're still an athlete."

I needed to hear that, and so did my ego.

═══════════

I wasn't the only one, though, who noticed my confidence had become as shaky as my right leg. Mom and Dad mentioned a couple of times that they were worried about my health. I told them to relax, that I just needed to get through the next month and everything would be fine. And then there were the guys at the Rock. They became so concerned about me that they asked Jimmy to talk me out of doing the race.

"Hey, Matt, I want to talk to you about this marathon," Jimmy began when he called me one day at the Rock.

"Yeah, what about it?"

"Maybe these injuries you're having, maybe they're telling you something."

"Huh? What are you getting at, Jimmy?"

"Look, if the marathon doesn't happen this year, it's not a big deal. You've done great. But maybe you should think about taking it easy. Let's push this back a year . . ."

Right then, I cut him off. Going back to our days playing basketball together as kids, when we used to bang each other in our backyard games of twenty-one, Jimmy was well aware that it took a lot for me to cry uncle. I never once beat him in a game of one-on-one, but I also never gave in, either. Now he was about to ask me to lie down. I gave him the elbow I used to lay on him under the boards when going after a rebound. "Jimmy, what did you do this morning? Get up and decide to give Matty a kick in the gut?"

"No, Matt, no."

"Well, don't. Don't bother telling me what I can and can't do."

"Matt, listen, that's not . . ."

"No, Jimmy, you listen. Nothing is keeping me from this race. Nothing. Not you. Not the pain. Nothing."

Then I did something I had never done before: I hung up on my best friend.

What was pushing me to run the marathon with all the mounting aches and pains? With the people closest to me asking me not to? With my own growing self-doubt?

When I first started down this road back in April, I had one goal in mind: to prove that I could be the athlete I was before my life changed so much. But when I chose to run with the Achilles Track Club, it was clear that I could never be that athlete again. So why bother putting myself through all the pain and anxiety?

Simple. Because now I was running for more than just myself.

When word spread that "the fireman who got run over by the bus" was training for a marathon, the local newspapers and TV stations pursued me for profiles and interviews. I had, it seemed, a heart-tugging story to tell. Then once the articles appeared, dozens of people, mostly strangers, began to contact me. They told me that my story had given them hope to deal with problems in their own lives. Every night, it seemed, whenever I returned home from work, I had another message waiting for me. Each one said someone was rooting for me and, no matter how long it took me to do the marathon, I was an inspiration just by taking part in the race.

Suddenly, the e-mail I got months back from John Kelly, my fellow Crony, the one telling me that someday the two of us would inspire people by the way we dealt with our respective problems, seemed all too on target. And as the number of well-wishers grew, my determination to finish the job mounted as well.

One call came from a friend of some fellow by the name of John Gleeson. The person asked me if I wouldn't mind visiting John, who was in a rehab facility north of the city recovering from a horrific accident. A car had hit John after he had completed a 120-mile bike ride. He suffered multiple broken bones, including a shattered hip, and he even had had a stroke during one of his operations.

When I went to see John, his room was filled with friends and family members. I asked everyone to leave for a few minutes while I spoke to him. Then I said, "John, a lot of people are going to tell you to hang in there and that everything will be all right. They mean well, and certainly thank them for their support. But the truth is, John, what you're going through right now is hell, and it's going to be awful for quite a while."

I watched as his eyes stared more intently at me. "But, John, I'm standing here talking to you now because I went through the same kind of hell. I know the pain and the helplessness you're feeling. I also know that if you keep pushing, it will get better."

"Yeah," John said finally, "but is it going to be what it used to be?"

"Nope, and that's the truth," I said to him. "But things will get better."

To prove my point, I told him what I had coming up. "John, in January I needed a cane to walk a city block. Now look at me. I still need a cane to get around, but I'm also running. And in a couple of weeks I'm running the marathon. You see, things can get better."

As I was leaving, I told John we'd stay in touch. He said, "Thanks for coming, Matt, and good luck with the marathon. I'll look for you on TV."

Running can be a very isolating sport. Something people do—something I did—to feel better about themselves. Maybe you run to keep the weight off or to lower the stress level. And often when you run a race, your only competition is you. It's a test of your own endurance and your own speed. So there can be a singular purpose to the sport. But now, with my goal of running the New York City Marathon nearing, I realized I was running for myself *and* for people like John Gleeson, strangers who were counting on me to give them, in a sense, a chance. If I could complete something as absurd as the marathon after what I had been through, then these people whom I barely knew would have reason to believe in their own prospects to survive and overcome.

And in some cases, even people I knew all too well could believe, too.

———

On the eve of the marathon, just before I went to bed, I checked my e-mail one last time. There was a message from my brother Robert. I opened it, not expecting much but a simple good luck. Instead, he wrote the following:

> *Matt, On Christmas Eve, a couple of days after your accident, the family was at the hospital. But that night, around 6 o'clock, I left to go to an Alcoholics Anonymous meeting. On the way back to the hospital from the meeting, I passed a bar. There were three old men sitting in it, and it would have been a perfect spot to go in and have a drink. I stood outside the bar for 20 minutes and kept thinking of going in. Finally I said, "No, Matt's dying up in that hospital. I can't be that selfish." Matt, there was definitely a power at work, and it was you—you brought me back to the hospital and kept me from going into that bar. You inspired me that night, and you inspire me now as you're about to run this marathon. I love you. Robert*

If I needed one more reason to run—and finish—the marathon, that was it.

# 17

# 26.2 MILES TO GO

It was a Saturday night in New York City, just after 9 p.m., and already I was in bed, trying to fall asleep but not having much luck. I stared through the top of my bedroom window at nothing but the corner of a neighboring building. The phone rang, but I didn't budge. I just kept staring. At this moment I didn't need any more phone calls or words of encouragement. Already today Mayor Bloomberg had called to wish me luck, and so did George Pataki, the former governor of New York. They were bold-faced names to receive calls from, especially when you're just a firefighter from Bay Ridge, Brooklyn. But it wasn't just the politicians who wanted to get a hold of me. All day long the cell phone kept ringing; I let most of the calls slip into voice mail.

"Matty, you're amazing. Can't believe you're doing this."

"Yo, bro, you're the man. Call me."

"Hey Matt, look for me. I'll be on the corner of 68th and First cheering for you."

*Look for you*, I thought after listening to that message, and then I shook my head. *I'm going to try and do something pretty damn impossible tomorrow—run the New York City Marathon—and you want me to look for you.*

When I couldn't fall asleep, I started to picture in my head what might happen on the marathon course the next day. I tried to visualize the race just as Anthony Carillo had told me to do the night before the Ironman years before. *Okay, mile one. Here you go. Move over to the side. Avoid the crowd. Don't get pushed. Stay between Noel and Frank. Deep breath. Don't fall . . . Mile three. Mom and Dad and Jimmy and the nephews and nieces will be waiting there. Be ready. It may get emotional.* And I planned for potential problems along the way. *Matt, what if you have to go to the bathroom? Then I'm screwed. No, no, no you're not. You packed some wipes. Just jump into a Portosan. It will be fine.*

The visualization did little to relax me; in fact, it only pumped me up more. So I decided to have a conversation with God. Every night—okay, almost every night—I prayed to Him. On this night He had every right not to listen to me, especially after all the cussing and bad-mouthing I had directed at Him for months. In those little talks, if I wasn't yelling at God, then I was asking Him— begging Him—to make me better again. "Please fix the colostomy, God," I would say, "and I'll be okay. I can handle the rest." The negotiating wasn't right, but I always suspected that God was just glad I had enough faith to ask for His help. My mistake all along was wanting Him to work on my timetable. I was Matty Take Charge; I gave the orders, and I wanted God to move on them. What I needed to learn was that God worked on His own schedule. And He let me realize that I could handle the injuries and their aftermath, but it took a lot of pain and tears and months before I did.

On the eve of the marathon I just said, "God, tomorrow is going to be a long day, but let's make it a good one. Just the fact that I'll be at the starting line means it will be. God, be with me. I hope I finish the marathon, but I don't need to. I've gone pretty far already." In my heart, of course, I was hoping He'd get me through all 26.2 miles. "Okay, I'll talk to you tomorrow when this is all done."

My prayers said, I looked at the clock one more time. 11:15 p.m. A few minutes later, I was finally asleep.

━━━━━━━━━

For the past few mornings, I had started getting up earlier and earlier so I could have my body ready to go—ready to go to the bathroom, that is.

Without the sensation that tells me it's time to clear the system, I lived with the constant anxiety that I could crap in my pants at any moment. I couldn't deal with that kind of stress during the marathon, when I expected to be on the course for six or seven or eight hours. That's why I was up by 3:30 a.m.; fortunately, on this morning everything worked out just fine.

Later I headed to the kitchen to make some breakfast: I spread some peanut butter on a bagel, as I had done the morning of my last marathon run. Then I poured a carbo-loading drink into five small bottles that I would carry on my fuel belt during the race. Again, I knew I might be out there a long time; I would need to replenish my energy supply throughout the day. When all was in order, I headed downstairs.

Waiting there in an FDNY van was Matt McSweeney, the same firefighter who had driven me so often to my rehab sessions during the first few months after I left the hospital. He had one more assignment: Get me to Staten Island and to the marathon starting line at the Verrazano-Narrows Bridge. He handed me that day's *New York Post*, and as we drove downtown to pick up Frank and Noel, I started flipping through the paper. I got to the op-ed page and there, right below an editorial on the upcoming Obama-McCain election, was a piece about me: "A Model of Courage." I started reading it to McSweeney. "He won't come close to winning the race, but the most significant victory in today's New York City Marathon already belongs to FDNY firefighter Matthew Long—who's competing just three years after a horrific traffic accident during the 2005 transport strike left him at death's door. Talk about survival." I liked where this piece was going. "Long, who had to learn to walk again after extensive reparative surgery and who still suffers from chronic pain, will be running today with two friends to balance and support him—but he nonetheless hopes to finish the entire 26.2-mile course. All New Yorkers should be cheered by his determination and dramatic recovery—and wish him a good race."

We got to the corner of 61st and First, where Noel and Frank were waiting. "Hey, guys, check this out," I said as they hopped in. "We made it into the *Post* already."

"Great, Matt, does that mean we don't have to run?" Frank said with a smile.

I gave it right back to him. "Frank, we haven't even started running and you're complaining. What are you going to do when we hit the wall?"

At that hour, a little before 6:30 on a Sunday morning, most of the city was still asleep, so McSweeney made good time driving through Manhattan and Brooklyn on our way to Staten Island. As we drove, we laughed about the crank phone call Noel and I had made to Frank the day before. We called to say I was pulling out of the race—"Sorry, bro, it's just going to be too painful," I told him, trying not to laugh—then listened as Frank jabbered on about how he understood. "But, Matt, this is something you've wanted for so long. Is this really your final decision?" He sounded so sincere and distressed.

"We got you pretty good, Frank," I said from the front of the van.

"Yeah, Matt, you did," Frank came back. "But listen—I got 26 terrible jokes to drop on you guys during the marathon, so be prepared."

As we approached the toll plaza of the Verrazano in the vicinity of the starting line, McSweeney zigzagged through traffic cones to get us closer and closer. It was nearly 7 a.m. when he came to a stop. I untucked myself from the van seat as Frank and Noel got out.

"Noel, see the guy in the yellow jacket?" I shouted from the door. "Ask him where the Achilles runners start."

"Yellow jacket? Where, Matt, where?"

"Bro, the yellow jacket . . . in front of you. Hurry, would you?" We now had less than 30 minutes to get to the start.

When Noel explained who we were and where we needed to be, the man in the yellow jacket weaved us through metal barriers, and between and around idling cars and buses, and around turnstiles to a sliver of land notched between delivery trucks and Portosans, the Gothic towers of the Verrazano-Narrows looming almost overhead. At that hour, three hours before the official start of the marathon, when 38,832 runners would take off, only a couple of dozen runners stood there. They were Achilles runners, mostly in wheelchairs or on crutches, or seeing-impaired and with a guide. We all would be starting with a two-and-a-half-hour lead on the rest of the field.

I stretched for a few minutes along a guardrail. A cool breeze blew through the bridge. Unlike the last time I ran this race, when warm temperatures made for an exhausting day, right now it was in the low 40s—and even with a bright sun rising, forecasts called for a pretty frigid day. I adjusted the black skullcap covering my head and tugged up my knee-high compression socks. I wore the socks for extra support, though at that moment they were also providing some added warmth. Just then, Sal Cassano, the chief of the FDNY, came over. Sal had run the marathon often in the past, including several times going under three hours. Today he was here to give me a pat on the back.

"Matty, you look great. How you feeling?"

"Good, Chief, good. A little nervous, but good."

"Matty, amazing. I haven't done one of these in years. I got to find more time to train. But good luck. And Frank, thanks for helping out."

"My pleasure, sir. Anything for Matty."

"Okay, fellows, I'll see you at the finish. We'll have some cold ones waiting for you."

As the start time neared, Frank, Noel, and I inched closer to the line with the other Achilles athletes. A photographer suddenly jumped in front of us.

"Hey, Matt, can I get a shot of you?" he asked.

"Sure, which newspaper you from?"

"No newspaper, wire service."

"Whatever, take what you need."

"So I hear you're going to walk the whole way; that's great."

"Walk? What do you mean walk? Who told you that? We're running."

"Yeah, sure, whatever you say. Thanks and, uh, good luck."

"Yeah, right, you jerk. Frank, did you hear that? He thinks we're walking."

"Matty, no worries. The guy's an idiot. Relax."

I looked at my watch. We would be off in seconds. Mary Wittenberg, the president of the New York Road Runners, the organization that puts on the marathon, waited at a podium ready to send us early racers off. Before she gave the orders, Mary said, "Matt Long, good luck! We'll be with you on the course."

There would be no boom from a cannon to start us. Just an "On your mark, get set, go."

My long run had begun.

━━━━━━━

"Damn, it's freezing on this bridge," I shouted over to Noel and Frank.

"Yeah, Matt, this wind is brutal," Noel shouted back. "Feels like we're climbing Everest."

We were just about a mile into the marathon and a little more than halfway across the Verrazano. We were also alone. The other early starters had already faded from sight, having rushed off on their crutches and in their chairs once they got the go-ahead.

"Hey, how did we do with that first mile?" I called out.

"Around 17:30. That work for you, Matt?"

"Yeah, pretty close to what I expected."

The last time I had run this race, I finished the first mile in seven minutes, 45 seconds, a bit slower than my goal pace of 7:15. Back then I didn't want to get caught up in the excitement of the start and go out too strong—and risk crippling myself later, when my chances of a Boston qualifier would be at stake. Today I had no time constraints to worry about. I had told everyone I wanted to finish in no more than eight hours; secretly, I hoped I could come in around six hours and 30 minutes, or double my previous marathon best. However I sliced it, it was going to be a long day—and not just for me. At this turtle-like pace, Frank and Noel already could feel how achy this run might be. They were taking micro-steps, not their normal half-body-length strides. In a sense, they were working two to three times as hard to cover the distance they usually made with one stride.

"Hey, where's Frank?"

"He's back taking a leak, Matty."

"Already? Noel, I need you guys near me in case I get knocked off balance."

"Matt, there's no one around right now."

"It doesn't matter. Stay close."

As we came off the bridge, Bay Ridge was the first section of Brooklyn we hit. After Mom and Dad had moved the family here from Cypress Hills, I would come out every year and watch the marathoners pass by. In a couple of hours locals would line both sides of Fourth Avenue to cheer on thousands of runners from all over the world. But right now—with just a firefighter from the neighborhood, a firefighter from Long Island, and a banker from Manhattan on the road—the streets were pretty empty and quiet, except for a gathering of people in front of Our Lady of Angels Church, near the three-mile mark. It was my family. Every last one of them. From Grandpa Mike to Charles, Jimmy's kid, the littlest of the nephews and nieces. I had told Mom and Dad that I would be in the vicinity of the church, where Mom had spent hours praying when I was in the hospital, by around 8:15 a.m. I said I would stop for 90 seconds or so; enough time for a picture or two.

As we got closer Noel asked, "Matty, geez, how many people are there?"

"Thirty, maybe 40," I said, as tears started to well behind the sunglasses I was wearing.

The closer we came, the louder the knot of people got. Finally, I shuffled to a stop in front of Mom and Dad and hugged them. Maureen and Eileen were off to the side, tearing up. Chris and Eddie were waving signs: "Matty, We Love You" and "Matty, You Will."

The 90 seconds passed quickly, and I started to move again, trying to give a glance to everyone there. I stopped a second, though, to high-five Jimmy. Any lasting memory of our phone conversation from weeks earlier had faded. When everyone was behind us, I could feel my eyes watering even more.

"Hey, Frank?"

"Yeah, Matt?"

"The allergies, bro. They're starting to kick in."

"I know. Mine are, too. Take it slow, Matty. Take it slow."

A few minutes later things brightened considerably when I heard Hell or High Water, the band from the Kenny Dolon run, start cranking my favorite tune, Neil Young's "Long May You Run." For the next couple of blocks, the pace picked up a bit.

═══════════

Through the better part of Brooklyn, we clicked off a mile every 17 minutes or so, a slow waddle on a beautiful fall Sunday in New York. We talked about some of our favorite bars in the area and the girls we once dated from around this part of the city. Frank told a couple of his jokes—he was right; they were awful, the only good thing about them was their length: Each one distracted us for at least a quarter-mile. I made sure to stop in the Portosans when I saw one (just in case) and to drink some of the fluid I was carrying. So far, nothing hurt. I felt good.

At mile nine, almost two and a half hours into our run, we looked back and saw the top elite women in the marathon not far behind us. They included Paula Radcliffe, the defending champion from England, and Kara Goucher, an American Olympian making her marathon debut. Finally, we were about to have some company. I had met Goucher at a dinner a few nights earlier; she had a bubbly personality, a cute smile, and, unfortunately, a husband. Still, we had a nice conversation that night and she seemed impressed when I told her of the comeback I was hoping to make.

As the women got closer, I said to Noel, "Run up ahead and get a picture of them passing me, okay, Noel? And try to get me in a shot with Kara."

"She's cute, Matty."

"Yeah, I know. Just get the shot."

"Okay, here they come. Smile."

The photo turned out to be a bit blurred. The women raced by us going at just over a five-minute-and-30-second-per-mile pace. They would finish the race by the time we hit mile 15.

Over the next few miles, we were passed constantly, first by the elite professional men and then by the everyday runners who could run a marathon as fast as I once had. As we approached the marker for mile 14, I took satisfaction from knowing that I had matched my longest distance since I first started training again. It was at this point that Shane McKeon and some of the other top firefighters caught up to us. Shane yelled out to me, "Go get 'em, Matty. I'll see you at the finish." I gave him a wave. Watching Shane zip by could have been demoralizing if I didn't keep in mind the odds I was trying to defy: from knocking on heaven's door to, now, 12 miles from finishing the New York City Marathon.

Before the day had started, my plan was to walk across the Queensboro Bridge, the dark, rolling, steel-grilled link between Queens and Manhattan that comes around mile 15. I figured the rise in the bridge might be too stressful on my heart rate, which I was trying to monitor so as not to tax my ticker too much. We had been going for four hours and 10 minutes. For the first time, I started to feel the effects of the mileage and the pounding. My right hip began to throb and so did my left foot, the one with the hammertoes that was absorbing most of my weight. I was hoping the slow walk across the mile-long bridge might calm things down a bit.

Frank and Noel took the opportunity to hang back and stretch out their legs. A few minutes earlier, I had heard Frank whisper "This hurts." I couldn't have asked for two better companions for a run like this. Basically, they were sacrificing their bodies for me. Frank may have been an Ironman several times over, but he never had to run a race this slowly and experience the extra body blows that come with so many more footfalls per minute. Noel, meanwhile, had originally hoped to make this marathon the one when he broke three hours for the first time—until I asked him to go with me at a pace twice as slow. He never asked out.

Running so deliberately when you're used to running so efficiently can touch off unaccustomed pangs. Norway's Grete Waitz won the New York City Marathon nine times, but she once said the most challenging marathon she ever did was in 1992, when she ran side by side with Fred Lebow, the former race director who was sick with cancer at the time. It took the pair over five and a half hours to finish. Afterward she admitted that being on her feet that long and running so slowly produced more pain than any of the races when she was fast enough to win.

Walking across the bridge, we were now being passed by the masses of runners. And every few seconds someone saw me and shouted out to me. Tommy Grimshaw caught up to us and gave me a "Way to go, Matty!" and a few minutes later Vicky Tiase was by my side.

"You're doing great, Cool Guy!"

"Thanks, Vicster!" I yelled back. "Hey, come back a second." She turned around and stopped in front of me. I gave her a kiss on the cheek. "I'll see you at the finish," I told her, "and thanks."

Finally, I made it to the 16-mile marker on the Manhattan side of the bridge, where you begin the descent down a ramp and continue on to First Avenue. That's when I started to run again.

Just as I had remembered from past marathons in New York, both sides of First Avenue were filled with people cheering and waving. The three of us stopped talking for the next few blocks and listened. Finally Frank said, "Can you believe this noise?"

"No way, Frank," Noel said. "I don't think I've ever heard it this loud."

I always thought of First Avenue as the spot in the race where runners received their congratulations from New Yorkers for all they had accomplished. Sure, there were many miles to go before you could take home a finisher's medal, but for this two-mile stretch you felt special, appreciated, immersed in this well of happy noise. On this day, though, I looked forward to First Avenue as a chance to say thank you to a lot of the people who had done so much to get me to this place. I wasn't going to stop and actually speak those words to anyone. The fact that I was running and had come this far was enough to show how much I appreciated the help they had given me and the faith they had placed in me—the kind of faith I often didn't have in myself.

As I approached First Avenue and 68th Street I looked down the block to New York–Presbyterian Hospital. The "allergies" kicked in again as I thought to myself that just three years ago, I arrived there on a bitterly cold December morning with a broken, bleeding body. At first the doctors had given me little chance to survive, but they never stopped trying to reverse the odds. They pumped 69 units of blood into me and operated dozens of times. And then they put me in the hands of nurses and therapists to see if I could get out of bed, walk, and then walk some more.

Now I was running up First Avenue, being passed by hundreds of fit, able-bodied runners and being cheered by these happy, rowdy faces that I didn't know.

Shortly after 70th Street a half dozen members of the Asphalt Green Triathlon Club joined our group; they said they planned to go the rest of the way with us. Then a few blocks later, Tom Nohilly, one of Jim Wharton's trainers, hopped in. For the next mile or so Tom trailed me, and he noticed how I had started to struggle, more so than normal. My right foot was barely getting off the ground and my head kept bobbing. "Matty, push off on your feet! Use your feet!" Tom yelled. "Pump your arms!"

At 103rd Street, just past mile 18, I had to pull over to the side of the road. "Tom, it's my left foot, it's killing me," I told him. Tom had me lean on Frank and Noel as he stretched out both my legs and flexed my foot.

"You okay, you okay?" Tom asked. I nodded, sort of. "Try to keep your shoulders and head from getting so far ahead of you, and lift your feet."

I nodded, and once again we were back on the road. For the next couple of miles, as we made our way in and out of the Bronx, I tried not to let anyone notice the pain I was in. For a while we all joked about the food we were going to eat when this was all over— "the fattest burger in Manhattan, that's what I'm planning on," Noel said—and just as we made our way back into Manhattan, I did a little moonwalk when I heard some rap music from a street-corner DJ. "I still got it," I told our band of runners.

But not for much longer.

———

As we made our way down Fifth Avenue and closer to Central Park, I leaned over to Noel. "Hey, this is it. You and Frank need to stay as close to me as you can. I'm scared I might fall at any moment." By now, a wisecrack or an attempt at a joke from someone in the group no longer got much of a response. In fact, as we entered the park, with less than three miles to go, I barked, "No more jokes!" Shuffling down the east side of the park the only noise you could hear from our group was me grunting—*Humph, humph, humph*—every few seconds.

We had been running for almost seven hours; my hope of finishing at double my previous best time was shot. Now, not only was every step an excrutiating jolt, but each one required more and more mental exertion to complete. I kept telling my legs, *Swing forward! You got to swing forward!* I had hit the wall somewhere in the Bronx, but a new wall seemed to pop up every few yards. I would have jumped at the chance to sit down if someone had offered me a chair. Luckily no one said a word, so I shuffled and hitched along, out onto Central Park South. There was less than a mile to go, and each step made the toes on my left foot burn a little more.

As our cluster ground its way up the last long street, Frank said, "Matt, just a half mile to go."

Then suddenly, I couldn't go any farther.

My legs just stopped.

Noel and Frank looked at me. "You okay, Matt?" Frank asked.

"Yeah, yeah, it's the foot," I said. "Let's just walk a bit."

*Walk now? With so little to go before I could say I was an athlete again? The family's waiting for me at the finish line. And so are some of my doctors. And the guys from the firehouse. Now's not the time to walk; it's the time to speed up.*

But I had to walk and let the pain subside. And let myself think.

———

For 50 feet I limped in silence, and for 50 feet I remembered the agony I went through and the pain I put others through after a

20-ton bus crushed me. I flashbacked to the surgeries and all the ugly stories people had told me of that day. Jimmy seeing the bloody emergency room and the nurse telling him it couldn't get any worse. And the hard time I gave Inna, my therapist, when she just wanted to help me get out of bed. And how scared I was when I saw my withered, aged face for the first time, and the two months' growth of graying hair on my usually clean-shaven head. And the afternoon when I yelled at Mom and she yelled back. And I thought about the torments of a bag that once hung from my side, and the scar on my left thigh, as wide as a pancake, from where my femur broke through my skin, a scar that reminded me every day of everything, as if I needed one more reminder. And then I thought about Fabio Selvig, who told me not to give up. And about John Kelly, who said something good would come of all this. And about John Gleeson sitting in a rehab room, waiting for me to finish this race. And the e-mail from my brother Robert. And I thought about how I never quit anything before in my life, except for the Boy Scouts—and only because I wanted to play basketball instead of tying knots. Otherwise I never ran away from a challenge or a game or a race. Even when I wanted to. Even when the challenge was worse than dying. I never quit.

And for 50 feet, maybe 30 seconds, I thought of all that as runners passed me on each side. They had gone as far as I had in half the time, and they were also exhausted. They were running, just as I had been doing for 25.5 miles. Technically what I was doing may not have been running; for sure, I hadn't been getting both feet off the ground, as the running books say you should. But in my heart I was running. And competing. And loving it. Until I hit the wall, and then another one, and then another one. And I had to stop. For 50 feet, maybe 30 seconds.

And then I said, "I have to finish this damn thing."

I began to shuffle again. And everyone followed. We ran the rest of Central Park South—*push, then slide; push, then slide; push, then slide*—up past Columbus Circle and then back into the park. There was no Boston qualifier to race for, just a finish line 385 yards away. We ran tighter together, Frank on my right, Noel on my left. And we all started to smile. I could see my family clustered just off to the side near the finish line. They were cheering and waving their signs. I could see Jimmy nodding me in.

Nothing, it seemed at that moment, was moving in real time. Even though I could hear people screaming and see their faces, it all seemed like a time warp. Everyone saying *ahhhh* in slow motion as I ran by them. In some ways, I felt just the same as when I was rushing to a 3:13 finish. I was moving toward something, something so close.

And then, with just yards to go, a streak of blue crossed between me and the finish line. At that moment I wasn't processing thoughts in real time; I didn't think it was another runner. It could have been anything. But something was suddenly in front of me. All I knew was that if it jumped back into me, I would go down, and I couldn't let that happen. I couldn't go down again. As I approached the finish line, with this image still bouncing in front of me, now just an arm's length away, I pushed it out of my way. It was another runner, and I made sure we didn't run into each other. I didn't need another collision, not today.

Then, with nothing else in the way, I crossed the line—in seven hours, 21 minutes, 22 seconds—and hit the ground.

# 18

## STARTING FRESH

Some days you wake up and you know the finish line is eight or nine or ten hours away, when you can come home from work and your real life—and the real fun—begins. You might head home to coach your kid's Little League team. You might meet up with a couple of buddies for a late-afternoon round of golf. You might tell your wife that you'll cook dinner that night so she can go out with her friends. Or you might just grab a beer out of the fridge, head to the back-yard, and watch the sky turn different shades of color as evening bends into night.

You do whatever it takes to make the hours between shifts yours, moments that will push you to tomorrow's finish line and the one after that.

My life up to that December day when a bus made a sudden turn on a New York City street had been a daily race to a finish line so that I could, well, *explode* through it and then get pumped up for the next one. It had been an ongoing 100-miles-an-hour chase to enjoy every-thing the world had to offer. I chased after the open spot on the basketball court, or after an opponent with the ball, looking to make a clutch basket, or a crucial steal. I chased down old friends and chased after new ones because I always wanted my circles—my Olympic rings—to get bigger and to make it easier for old friends to meet new friends. I chased the ladies, hoping someday to catch up with the right one, the one who had as much energy and enjoyed the silliness and pleasures of life as much as I did. I chased adventure and wasn't afraid to take a risk or two along the way. I opened a bar in New York City, a city where bars open and close as fast as elevator doors. But Third & Long had made it big, big enough to try opening a few others. Some worked, others didn't, but no worries. If you looked at all the possible consequences, all of the time, of every opportunity that came your way, you'd pretty much talk yourself out of doing anything. And that wasn't me. Yes, I avoided roller coasters, but otherwise I was up for any challenge and any chance to learn new things. I tried triathlons even though when I started training for them I could barely swim a lap of a pool. I joined the New York City Fire Department and in my first 12 years I took in more adventures than any recruitment flier promised. I once pulled a man from a burning building, saving his life. And I saw, up close, too many people die when a pair of 110-story buildings crumbled on September 11, 2001.

I was no wallflower. In fact, I liked being the life of the party. At the bar some nights, when the scene seemed too mellow, I'd rush to the middle of the dance floor and get the place hopping. I'd make sure everyone went home with a smile wider than my own. An empty glass? I filled it. A party needed some life? I cranked up the music. A pretty girl looked lonely? I gave her a goofy grin and started chatting with her. Someone else needed a laugh? I pulled up a stool and told a story. *Have you heard the one about the time I did stand-up with Billy Crystal at the Garden? Well, it goes like this . . .*

I enjoyed my life. Maybe I enjoyed it more than you're supposed to. I lived it to the fullest, made it a journey that I approached head-on and traveled as fast as I could. Each day I was up and out, sometimes early, sometimes late, but always looking for something new to do.

And one more finish line to cross.

When I hit the ground after finishing the marathon, it wasn't because I was exhausted or in pain, although I certainly was both. No, with my family, friends, and fellow firefighters yards away, watching from just beyond the finish area, I lay down. And started doing push-ups.

*One, two, three, four, five, six, seven, eight, nine, ten.*

Why? Because I liked to play to a crowd. And at that moment, if running 26.2 miles wasn't enough, I wanted to show everyone that I was, once again, Matty Long.

After the tenth push-up I got up and hobbled over to the group. They were smiling but they all looked chilled, with a cool breeze blowing and Central Park's maples shading what was left of the midafternoon sun. They had put in a long day, too, rushing around the city—from early in the morning, when they had congregated in front of the family church in Bay Ridge, to now, nearly 3 p.m., in this corner of the park. I gave my mother a hug. "Mom, this was for you," I whispered to her. And it was, for all her prayers and worries and for the tough love she finally showed me one day over lunch. She didn't say much—maybe just "Matthew"—but she was crying. Then I grabbed Dad and threw my arms around him. The marine was crying, too. I said, "I love you," and he said the same. Then I reached out to everyone there. Jimmy, Maureen, Michael, Chris, Frank, Eddie, and Eileen. They each got a sweaty, smelly squeeze. I looked down at Eileen's wrist. Back when I was in the hospital, she had ordered dozens of red wristbands with the words "IronMatt, 43 Truck" embossed on them. She would pass them out to people who came to see me. When I told Eileen I was training for the marathon, she said she would take her band off after I completed the race. Secretly, I was looking forward to seeing her empty wrist.

Everyone was hopping around trying to stay warm while listening to me give highlights of the run. Then I saw Robert, whom I hadn't gotten to yet. I squeezed him the tightest of all. "Robert, that e-mail you sent last night, bro?" I said quietly into his ear so no one else could hear. "It helped me a lot. It kept me going out there. You might be proud of me, Robert, but don't ever forget how proud we all are of you."

"Thanks, Matt, thanks a lot. And, hey, that was pretty incredible what you just did."

"Yeah, not bad for a 42-year-old."

For the next 15 minutes or so we stayed huddled near the finish line, and I kept seeing more people I knew who wanted to congratulate me. There was Sal Cassano, the FDNY chief, who had sent us off at the start of the race in Staten Island. I joked with him that it would be a long time before I went under three hours and beat his best time. "Don't worry about that, Matt. I could never do what you just did." Two of my doctors, Dr. Eachempati and Dr. Lorich, had come to watch the finish as well. Dr. Lorich was there with his wife and three daughters. "Matt, that was just unbelievable," he said as we embraced. When I got home that night, I thought about that moment. Three years ago I knew neither of those men, and Dr. Lorich's third child was weeks from being born on the day he rushed to the hospital, with the rest of his family, to save my life. Today his youngest sat in her stroller, watching her dad hug a stinky firefighter.

We talked a little more, but I needed to stretch and work out some of the cramps and pain. From the teetering that came with running 26.2 miles, my hips felt like they were being pierced by nine-inch nails. But it was the toes on my left foot that made me cringe the most. When I took off my left shoe, my sock was caked in blood and two toenails were missing. Tom Nohilly stretched me under a tent for a few minutes and told me to make an appointment for a longer session tomorrow.

"You're not working tomorrow, are you, Matt?" he asked.

"No, Tom, I'm taking it off."

"Good thinking," he said, and we both laughed.

Later I made a brief stop at the FDNY marathon party, where the guys cheered my arrival. Again I thought about the day three years earlier when I ran my fastest marathon, finishing fourth among all of the 150 firefighters in the race—and qualified for the Boston Marathon. Today I got staked to a two-and-a-half-hour lead on the guys, and most of them still passed me. No worries. We beat the NYPD again.

When I got home that night, I took a very long shower and, for the first time in a while, popped some painkillers. Early on in my rehab I had read a book by a well-known American marathoner, Dick Beardsley, who told of his addiction to painkillers after being injured in a series of near-fatal accidents. After reading Beardsley's account, I feared becoming dependent on the medication, so I weaned myself from it as quickly as I could. But tonight, after the day I had put in, my body deserved a little something extra.

Then, just before crashing for the night, I went to my computer and logged on to the Web site of my triathlon club. I went to the page where Asphalt Green members could post their most recent racing results. I typed the following: "I have looked at this page for three years now, waiting for the day when I would post a finishing time. Here it is: 7:21:22."

I looked at my time one last time, then shut off the computer and went to bed.

━━━━━━━━━

Once again I may have had a finishing time to talk about, but now it was time to start something new.

A few weeks before the marathon, I was at work at the Rock when I overheard some of the trainers telling our boss, Mike Cacciola, that the probies seemed to be slacking off in their daily workouts. They weren't sure what the cause might be; maybe it was just the typical lull that comes after  weeks of intense training. Lieutenant Cacciola said he would talk to the probies and get them in line.

When I saw the lieutenant later that day, I told him that I had heard about the situation and asked him if I could speak to the class.

"Sure, if you want to, Matt," he said. "But what are you going to tell them?"

"I'm not sure, but I think I have an idea."

The next day, when we had gathered the 275 probies together before the morning training session, the lieutenant told the group that Firefighter Long had some words for them. I stood before them, a bunch of men who were mostly younger than my kid brother Eddie. They didn't know my story. They just knew me as the bald trainer with the funny limp.

"Guys, word has it that some of you are slacking off, not working as hard as you could be. That some of you are complaining about minor aches after the daily run. Well, guys, let me tell you: Don't let that stuff keep you from being fit. This is the time to work hard and get in the best shape possible. We need you at your best. One day, very soon, you're going to leave the Rock, and you're going to be at a firehouse with a bunch of other firefighters.

A call is going to come in and you'll be off to a fire where you're going to have to perform a search and rescue. It's going to be five firefighters working as one, and let me tell you, because I've been there, the search team is only as strong as its weakest link. Don't be the weak link. Stay in shape. If you don't, you're cheating. You hear me: You're cheating. And who are you cheating?"

I stopped for a second and waited for someone to give me an answer. And waited. No one did. "Men, you're cheating the person sitting right next to you. You've just spent five months training with that guy. Imagine how you would feel if you had to go tell his wife, 'Sorry, your husband came back to get me during the fire because I was out of breath. And, well, I'm sorry, but he died and I lived.' Guys, you don't want to have that conversation."

Then I paused again and took off my shirt. I stood in front of the probies for several seconds so they could see my chest, with the 18-inch scar running down it. For the next few minutes I shared my story with them. It was the first time I had told it in public like that. And then I said I was hoping to run the marathon in a few weeks. I watched as one probie after another craned his neck to look at my scar. "Guys, I'm not telling you to go out and get run over by a bus and then run a marathon. But come on: Give us an honest effort every day. When you joined the department, you took a job where people depend on you, and not just people trapped in burning buildings. Your fellow firefighters depend on you."

When I finished, there was no clapping or cheering. No let's-go-run-a-mile-for-Matty chant. But throughout the day several probies came up to me and said "Thanks." And a few followed with, "Good luck in the marathon."

That talk became the first of many I have given about my life and the unexpected journey that started on December 22, 2005. I've spoken to teenagers in a tiny high school auditorium and to hundreds of college seniors on the floor of Madison Square Garden. I've talked before Wall Street bankers and to Olympic athletes. And I've visited dozens of hospital rooms and privately met with many anguished patients. Like John Gleeson.

So many of these people sought me out when they heard of my story—and so many of them, as it turned out, had their own stories of being injured in catastrophic ways. Some of them were athletes like me, trying to reclaim their sporting lives, while others were just regular folks looking to get back on their feet. I realized I had an opportunity to do more than inspire them—though inspiration and hope, as I discovered, are essential to making that first step out of a hospital bed or down a dusty road alongside an Arizona canal.

Just before the marathon I launched a foundation that I called simply I Will. It's a program to help people come back from life-altering illnesses or traumatic injuries and to enjoy their lives to the fullest. My trainers in Tempe, Mark D'Aloisio and Kyle Herrig, and fellow members of the Asphalt Green Triathlon Club, including Noel and Vicky, have made themselves available to bring their specialties—from rehab training to nutrition—to those who need it. And we have raised money to provide entry fees for disabled athletes who want to compete in races and wheelchairs for returning veterans of the wars in Iraq and Afghanistan.

The foundation's name, I Will, comes from the night when I told my brother Eddie that I was tired of wallowing in the misery of my injuries and moaning over how those injuries stole my dreams. The night I told Eddie that somehow, someday, "I will run again." And I did run, farther than many people—including myself—ever dreamed possible.

Now I want my story to help infuse other people with that same kind of determination—because at its heart my story is really about an ordinary person who just happened to have extraordinary challenges come his way. And I dealt with those challenges just as any person might: unprepared and with a lot of uncertainty.

At times after my accident I regrettably let bitterness and self-interest and poor judgment get the better of me, and I isolated myself from people who just wanted to help. Maybe I had the right to behave like that—*I got run over by a bus!*—or maybe it was because of my personality and who I had always thought I was. I was Matty Take Charge, and I liked that person and wasn't ready to let go of him. Ultimately, though, I had to discover and appreciate that life is a journey that, quite frankly, you're not in charge of. Trust me, I wish there had been another way to learn this lesson. But the fact that I made it through a lot of physical and emotional pain to the point where I could run a marathon again—and walk around the city with a smile again, and have a zest for life again—showed me the reason why I was meant to survive the accident. It was so that the old Matt Long and the new Matt Long could merge into one person who helps others recover their lives and their desires.

I feel comfortable telling my story, maybe because there is a nice finish attached to it. And we all like a happy ending. When I crossed that finish line on Marathon Sunday in New York, I conquered something and achieved something. And the next day the newspapers told New York all about me. "Firefighter Proves He's More Than a Long Shot" proclaimed the *Daily News*. "Bravest Runs Amazing Race" shouted the *Post*. Marathon day was a great day with a great ending.

But the story didn't end there. When the marathon was over and the newspaper articles were written, I knew that the next day, and every day after that, would bring another marathon for me to take on.

And I knew I would always need to glance to my left when moving ahead on my journey.

My life is a struggle. I can't sit in a chair for more than a few minutes before I have to get up and stretch the nagging tightness out of my upper right thigh. Walking the streets of New York can be so onerous that sometimes I'll hop in a cab just to go three or four blocks. My doctors tell me I can expect an early onset of arthritis because of the complex injuries my joints sustained. On top of the more than 40 surgeries I've already had, it's likely that I'll face more in the not-too-distant future to retouch and redo work that has already been done. I agonize constantly about how my body feels.

Those are just the physical struggles. I live with the anguish that the accident I endured was the result of an ill-conceived and illegal job action. When I sued the transport union for its role in my accident, a judge dismissed the case because the Taylor Law, which prevents public employees from striking, is not "intended to protect individuals from the negligent acts of third parties—such as the traffic accident, in this case." If that is the law, then I will live by it, but it doesn't mitigate the consequences or the hurt.

I also live knowing that my career as an active firefighter is over. In the rank and file of the FDNY, you strive for one designation. You want your fellow firefighters to speak of you as a "good firefighter." Nothing fancy to that title, but it says plenty. Among the men of Ladder 43, I was considered a good firefighter. I'm satisfied with that achievement. But I wanted to be so much more to the house. I wanted to be the guy who the newest rookie could go to if he wanted to learn how to better tie a lifesaving rope or to prank one of the middle guys with a bucket of water. I'll never be a senior man.

And I live knowing that because of the physical shape I am now in, it may be difficult to find the woman who will join me through the rest of my days and the challenges I'll be facing.

I live with these and other frustrations. They are part of my daily marathon. But as any marathoner will tell you, part of the sport is realizing that not every race day is going to end with your best time. Sometimes you have to accept that the unexpected might trip you up. You train 16, 20, 30 weeks, getting your body into the best shape possible, and then you arrive at the starting line, and the rain begins to fall, then never stops, and your shoes get soggy, and your body feels raw, and your legs just don't feel like going anymore.

You finish the race and you look at your time, and you think, *Wow, rough day.* And then, if you love the sport and all that it offers, you think, *When is the next race?*

I loved running. I loved it as much as I love a medium-rare New York strip at Smith & Wolly's, or a long jump shot on the basketball courts of Breezy Point, or Christmas breakfast at my parents' house, or a phone call in the middle of the afternoon from one of my nephews or nieces. I woke up each day thinking of how I could squeeze my workout in, what time I could get to Central Park to run its hills and straightaways as hard as possible. To hear the chatter of other runners. To feel the sensation of legs that never seemed to want to quit. And to try to go faster and faster and faster, so in that next race, and the one after that, and the one after that, my time might get better and better and better.

Then my legs went dead for a stretch, and I wondered what would happen to me.

I discovered the answer one Sunday, when I ran a race and went slower than I had ever run before. And at the end, I stood among a circle of people whose memory of 7:21:22 would last but the length of a hug. They were just glad to see a race completed.

I couldn't have asked for a better time.

# EPILOGUE

As it turned out, I had one more finish line to cross.

On July 26, 2009, at 7 a.m., nearly 2,300 people waded into Mirror Lake in Lake Placid, New York. I was one of them, wearing bib number 43. I was about to try to become an Ironman once again.

Similar to what had happened when I told people I wanted to run the New York City Marathon, I received a lot of curious looks and questions when word spread that I was training for the Ironman throughout the spring and early summer of 2009. "Matt, are you off the wall?" My answer seemed logical, at least to me. As I pursued my goal of becoming an athlete again, I managed to clear each of the major hurdles that I had passed prior to my accident: I had run a mile, 5 kilometers, 10 kilometers, a half-marathon, and, of course, a full marathon. The only missing link to my past was the Ironman. Did I need to do the killer event with its 2.4-mile swim, 112-mile bike, and 26.2-mile run in order to prove anything? Not really. In my mind, I always maintained that by completing the marathon I was whole again, as a person and as an athlete. What drove me back to the Ironman was mostly a desire to take part in an event that I enjoyed a lot.

Yes, to someone who has never attempted an Ironman, the sport sounds beastly. But once you have tested yourself against the race's varying disciplines and against athletes intent on pushing their strength and skills to the most extreme level, you need to do it again. And again. That's what I wanted. I wanted to push myself one more time. I wanted the thrill of the Ironman.

My preparation for this Ironman bore little resemblance to the one that I had trained for in 2005 and had completed in 11 hours and 18 minutes. After the beating the marathon put on me, I could not let my body sustain the repeated blows that running dealt it; the toes on my left foot could take only so much cruelty. So between January and mid-July, which I had blocked out for my buildup to the Ironman, I ran only a dozen or so times, and in most cases I logged just one mile per outing. That mile would come at the end of a 20-mile bike ride that I did every Wednesday with the Asphalt Green Triathlon Club. Otherwise, except for a weekly swim, most of my Ironman training took place on the bike. Some weeks I cycled more than 300 miles, twice the amount I did when I was training in 2005.

On race day I had to hope that work would enable my legs to run 26.2 miles with the clock bearing down on me.

To earn Ironman status, you need to complete the course in 17 hours. Finish one second past midnight and, well, it's a very long trip home from Lake Placid, the serene town in the Adirondack Mountains of upstate New York. Lake Placid is perhaps best known in the sporting world as the site of the 1980 "Miracle on Ice," when the underdog USA hockey team defeated the overwhelming favorites from the Soviet Union en route to the gold medal.

On race day I knew I might need a miracle or two to finish by midnight.

My plan was to go as hard as I could in the swim and bike portions of the event, and then gut it out in the marathon with whatever

I had left. With my right shoulder's limited range of motion, a lingering aftereffect from the bus accident, my swim stroke was compromised. Still, I was pleasantly surprised when I finished the swim only 13 minutes behind my 2005 pace.

It had been raining a good portion of the time I was in the water, so I crawled out of Mirror Lake onto a soggy lakefront. As I hustled to get my bike in the transition area, hobbling as I normally do, I heard someone in the crowd say, "Ooh, that guy's cramping up." I turned and smiled at him. "Cramping up?" I said. "I'm like this every day."

Early on in the bike leg, I fed off the energy of the crowd that lined much of the course. I also had members of my family positioned at different mile markers along the 56-mile loop, which you do twice. Knowing they were out there gave me motivation to keep pushing. Unfortunately, the last 12 miles of each loop end with a climb up Whiteface Mountain. On my first loop I handled the uphill with relative ease. But on my final go around, I struggled for more than an hour climbing the ridge, my left foot screaming with each pedal. I finally finished the bike in seven and a half hours, 90 minutes longer than it took me in 2005.

My cumulative time after the first two disciplines was nine hours. That meant I had eight hours to complete the run. The last time I did a marathon was my seven-hour, 21-minute run in New York City. Now I had to nearly duplicate that effort—after already tackling 114 miles.

Like the bike course, the marathon in Lake Placid comprises two loops. Through the first 12 miles or so I ran alone, just teetering my body forward with the strength I had left. At that point my friend Shane McKeon caught up with me—he was finishing his 24th mile. I ran with him until he had to peel away for the finishers' chute. Before we split, though, I asked him for his time.

"It's just about 13 hours, Matty," Shane said.

"Bro, I'm not going to make this."

"What do you mean?"

"Shane, I just did 13 miles in three and a half hours. There's no way I'm going to do the next 13 miles in four hours. I'm dead."

"Well, what are you thinking?"

"Well, I think I've accomplished a hell of a lot. So do I quit now and save my body from any extra pain, or do I continue and run until midnight?"

"Well, what did you come here to do?"

I said, "I came here to be called an Ironman again."

Shane looked at me. I looked at him. I kept on running.

Little did I know what was in store.

As I was running alone on the road, a stranger started shuffling alongside me. It turned out to be Aaron Azevedo, who worked for Zoot Sports, which made my running shoes. I had only spoken to him over the phone and had never met him in person. Aaron asked how I was doing.

"I'm hurting pretty bad," I told him.

"Well, do you want to be left alone or would you like some company?"

"No, come along," I said. "Let's go."

Aaron and I ran and we talked, barely noticing how dark the course had become. It was now close to 10 p.m. With about seven miles to go, Noel Flynn came out with Tara Rasch, another member of our triathlon club, on their bikes. They had finished the race already but now were looking to get a progress report to send back to my family.

"We're going as fast as we can," I told them.

Over the next 90 minutes our pack kept growing the closer we moved toward the finish. Some 50 local residents and competitors who had completed the race hours earlier—and who knew of my comeback story—joined our posse. But the march was a slow one; I was completing miles in 20 minutes and finding myself walking more and more. As I hit mile 23, a good stretch of which was an uphill switchback, Aaron told me we needed to cut out the walking and make up time. At the pace we were going, we had no shot of finishing by midnight. "Matt, forget about staying on the right side of the road, and just follow the S's," Aaron said. "Just keep running straight. If you find yourself on the other side of the road, don't worry about it."

I followed his orders, and the pack behind me inched forward. When we were about two miles out, I could hear the race announcer, Mike Reilly, calling out the names of finishers as they crossed the line, following each name with the words: "You are an Ironman." Suddenly, though, I could hear Reilly tell the spectators at the finish, which included my family, "Matt Long is still on the course. He's moving, but he may need some help." That news prompted the crowd to start chanting "Matt! Matt! Matt!"—which pushed me to another gear for at least the next 100 yards.

I tried not to look at my watch; I needed no reminders of what little time I had left. What I had was this pack of runners following me as if I were Forrest Gump. But there was room for one more. A mile and a half from the finish, a race official asked me if there was anything I needed.

"I know I have all of Lake Placid running behind me," I said to him. "But could you get Heather Fuhr to come join us, too?"

"I'll see what I can do," the guy said.

A few minutes later Fuhr was with us. She was the top female finisher at the Ironman World Championship in Hawaii in 1997, and she once ran the marathon leg of the Ironman in an impossibly fast two hours and 51 minutes. Now she was at my side, basically walking, as I tried to leg out the remainder of the course in the time remaining.

"How you doing, Matt?" Heather asked.

"I'm hurting, and I don't think I have another gear."

"Matt, you're not going to make it unless you find one. You need to get moving. Can you give me surges?"

"What do you want?"

"Listen. Take a couple of deep breaths, and then I'm going to start counting. We're going to take 10 big strides."

"All right, I'll try, I'll try." So I took three breaths.

"You ready?" Heather asked.

"Yep," I said.

"Okay, one, two, three—" and she kept counting to 10 as I stretched out each stride as much as I could. "Good, good, good, Matt. Take a break."

I went back into my very slow shuffle. But after 30 seconds, Heather said, "Time for another surge. Deep breath, then stride."

We did that four or five times in the last mile, until we got to the oval where you run the final 400 meters in front of the crowd. Heather called back to the pack: "The oval is Matt's. No one enters the oval." My band of runners went off to get seats in the grand-stand at the finish line, and I had the oval all to myself. If I never compete in a race again, this moment would leave me with enough memories. In this town in the northern reaches of New York State, where people have seen miracles, I hunched and lurched and rocked my way over the final stretches of this race, which at one point seemed endless. I raised my arms as hundreds of people who didn't even know me or my story cheered. With 100 yards to go, I could see the clock. I was going to finish, and with time to spare.

At 11:58 p.m. on July 26, 2009, after 16 hours, 58 minutes, and three seconds, Mike Reilly announced to those there, including a tired but deliriously happy firefighter from New York City, "Matt Long, you are an Ironman."

# ACKNOWLEDGMENTS

I am forever grateful to those who supported me at the time of my accident and throughout my recovery. Your kindness and compassion will never be forgotten. I have known many of you for years; others came into my life after the events of December 22, 2005. In your own way, each of you has helped me become the man I am today—and let me live *The Long Run*.

To Mom and Dad and all my brothers and sisters: We have endured so much together, and for me to triumph in my quest to cheat death and become an athlete again would not have been possible without all of you. The same goes to Grandpa Mike and Nana, Aunt Anke and Uncle Tom, Aunt Cathy and Uncle John, and all the cousins. I love you all.

To the members of Engine 53, Ladder 43: As firefighters, we are taught to take the high road by those who came before us. I don't know if there is a higher road to take than how you treated my family and me during this tragedy. When I tell someone where I worked as a member of the New York City Fire Department, I could not be prouder. I am fraternally yours, always. God bless all of you and those who will come after us.

To my A-Team of medical professionals, Dr. Soumitra Eachempati, Dr. Dean Lorich, Dr. Darius Paduch, Dr. David Helfet, Dr. Bryan Kelly, Dr. Jeffery Milsom, Dr. Lloyd Gayle, Dr.

Rock Positano, and Dr. Toyooki Sonoda: I was told that your first concern is life, not the quality of life. I want you all to know that I have returned to the fullest quality of life that God would allow. In my eyes God made that possible through your hands and talents. Thanks for saving my life.

To the residents of New York–Presbyterian Hospital/Weill Cornell Medical Center and the Hospital for Special Surgery. There are too many of you to name individually, but I hope I can be a symbol of what you will forever call job satisfaction. You have spent much of your life studying so that you can help others live healthy lives. Your sacrifices have not gone unappreciated.

To the nurses of Two South, the intensive care unit of New York–Presbyterian: Because I was barely conscious while I was in your care, I don't know most of you by name. But the fact that I can express my appreciation to you means that you did your job extremely well. I will return often to let others see how your work plays a vital role in the future happiness of those who spend time in the ICU. Thanks for caring about others.

To all the other nurses and aides on the various floors where I spent time: I am indebted to your service, kindness, and respect. I would especially like to thank Anna Vacco, the head nurse on the 17th floor during my stay. When I finally learned that you were coming in on your day off to care for me, I knew God had sent an angel to my bedside. Also, thank you, Anna Miller, who held me when I couldn't stand for an x-ray—and despite what that deed could have done to you. You, my friend, are a special person. May that act of selflessness come back to you 100 times over.

To all who gave blood in my name: Your generosity, I'm sure, has made a difference. I can only ask that you continue to donate. As I can attest, you never know who might need it someday.

To Inna Tsykun, Tammy Noren, and Hope Hunter, who were the first therapists to work with me during my rehabilitation: I am sorry you encountered so much early resistance from me. At the time my life was turned upside down, but your commitment to helping me get stronger is evident daily. Friendships have been forged for a lifetime. The same goes to Loreen Acevedo and Julie Khan, my therapists in the rehabilitation ward at New York–Presbyterian: What a journey. I could never have accomplished what I have without your help. I love you both.

To Fabio Selvig, Anne Christine Kreter, and Jim MacLaren: Your encouragement was a constant source of inspiration. Thank you.

To those who worked to get my body in running shape: Your efforts went a very long way. I would like to especially thank Lucy Diaz, Louis Vasquez, Jim Wharton, John Alsop, Tom Nohilly, Mark D'Aloisio, Kyle Herrig, Janna Nelson, Pam Wilson, Adam Lake, Anthony Carillo, and Neil Cook.

To the companies that provided assistance as I mounted my athletic comeback and that continue to support the I Will Foundation. They include Zoot Sports, Nestlé Waters, SunGard, Tri-Life Coaches, Zipp Wheels, Serrota Bicycles, Shimano Bikes, Signature Cycles, Hammer Nutrition, Bike Cycles, and Larry and Jeff's Bike Shop.

To Stephen Breen, Terry Brennan, Sean Scott, Jim Long, Eddie Long, Rob McGovern, Curtis Lanton, and everyone who kept the bars running during my absence. Well done, fellows.

And finally, and with my never-ending gratitude, I recognize and praise the first responders at the scene of my accident: the New York City Police Department, the New York City Fire Department, and the Emergency Medical Services unit. You are the best the world has to offer, and on a very cold winter morning, you proved it. My thanks, always. —*Matt Long, July 2010*

In April 2007, at a Starbucks in midtown Manhattan, I first met Matt Long. He had been out of New York–Presbyterian Hospital for about a year. He arrived on crutches and shimmied his way around the tables and chairs to the front counter. He ordered a Grande Soy Mocha and I had an iced tea. We then sat down for the first of many conversations we would have over the next three years. It was during that first talk, though, that Matt mentioned his dream of one day running the six-mile loop of Central Park with his friends, and then celebrating with a round of beers. I asked him when he thought that run might happen. "I have no idea," he told me.

I relayed that conversation to David Willey, the editor-in-chief of *Runner's World*. David told me to follow the story and see where it led. "It could be something good."

You were right, David. In March 2009 *Runner's World* published "A Second Life," which told of Matt's remarkable journey from intensive care unit to marathon finish line. Later, David greenlighted the writing of this book, providing me with the time to dig deeper into Matt's emotional and physical comeback. David, thank you very much for your continued support (as well as your careful reading of *The Long Run* manuscript). Your help and encouragement have made this a memorable and fulfilling experience.

As well I'd like to thank the entire staff of *Runner's World*. You are an incredibly talented, creative group with a dedication to the sport of running as inspiring as Matt's. I would especially like to recognize Peter Flax for his expert editing of "A Second Life"; Andrea Maurio, Nick Galac, Kory Kennedy, and Marc Kauffman for their work in capturing Matt in pictures; Brian Sabin and Glenn Osten Anderson for capturing Matt in video; and Chris Evans Gartley for keeping everything moving just fast enough.

The editing team at Rodale Books—Karen Rinaldi, Colin Dickerman, John Atwood, Stephanie Knapp, Zachary Greenwald, Chris Rhoads, and Amy King—took a chance on this project, and Matt and I are grateful for all the energy and support you put behind it. You are a busy crew, but your patience, precision, and good spirits were always appreciated.

Farley Chase, our agent at the Waxman Literary Agency, took the idea of *The Long Run* and, well, ran with it. You turned a sketchy idea into a hardcover reality. Thanks.

To bring Matt's multifaceted world to life required the insights of many people (in addition to the main subject). Matt's family proved indispensable. At times, I know, it was painful to recall the moments when your son and brother had been suffering, but for all the tolerance you showed me when I asked (and asked again) for details, I thank you immensely.

Like Matt, I want to recognize the staff and professionals of New York–Presbyterian Hospital. Your willingness to share the most intimate facts about the care you provided Matt made my job much easier. I would especially like to thank Dr. Eachempati, who not only took hours answering my questions but later read through drafts to ensure their accuracy. Also, I would like to thank Vicky Tiase, OR nurse and accomplished athlete, for always being available to answer "another question."

Terry Brennan, Matt's partner in the bar business, saved many of the e-mails he sent to friends about Matt's time in the hospital. He shared those e-mails with me, which gave me a better sense of his friend's fragile state early on. Thanks, T-Red.

Anne Alonzo, one of the finest editorial researchers I know, meticulously verified my reporting on Matt's diverse worlds. Well done, Anne.

I met Alison Lowander 25 years ago. At the time I was amazed at how easily she could turn clunky sentences into polished copy. You haven't lost your touch, Alison. Thanks for a deft edit.

Judd Hark shared his technological skills when I needed them most. His help uncovered new views into Matt's tragedy. Much appreciated, Judd.

While writing this book, I drew upon the friendship, inspiration, and encouragement of many. They include Chris Grant, George Kendall, Mark Bernstein, Jeff Plaza, Fred DeCaro, David Diehl, Robert Sullivan, John Capouya, Jon Orlin, Dan O'Shea, Brian Silverman, John Mulvey, Andrea Witzig, Rich O'Connor, Ian Winograd, Bill Steinman, Geoff Brewer, Tim Vaughan, Rob Zeiger, Erin Strout, Joy Scharfstein, Alyce Lubitz, Brian Trusdell, Donna Rosato, David Craig, Dave Rubel, John Hanc, Lori Adams, Barbara Lorge, Dan Lorge, Abby Lorge, Bart Yasso, Budd Coates, Steve Friedman, John Brant, Rich Berlin, Charlie Competello, Noah Rothbaum, and Robert McCord. Thanks, folks.

Like Matt, I grew up in a large family. And like Matt, each brother and sister—John, Jane, Amy, Edward, Claire, Mary, and Meg—found a way to nudge this book to the finish line. To all of you, keep being the special people that you are.

Mom, thanks for saving all the clips; Dad, thanks for making me read Red Smith.

Matt ran his comeback marathon in seven hours and 21 minutes. At points it felt like that was all the time we had to write his life story. Fortunately, the team didn't mind too much. To Sarah, my patient, cheerleading wife, thanks for everything you did (and always do) to make this happen; you're awesome. Dinner's on me. And to Leah and Ben—yes, it's done.

Finally, I want to thank Matt Long for sharing his story. You've come so far from a very dark morning, and continue to show that the smallest steps can lead to great achievements. Long may you run.

—*Charles Butler, July 2010*